D0528787

The Complete Keto Cookbook
for Beginners #2019-2020

600 5-Ingredient Low-Carb Ketogenic Diet Recipes to Lose

Weight Quick & Easy (28 Days Meal Plan Included)

By Emily Walton

Copyrights©2020 By Emily Walton
All Rights Reserved

This document is geared towards providing exact and reliable information in regards to the topic and issue covered. The publication is sold with the idea that the publisher is not required to render accounting, officially permitted, or otherwise, qualified services. If advice is necessary, legal or professional, a practiced individual in the profession should be ordered.

Legal Notice: The book is copyright protected. This is only for personal use. You cannot amend, distribute, sell, use, quote or paraphrase any part or the content within this book without the consent of the author.

Under no circumstance will any legal responsibility or blame be held against the publisher for any reparation, damages, or monetary loss due to the information herein, either directly or indirectly.

Disclaimer Notice: Please note the information contained within this document is for educational and entertainment purpose only. Every attempt has been made to provide accurate, up to date and reliable complete information. No warranties of any kind are expressed or implied. Reader acknowledge that the author is not engaging in the rendering of legal, financial, medical or professional advice. The content of this book has been derived from various sources. Please consult a licensed professional before attempting any techniques outlined in this book.

Table of Content

Introduction

Anyone wants to go on a diet. The problem is that not all diets are effective in helping you achieve your goals. If your goal is to shed off your unwanted pounds so that you can look and feel great again, then you need a diet that is not only based on science but can also deliver realistic results. The Ketogenic Diet is considered as the most popular diet today because it brings in fast and sustainable weight loss results. While simple and straight-forward as it seems, there are still so many who fail on this diet because there are many misconceptions that shroud this particular diet regimen. Thus, this is where this book comes in. I am writing this book to shed light to readers on how easy you can achieve your goals using the Ketogenic Diet as long as you have the right information. This book is specifically targeted to individuals who want to follow this diet regimen but do not know where to start as well as those who have started with the diet but want to further their knowledge about this diet program. With this book, readers will be able to know not only about the basics of the Ketogenic Diet, foods to consume and avoid, as well as important tips to stay on ketosis and be successful in their weight loss journey. The thing is that this book aims to be your ultimate guide staying in shape through the Ketogenic Diet.

Chapter-1 | The Basics About Keto Diet

What Is Ketogenic Diet

The ketogenic diet basically all about consuming fewer carbs, moderate protein, and lots of healthy fats. Following a normal carb-rich diet, the cells, tissues, and organs use up glucose (from carbohydrates) and convert into energy. While this is the ideal biochemistry of the body, consuming too many carbs leads to an excess in glucose in the blood. If the cells are no longer able to use the excess, it gets stored in the liver as glycogen and eventually converted into fats. This means that if your physical activity is too little, you end up accumulating fats in your body, leading to chronic problems such as high blood pressure, obesity, diabetes, and others.

How Does Ketogenic Diet Work?

Under this particular diet regimen, your body bypasses glucose and instead uses fats as its main source of fuel. When the body detects little carbohydrates in the bloodstream, it automatically turns on another pathway that burns the stored fat into energy. This process is called ketosis. In most cases, this usually occurs during prolonged fasting periods. However, not everyone can go through long periods of fasting. Thus, the ketogenic diet mimics fasting, but individuals still consume foods that do not break ketosis, so you still eat good food, but you lose fat at the same time.

Entering Ketosis

In order to understand the ketogenic diet, it is crucial to understand ketosis. Ketosis is the process when the body burns off fat as an alternative source of energy in the absence or deficit of glucose. Under normal circumstances, the body utilizes the hormone glucose to push glucose (converted from carbohydrates) into cells to provide energy. Low levels of glucose switch another metabolic pathway in the body, which is ketosis to burn off fats as an energy source. Ketosis is a normal process and it plays a very vital role in the evolutionary success of humans. In ancient times, our ancestors rely on ketosis to survive for days when they cannot hunt or forage for food. But while fasting is the best way to push the body into ketosis, it is important to take note that not everyone can withstand going for three days without having something to eat. So instead of starving yourself, the ketogenic diet can help induce ketosis without the need for people to go hungry.

Measuring Your Ketones

Unlike other types of diets, the Ketogenic Diet can be measured by quantifying the number of ketones found in the blood. It is important to take note that when the body is pushed into ketosis, it releases ketone bodies in the bloodstream. There are three types of ketone bodies, including acetone, acetoacetate, and beta-hydroxybutyrate. The baseline of ketones in the Ketogenic Diet is important in achieving weight loss. Thus, there are several ways on how to measure ketone levels, and you don't even need sophisticated technology for that.

- **Blood Testing:** Blood testing for ketones is the most accurate way to measure ketosis. It measures Beta-hydroxybutyrate instead of acetone and acetoacetate. To use this particular method, you need a handheld ketone reader and test strips that can be expensive.
- **Urine Testing:** Unlike blood testing for ketones, urine testing is relatively cheaper and less invasive, thus making it perfect among people who do not like needles. It can measure acetoacetate. Moreover, you can also get urine test strips easily in drug stores. However, the reading is less accurate than blood tests, and over time, the body adapts to excreting fewer ketones in urine even during the state of ketosis.
- **Breath Testing:** Ketone bodies can also be tested using a specialized breath analyzer. It is the most convenient because you don't need to draw blood or get a urine sample as you only need to breathe to the device. However, breath ketone meters are relatively new to the market; thus they are less accurate than blood ketone meters.

Understanding Your Ketone Levels

How do you know that you have achieved ketosis when following the Ketogenic Diet? When starting with the keto diet, you need to know your ketone levels so that you can measure your progress. But when it comes to the keto diet, it is important to take note that the ketone levels are a spectrum and that different levels of ketones in the blood indicate what type of ketosis you are in. It is suggested that ketosis starts when the molecular concentration of ketones is at 0.5mmol/L The moment that your body crosses more than that amount, you are in ketosis. From a nutritional vantage point, ketosis is considered light if the value is at 1 mmol/L then becomes optimal between 1.1 mmol/L and 3 mmol/L. These levels allow you to lose weight. But if you want to use the ketogenic diet for therapeutic use to treat epilepsy and other metabolic disorders, a ketone level of between 3 mmol/L and 5 mmol/L is highly advisable.

Chapter-2 | The Keto Diet Action Plan

Succeeding in the Ketogenic Diet relies not only on knowing about the right information but creating an actual diet plan. Your action plan does not only involve knowing about the right foods to avoid and eat but also many other things. This chapter will discuss the right Ketogenic Diet action plan to ensure that you become successful with your weight-loss saga.

What Food to Eat

The Ketogenic Diet is a very straight-forward diet regimen that you can follow. While the principle behind this diet regimen involves the consumption of fats, it is crucial to take note that not all foods are created equally. Thus, below are the foods that you are allowed to eat under the Ketogenic Diet.

- **Fats and oils:** This diet encourages the intake of healthy fats to drive ketosis in your body. However, there are certain amounts of fats that you should consume, and these include animal fat, butter, eggs, olive oil, sunflower oil, fatty fishes, nuts, avocado, peanut butter, and seeds.
- **Proteins:** Proteins should be consumed moderately when following this particular diet. It is crucial to choose protein sourced from free-range, organic, or grass-fed livestock. Under this diet regimen, you can consume fish, shellfish, eggs, meat, and poultry.
- **Vegetables:** Vegetables are encouraged in the Ketogenic Diet to include dark and leafy green vegetables as they contain high amounts of minerals but minimal amounts of carbs.
- **Water:** To avoid dehydration, you are encouraged to drink a lot of water. However, if you want to drink other beverages, you can do so as long as they are not alcoholic and unsweetened.
- **Sweeteners:** Sweeteners can also be consumed but make sure that they are sugar-free. Go for liquid sweeteners as they do not contain any carbohydrates binders such as maltodextrin or dextrose. You can try stevia, sucralose, and erythritol.

What Food to Avoid

Similar to other weight-loss diets, the Ketogenic Diet is also restrictive to certain types of foods, particularly those that contain high amounts of carbohydrates. But other than carb-laden foods, there are other foods that you should avoid if you are going to follow the Ketogenic Diet.

- **Fruits:** Although fruits are healthy, the Ketogenic Diet discourages the consumption of fruits as they contain high amounts of sugar – fructose.
- **Processed foods:** Processed foods contain high amounts of sugar as well as trans-fat. Trans fat is a bad type of fat that should be avoided at all costs.
- **Root vegetables:** Root vegetables such as potatoes, beetroot, and carrots, to name a few, contain high amounts of carbohydrates.

Keto Diet Pantry Stock and Store Cupboard

When it comes to shopping for your ingredients, it is crucial that you stock up on ingredients that are keto-friendly. The best thing about your ketogenic pantry is that ingredients are now easily available from your local food stores. Make sure that your ingredients are fresh and opt for those that are not processed. Below are some of the food items that you need to stock up on in your pantry.

- **Low-Carb Vegetables:** Stock up on low-carb vegetables such as spinach, arugula, mushrooms, cauliflower, broccoli, kale, cabbages, zucchini, and bell peppers. Not only do they contain fewer carbs, but they are also high in fibers, vitamins, and minerals.
- **Low Sugar Fruits:** You can still enjoy fruits as there are fruits that are low in carbs. These include citrus fruits, avocado, blackberries, blueberries, and strawberries. Stay away from bananas, pineapples, apples, papaya, grapes, and pears.
- **Seafood:** Seafood is a good source of fats as well as high-quality proteins. Stock up on wild salmon, sardines, mackerel, crab, shrimps, tuna, and mussels. Avoid anything that is farmed and opt for wild-caught seafood.
- **Meat, Poultry, And Eggs:** Stock up on fatty meats, turkey, venison, chicken, and beef as long as they are organic and grass-fed.
- **Nuts and Seeds:** Nuts and seeds are good sources of fats. You can stock up on peanuts, walnuts, sesame seeds, Macadamia nuts, Brazil nuts, chia seeds, almonds, pumpkin seeds, and many others.
- **Dairy Products:** Dairy products such as cottage cheese, plain Greek yogurt, butter, and cream are high in fat but make sure that they are not made with any form of sugar.
- **Oils:** Oils from fruits and nuts are good for the body. Opt for healthy oils sourced from coconut butter, olive oil, avocado oil, nut oil, and MCT oil.
- **Keto Approved Condiments:** Keto-approved condiments such as olive oil mayonnaise, mustard, and oil-based salad dressing are not highly processed and do not come with added sugar.
- **Keto Approved Snacks:** Keto-approved snacks such as nut butter, sugar-free jerky, dried seaweeds, nuts, and low-carb crackers are approved for this particular diet.
- **Chocolate:** As long as you consume dark chocolates, then this is approved for the Ketogenic Diet.

The Guide to Keto Diet Meal Plan

When it comes to starting with this particular diet, it is important that you create a meal plan. But the Keto Diet meal plan does involve not only planning your meals way ahead of time but also other things. Below are the things that you need to do in order to be successful while following the Ketogenic Diet.

- **Cut The Worst Carbs Out Of Your Diet:** The first thing that you need to do is to do an inventory of the foods that you consume. Once you have already created an inventory, the next thing to do is to cut the worst carbs out of your diet completely. These include sweets, bread, pastries, snacks, and many others.
- **Try Some Light Exercise:** Exercising is very important if you want to push your body to ketosis faster. Exercises allow the body to use up the free glucose in your bloodstream so that you can switch on ketosis.
- **Don't Ignore Your Macros:** The dietary macronutrients for this particular diet is divided into 60% fats, 35% proteins, and 5% carbohydrates. Moreover, a dieter needs to consume no more than 2000 kcal per day and that the carbohydrates should be kept at a minimum consumption of 20 grams per day.
- **Don't Skimp On Protein:** Protein is important for muscle building, so don't skimp on them when following this diet.

However, make sure that you choose the right protein choices. Ideally, you need to consume lean and organic meats sources from grass-fed livestock.

- **Do Not Obsess Over Your Ketone Levels:** When you are still starting out with the Ketogenic Diet, it is important that you don't obsess over your ketone levels. Whether your ketone levels are high or low, what matters is that you achieve ketosis.

Your Body Reaction to The Meal Plan Along the Way

The increasing levels of ketone bodies in the body due to ketosis can bring about many effects to the body. The collection of the symptoms and side effects is called the Keto Flu. Below are the things that you will expect if you follow the Ketogenic Diet.

- **Weight Loss:** The most evident reaction to following the Ketogenic Diet is weight loss within the next few days following the diet.

- **Thirst:** Many people who follow the Ketogenic Diet feel thirstier than usual due to water loss. In fact, high levels of ketone bodies can lead to dehydration as well as electrolyte imbalance, so be sure that you drink a lot of water.

- **Muscle Cramps And Spasms:** Because it is easy for people following the Ketogenic Diet to become dehydrated, muscle cramps and spasms may be common side effects due to electrolyte imbalance.

- **Headaches:** Headaches can be common side effects once you switch to this diet regimen. It can happen due to the consumption of fewer carbs. However, the side effects usually last for only a few days after starting the diet.

- **Fatigue And Weakness:** During the initial stages of the Ketogenic Diet, you might feel tired and weak than usual. This happens because the body is still adjusting after making the switch to a low carb diet.

- **Stomach Upset:** Making any changes with your diet can increase the risk of digestive complaints. To reduce the risk, make sure that you drink plenty of liquid.

- **Disrupted Sleep:** Disrupted sleep is a common side effect among people who switch to the Ketogenic Diet. However, this side effect usually goes away after a few weeks.

- **Bad Breath:** Bad breath is a common side effect due to ketosis. As the ketone bodies leave the body, it produces a certain type of smell. Now, if the ketone body produced by the body is acetone, then the breath can smell fruity or sweet. However, acetophenone and BHB can contribute to bad breath.

- **Better Concentration:** As the symptoms fade over time, most people notice that they have better concentration following the Ketogenic Diet.

South Dublin Libraries
www.southdublinlibraries.ie

The Ketogenic Diet can help a lot of people achieve their weight loss goals. While it encourages the consumption of fewer carb-rich food, there are other things that you can do to drive ketosis in your body. This chapter will discuss tips and tricks to enjoy and optimize your results for this particular diet regimen.

Tips to Have A Great Keto Experience

1.) Increasing your physical activity can help fast-track the process of ketosis. You don't need to perform complicated exercise routines. You can do simple aerobic exercises or even jog daily to deplete the glycogen stores in the body.
2.) Significantly reduce the carbohydrate intake so that you can drive ketosis in your body. Aim to reduce your consumption of carbohydrates to 20 grams daily or even less.
3.) Do fasting. The thing is that going without food for a longer period of time can help you achieve ketosis faster. As a general rule, you can go fasting for 24 to 48 hours.
4.) Increase the intake of healthy fat by consuming more coconut oil, olive oil, avocado, and flaxseed oil, to name a few.

FAQs

#1 – How Long Does It Take For One To Get Adapted To The Ketogenic Diet?

Many research papers and anecdotal evidence noted that an individual can adapt to this particular diet after three to four weeks. But if you want to adapt to this diet and dispel the side effects faster, you can engage in physical activities so that your body can tap into its fat stores.

#2 – How Do i Know If i Am In Ketosis?

You don't really need to test your urine, breath, or blood to know if you are in ketosis or not. In fact, there are few tell-tale signs that tell you that you in ketosis. One of the most important signs is when you wake up with a fruity or unusual odor in your breath. Another sign is when you experience mental sharpness than usual.

#3 – What Can Put Me Out Of Ketosis?

Getting out of ketosis is very easy. This happens when you consume any amounts of carbohydrates, and it can usually last for a few hours.

#4 – How Do i Promote Ketosis Aside From Exercise?

Aside from exercise, there are other ways to promote ketosis. It is recommended to use MCT oil to improve periods of ketosis. We would like to discourage the use of keto esters as they are not clinically tested yet.

#5 – Can i Still Do My Usual Exercise Routine?

While you can exercise to push your body to ketosis, the Ketogenic Diet encourages one to reduce the intensity of your workout. This is especially true if you are still dealing with the keto flu.

Chapter-4 | 28-Day Meal Plan

The success of following this diet does not only rely on knowing the right information. It is also important that you plan your meals ahead of time. Planning your meals is very crucial so that you know what goes into your food so that it still follows the principle of the Ketogenic Diet. Moreover, it also makes your life easier so that you don't eat anything that will kick you off the diet.

28-Day Meal Plan

Day #	Breakfast	Lunch	Snack	Dinner
1	Mini Eggs in Cups	Eggs Baked in Avocado	Appetizing Lemon Pepper Chicken Wings	Grilled Cauliflower
2	Keto Caprese Salad	Middle East Vegan Falafel	Chili-Lime Shrimps	Grilled Spicy Eggplant
3	Bacon and Swiss Omelet	Tomato and Burrata Salad	Roasted Buffalo	Cheese and Broccoli Balls
4	Stuffed Jalapeno	Simple Chicken Garlic-Tomato Stew	Cajun Spiced Pecans	Easy Kale Salad
5	Eggs and Sausage Crescent Roll Casserole	Citrus Avocado Spinach Salad	Tuna Topped Pickles	Mustard-Crusted Salmon
6	Caprese Salad	Pork Chops and Peppers	Salad Lettuce	Cucumber and Red Onion Salad
7	Italian Cloud Eggs	Easy Asian Chicken	Middle Eastern Style Tuna Salad	Boiled Garlic Clams
8	Ricotta and Pomegranate Bruschetta	Bacon Tomato Salad	Walnut Butter on Cracker	Italian Shredded Beef
9	Cream Cheese Chive Omelet	Thai Coconut Pork	Crab Stuffed Mushrooms	Easy Chicken Vindaloo
10	High Protein, Green and Fruity Smoothie	Lemon-Rosemary Shrimps	Homemade Apricot and Soy Nut Trail Mix	Celery Salad

11	Yogurt with Rhubarb Compote and Almonds	Beefy Cabbage Bowls	Guac Deviled Eggs	Express Shrimp and Cauliflower Jambalaya
12	Cauliflower Mash	Cauliflower Fritters	Baba Ganoush Eggplant Dip	Chicken and Mushrooms
13	Spanish Omelet	Beefy Scotch Eggs	No Cook Choco and Coconut Bars	Provolone Over Herbed Portobello Mushrooms
14	Garlic and Greens	Blue Cheese, Fig and Arugula Salad	Easy Baked Parmesan Chips	Thyme-Sesame Crusted Halibut
15	Almond Vanilla Yogurt Parfaits	Easy Asian Style Chicken Slaw	Crunchy Kale Chips	Easy Thai 5-Spice Pork Stew
16	Nutritiously Green Milk Shake	Garlic Lime Marinated Pork Chops	Cheese and Broccoli Balls	Steamed Lemon Mustard Salmon
17	Spinach and Mushroom Omelet	Chili-Garlic Salmon	Cauli Mac and Cheese	Stir Fried Bok Choy
18	Scrambled Eggs with Mushrooms and Spinach	Easy BBQ Chicken and Cheese	Cauliflower Fritters	Chili-Garlic Salmon
19	Toad in A Hole	Curried Tofu	Fat Burger Bombs	Roast Rack of Lamb
20	Green Beans and Radish	Easy Baked Shepherd's Pie	Crispy Keto Pork Bites	Steamed Herbed Red Snapper
21	Feta Scrambled Eggs Wrapped	Green Jalapeno Sauce	Basil Keto Crackers	Lettuce Taco Carnitas
22	Coconut-Mocha Shake	Oven-Baked Skillet Lemon Chicken	Bacon Jalapeno Poppers	Grilled Parmesan Eggplant
23	Strawberries and Cream	Shrimp Scampi	Sautéed Brussels Sprouts	Grilled Marinated Flank Steak
24	Italian Greens and Yogurt Shake	Mushroom Pork Chops	Air Fryer Garlic Chicken Wings	Steamed Asparagus and Shrimps
25	Basic Poached Eggs	Beefy Burritos	Old Bay Chicken Wings	Coconut Curry Cod
26	Gritty and Nutty Shake	Golden Pompano in Microwave	Soy Garlic Mushrooms	Greek Chicken Stew
27	Maple Toast and Eggs	Ginger Asian Beef Stir Fry	Shrimp Fra Diavolo	Filling Beefy Soup
28	Basic Poached Eggs	Steamed Ginger Scallion Fish	Baked Vegetable Side	Pork Chops with Black Currant Jam

Beyond 28 Days

While this eBook only provides you with a 28-day meal plan, what do you do after 28 days? The thing is that we want you to be able to continue following this diet regimen. What you need to do is to learn how to make your own meal plans using recipes found in this book. By doing so, you will be able to enjoy delicious meals without being kicked out of ketosis.

Chapter-5 | 5-Ingredient Eggs & Dairy Recipes

Blueberry Pancakes

Prep time: 5 minutes, cook time: 10 minutes; Serves 1

5 Ingredients:

¼ cup blueberries

1 teaspoon vanilla extract

2 large eggs

4 to 6 tablespoons coconut flour

2 teaspoons baking powder

What you'll need from the store cupboard:

4 to 5 tablespoons of cooking oil

Instructions

1. In a large mixing bowl, mash the blueberries until only small bits remain. Add the vanilla extract and eggs. Mix until well incorporated.
2. Stir in the coconut flour and baking powder.
3. Add in the cooking oil if the mixture is too dry.
4. Heat a non-stick pan over medium flame and add a little cooking oil.
5. Spoon ¼ cup batter and reduce the heat to low.
6. Cook for 2 minutes on each side.
7. Top with any available toppings you desire.

Nutrition Facts Per Serving

Calories: 341; Fat: 29g; Carbs: 11g; Protein: 8g

Eggs and Sausage Casserole

Prep time: 15 minutes, cook time: 40 minutes; Serves 6

5 Ingredients:

1-pound bulk pork sausages, sliced

2 cups mozzarella cheese, shredded

8 large eggs

2 cups milk

¼ cup green onions chopped

What you'll need from the store cupboard:

Salt and pepper to taste

Instructions

1. Preheat the oven to 375⁰F.
2. Cook the skillet over medium flame for 6 minutes or until no longer pink. Break them into crumbs and drain the oil.
3. Spread the sausage evenly in a cast-iron skillet and sprinkle cheese evenly.
4. In a mixing bowl, combine the eggs and milk. Season with salt and pepper to taste.
5. Pour the egg mixture over the sausage and cheese.
6. Place inside the oven and bake for 35 minutes or until a knife inserted in the middle comes out clean.
7. Sprinkle green onions before serving.

Nutrition Facts Per Serving

Calories: 557; Fat: 45g; Carbs: 7g; Protein:30g

Keto Parfait

Prep time: 5 minutes, cook time: 10 minutes; Serves 4

5 Ingredients:

4 cups coconut cream

¼ cup heavy cream

½ cup almonds, slivered

16 blueberries

What you'll need from the store cupboard:

None

Instructions

1. In a bowl, mix together the coconut cream and heavy cream.
2. Layer the glass with cream mixture, almonds, and blueberries. Put four blueberries on each glass.
3. Place in the fridge to chill for at least 10 minutes.

Nutrition Facts Per Serving

Calories: 619; Fat: 56g; Carbs: 12g; Protein:9g

Italian Cloud Eggs

Prep time: 10 minutes, cook time: 20 minutes; Serves 4

5 Ingredients:

4 large eggs, white separated
¼ teaspoon Italian seasoning
¼ cup shredded Parmesan cheese
1 tablespoon minced fresh basil

What you'll need from the store cupboard:

Salt and pepper to taste
Cooking spray or oil

Instructions

1. Preheat the oven to 450⁰F.
2. Place the eggs whites in a bowl and the yolks in 4 separate small bowls.
3. Beat the egg whites and add in the Italian seasoning, salt, and pepper until stiff peaks form.
4. Coat the skillet with cooking spray. Drop the egg white mixture to create four mounds. Using the back of the spoon, create a small well in the middle of each mound.
5. Sprinkle cheese inside the mound.
6. Bake until light brown. Slip an egg yolk into each of the mounds and bake again for another 5 minutes.
7. Sprinkle with basil.
8. Serve immediately.

Nutrition Facts Per Serving

Calories: 96; Fat: 6g; Carbs: 1g; Protein: 8g

Cream Cheese Chive Omelet

Prep time: 5 minutes, cook time: 10 minutes; Serves 2

5 Ingredients:

4 large eggs
2 tablespoons minced chives
2 ounces cream cheese, cubed
1 tablespoon olive oil

What you'll need from the store cupboard:

Salt and pepper to taste
Water

Instructions

1. Heat the olive oil in a skillet over medium flame.
2. In a bowl, whisk the eggs, chives, salt, and pepper. Add water to adjust the consistency.
3. Add the egg mixture into the skillet and allow it to set.
4. Once the edges are set, push the cook eggs towards the center so that the uncooked part flows underneath.
5. When the eggs are cooked, sprinkle cheese on one side and fold the eggs.
6. Slide into a plate and cut in half.
7. Serve.

Nutrition Facts Per Serving

Calories: 287; Fat: 24g; Carbs: 2g; Protein:15g

Yogurt with Rhubarb Compote and Almonds

Prep time: 10 minutes, cook time: 15 minutes; Serves 4

5 Ingredients:

1 cup finely chopped fresh rhubarb
1 packet Stevia
3 cups plain coconut cream
¾ cup sliced almonds, toasted

What you'll need from the store cupboard:

Water

Instructions

1. In a small saucepan, combine the rhubarb, stevia, and water.
2. Bring to a boil and reduce the heat. Allow simmering for 15 until the rhubarb is tender. Stir constantly. Transfer to a bowl to cool slightly.
3. Spoon coconut cream into serving dishes and layer with the rhubarb compote.
4. Sprinkle with almonds on top.

Nutrition Facts Per Serving

Calories: 602; Fat: 62g; Carbs: 9g; Protein:11g

Spanish Omelet

Prep time: 5 minutes, cook time: 15 minutes; Serves 4

5 Ingredients:

6 large eggs

¼ cup chopped red onion

½ cup Mexican cheese blend, divided

2 tbsp cilantro, chopped

What you'll need from the store cupboard:

1 tbsp oil

Instructions

1. Heat oil in a skillet over medium heat.
2. In a bowl, whisk the eggs. Add the egg mixture into the skillet and allow it to set.
3. As the eggs set, push the eggs towards the center to let the uncooked portion flow underneath.
4. When the eggs are set, spoon the onion on one side. Sprinkle with cheese. Fold the eggs and allow them to cook.
5. Slide the omelet onto a plate and garnish with salsa.

Nutrition Facts Per Serving

Calories: 165; Fat:14g; Carbs: 2g; Protein:7g

Almond Vanilla Cream Parfaits

Prep time: 5 minutes, cook time: 15 minutes; Serves 4

5 Ingredients:

4 cups heavy cream

1 teaspoon vanilla extract

1 cup toasted almonds, chopped

What you'll need from the store cupboard:

None

Instructions

1. In a large bowl, mix the cream and vanilla extract.
2. Layer a glass with cream and almonds. Repeat the layers.
3. Serve immediately.

Nutrition Facts Per Serving

Calories: 624; Fat: 62g; Carbs: 10g; Protein:11g

Spinach and Mushroom Omelet

Prep time: 5 minutes, cook time: 15 minutes; Serves 2

5 Ingredients:

4 large eggs

1 teaspoon butter

½ cup thinly sliced fresh mushrooms, chopped

½ cup baby spinach, chopped

2 tablespoons shredded provolone cheese

What you'll need from the store cupboard:

Salt and pepper to taste

Instructions

1. Beat the eggs in a bowl until fluffy. Season with salt and pepper to taste. Set aside.
2. Heat butter in a skillet over medium flame and sauté the mushrooms for 3 minutes.
3. Add in spinach and cook until wilted.
4. Stir in the eggs and the provolone cheese.
5. Cook until the eggs are done.

Nutrition Facts Per Serving

Calories: 162; Fat: 11g; Carbs: 2g; Protein:14g

Eggs Chorizo Kale Wrap

Prep time: 10 minutes, cook time: 15 minutes; Serves 6

5 Ingredients:

12 ounces fresh chorizo

6 large eggs

2 tablespoons full-fat milk

1 cup shredded cheddar cheese

6 large kale leaves, blanched

What you'll need from the store cupboard:

Commercial salsa if available

Instructions

1. Remove the chorizos from the casing. Set aside.
2. Cook the chorizo in a skillet over medium heat. Be sure to break the chorizo into tiny pieces.
3. In a small bowl, beat the eggs and milk until blended. Add egg mixture and cheese into the chorizo mixture. Cook until the eggs are set.
4. Assemble the wrap by placing on one side of the blanched kale leaves the egg and cheese mixture.
5. Top with salsa if desired.
6. Fold the kale wraps.
7. Serve.

Nutrition Facts Per Serving
Calories: 407; Fat: 34g; Carbs: 3g; Protein:20g

Toad in A Hole

Prep time: 10 minutes, cook time: 30 minutes; Serves 6
5 Ingredients:
6 large eggs
1 cup whole milk
6 tablespoons almond flour
1 package (12 ounces) sausage links
What you'll need from the store cupboard:
Salt to taste
3 tablespoons olive oil
Instructions
1. Preheat the oven to 400⁰F.
2. In a bowl, mix the eggs and milk. Season with salt to taste and add in the almond flour until well-combined. This will be the batter. Allow standing for 30 minutes.
3. Meanwhile, cook the sausages on a skillet over medium heat. Slice thick and set aside.
4. Grease a baking dish with cooking oil and place in an oven for 4 minutes or until hot.
5. Pour in the batter and top with the sausages into the hot baking dish.
6. Bake inside the oven for 20 minutes or until brown and puffed.
7. Remove from the baking dish.
8. Serve.

Nutrition Facts Per Serving
Calories: 210; Fat:18 g; Carbs:3g; Protein:9g

Spinach and Cheese Scrambled Egg

Prep time: 10 minutes, cook time: 15 minutes; Serves 6
5 Ingredients:
4 large egg whites
2 large eggs
¼ cup chopped fresh spinach
2 tablespoons shredded cheddar cheese
What you'll need from the store cupboard:
Pepper to taste
Cooking oil
Commercial salsa
Instructions
1. In a large bowl, beat the eggs white and eggs. Season with pepper to taste.
2. Stir in the spinach and cheddar cheese.
3. Heat a skillet over medium heat and add in the eggs.
4. Continue stirring until the eggs are cooked.
5. Serve with salsa if desired.

Nutrition Facts Per Serving
Calories: 68; Fat: 6g; Carbs: 0.5g; Protein:4g

Chorizo Salsa Omelet

Prep time: 10 minutes, cook time: 25 minutes; Serves 1
5 Ingredients:
1 tablespoons butter
3 eggs
2 tablespoons milk
¼ cup cooked chorizo
2 tablespoons chunky salsa
What you'll need from the store cupboard:
Salt and pepper to taste
Water

Instructions

1. In a small skillet, melt the butter over medium heat.
2. Whisk the eggs and milk. Season with salt and pepper to taste.
3. Pour in the egg mixture into the skillet and cook until the eggs have set.
4. As the eggs set, push the edges towards the center to allow the uncooked portion to flow underneath.
5. Spoon the chorizo and salsa on one side and fold the other side of the egg.
6. Slide the omelet into place.

Nutrition Facts Per Serving
Calories: 588; Fat:48 g; Carbs:3 g; Protein:34g

Berries in Yogurt and Cream

Prep time: 10 minutes, cook time: 30 minutes; Serves 10

5 Ingredients:
1 ½ cups plain yogurt
2 ½ cups heavy whipping cream
½ packet stevia powder
3 cups assorted fresh strawberries
1 tablespoon coconut oil

What you'll need from the store cupboard:
1 teaspoon orange zest

Instructions

1. Place the yogurt in a bowl and add in the cream, orange zest, and coconut oil. Whisk until well-combined.
2. Sprinkle half of the stevia packet but do not stir into the cream. Cover and refrigerate for at least 30 minutes.
3. Place berries in cups and add in the cream.

Nutrition Facts Per Serving
Calories: 149; Fat: 14g; Carbs: 4g; Protein:6g

Cottage Cheese Fluff

Prep time: 10 minutes, cook time: 35 minutes; Serves 6

5 Ingredients:
3 cups cottage cheese, full fat
3 ounces sugar-free lemon-flavored Jell-O mix, mixed in warm water
8 ounces whipped cream
½ cup berries of your choice
2 tablespoons toasted almond nuts, chopped

What you'll need from the store cupboard:
None

Instructions

1. Place the cottage cheese in a food processor and blend until creamy.
2. Whisk in the flavored gelatin and fold.
3. Place in molds and allow it to set in the fridge.
4. Before serving, top with whipped cream, fruits, and nuts.

Nutrition Facts Per Serving
Calories: 183; Fat: 12g; Carbs: 6g; Protein:10g

Cheesy Andouille Sausage with Cauliflower

Prep time: 20 minutes, cook time: 30 minutes; Serves 8

5 Ingredients:
1 onion, minced
1-pound andouille sausage, sliced
3 ounces cauliflower, shredded and wrung dry
2 cups cheddar cheese, shredded

What you'll need from the store cupboard:
1 tablespoon canola oil or any kind of cooking oil
3 tablespoons hot sauce

Instructions

1. Preheat the oven to 425°F.
2. In a skillet, heat the cooking oil and stir in the onions. Sauté for 2 minutes.
3. Add in the sausages and cook for 6 minutes while stirring occasionally.
4. Transfer into a greased baking pan and layer the shredded cauliflower.

5. Top with shredded cheddar cheese.
6. Drizzle with hot sauce.
7. Place in the oven and bake for 22 minutes.

Nutrition Facts Per Serving
Calories: 307; Fat: 22g; Carbs: 8g; Protein:19g

Peanut Butter Parfait

Prep time: 5 minutes, cook time: 10 minutes; Serves 4
5 Ingredients:
3 cups heavy cream
¼ cup smooth peanut butter
1 cup slivered almonds
1/4 cup unsalted roasted peanuts, chopped
What you' ll need from the store cupboard:
None
Instructions
1. In a bowl, combine the cream and peanut butter until well combined.

2. In a glass, layer the peanut buttercream, almonds, and peanuts in an alternating manner.
3. Put in the fridge to chill for at least 10 minutes to set.

Nutrition Facts Per Serving
Calories: 455; Fat: 45g; Carbs: 8g; Protein:12g

Mini Eggs in Cups

Prep time: 10 minutes, cook time: 20 minutes; Serves 6
5 Ingredients:
6 eggs, beaten
1 tablespoon Dijon mustard
¾ cup smoked salmon, finely chopped
½ cup cheddar cheese, shredded
¼ cup green onion, chopped
What you' ll need from the store cupboard:
Cooking oil
Instructions
1. Preheat the oven to 400⁰F.
2. In a bowl, whisk the egg together with the mustard. Set aside.

3. In another bowl, mix the smoked salmon, cheese, and green onions.
4. Grease a mini muffin pan with cooking oil.
5. Place mixture and salmon mixture into the muffin pan.
6. Bake for 20 minutes until the eggs have set.
7. Allow cooling before taking out of the muffin cup.

Nutrition Facts Per Serving
Calories: 98; Fat: 6g; Carbs: 0.5g; Protein:9g

Strawberries and Cream

Prep time: 10 minutes, cook time: 45 minutes; Serves 12
5 Ingredients:
6 ounces packaged cream cheese, softened
1 packet stevia powder
2 tablespoons coconut oil or MCT oil
3 pints fresh strawberries, hulled and sliced
12 ounces whipped cream
What you' ll need from the store cupboard:
None
Instructions

1. In a bowl, mix the cream cheese, stevia powder, and oil. Whip topping in a bowl until smooth.
2. In a glass, place a layer of cheese mixture. Add a layer of strawberries and cream on top. Repeat the layers.
3. Place in the fridge to cool for at least 35 minutes.

Nutrition Facts Per Serving
Calories: 147; Fat: 13g; Carbs: 8g; Protein: 9g

Keto Crème Brulee

Prep time: 15 minutes, cook time: 52 minutes; Serves 2

5 Ingredients:

1 packet stevia powder

1 cup heavy cream

3 eggs

¼ teaspoon vanilla extract

What you'll need from the store cupboard:

None

Instructions

1. Preheat the oven to 3500⁰F.
2. In a bowl, whisk the packet of stevia and cream until well-combined.
3. Heat the mixture in a saucepan for 2 minutes until warm and to dissolve the stevia.
4. Remove from the heat and stir in the egg yolks and vanilla. Whisk until smooth.
5. Place the cream mixture into ramekins.
6. Place the ramekins into a roasting pan with enough hot water to reach half of the sides of the ramekin.
7. Place in the oven and bake for 50 minutes.
8. Remove the ramekins from the hot water and allow it to chill in the fridge for 2 hours.

Nutrition Facts Per Serving

Calories: 411; Fat: 37g; Carbs: 4g; Protein:15g

Keto Bacon and Egg Casserole

Prep time: 20 minutes, cook time: 20 minutes; Serves 6

5 Ingredients:

12 bacon strips, diced

¼ cup butter

12 large eggs, beaten

What you'll need from the store cupboard:

Salt and pepper to taste

Instructions

1. Cook the bacon on a skillet over medium heat until the fat has rendered. Take the bacon out and place on paper towels to drain excess fat.
2. In a saucepan, heat butter until melted.
3. Pour in the egg and season with salt and pepper to taste.
4. Stir in the bacon.
5. Cover with foil and bake in the oven at 4000⁰F for 20 minutes or until the eggs have set.

Nutrition Facts Per Serving

Calories: 208; Fat: 20g; Carbs: 2g; Protein:7g

Eggs Baked in Avocado

Prep time: 5 minutes, cook time: 30 minutes; Serves 2

5 Ingredients:

2 eggs

1 teaspoon olive oil

1 avocado, halved and pit removed

1/8 teaspoon salt

1 teaspoon chopped mint leaves

What you'll need from the store cupboard:

None

Instructions

1. Preheat the oven to 400ºF.
2. Separate the egg yolks from the whites and put them in separate bowls.
3. Add salt into the egg whites and mix well.
4. In a skillet, sear the avocado halves under medium flame.
5. Place the egg whites into the depression made from the pit of the avocado.
6. Place the avocado in the oven and cook for 15 minutes.
7. Slide in the yolks and put in the oven to cook for another 15 minutes.
8. Garnish with chopped mint leaves before serving.

Nutrition Facts Per Serving

Calories: 310; Fat: 27g; Carbs: 10g; Protein:11g

Baked Egg Stuffed Cups

Prep time: 10 minutes, cook time: 28 minutes; Serves 4

5 Ingredients:

1 cup ground beef, fat not removed

4 eggs

¼ teaspoon salt

¼ teaspoon pepper

Chopped sage leaves for garnish

What you'll need from the store cupboard:

Cooking spray

Instructions

1. Preheat the oven to 325⁰F. Grease ramekins then set aside.
2. In a skillet heated over medium flame, stir the beef for 3 minutes until golden.
3. Press the ground beef into greased ramekins. Form wells in the center.
4. Break and slip the egg at the center of the beef.
5. Season with salt and pepper to taste.
6. Bake in the oven for 25 minutes.
7. Garnish with chopped sage.

Nutrition Facts Per Serving

Calories: 177; Fat: 14g; Carbs: 1g; Protein:11g

Keto Broccoli and Eggs

Prep time: 10 minutes, cook time: 35 minutes; Serves 2

5 Ingredients:

2 teaspoons coconut oil

1 medium broccoli, chopped

3 large eggs

1 cup shredded cheddar cheese

Salt and pepper to taste

What you'll need from the store cupboard:

None

Instructions

1. Set your oven to broil on high.
2. Brush a baking dish with oil.
3. Spread the chopped broccoli in a baking dish and create wells.
4. Crack one egg for each well created and sprinkle with cheddar cheese.
5. Season with salt and pepper to taste.
6. Bake in the oven for 35 minutes.

Nutrition Facts Per Serving

Calories: 364; Fat: 31g; Carbs: 4g; Protein:17g

Creamy Apple and Nuts

Prep time: 10 minutes, cook time: 10 minutes; Serves 4

5 Ingredients:

1 ½ cups heavy cream

½ cup mixed nuts, toasted and unsalted

½ cup applesauce, unsweetened

A dash of ground nutmeg

What you'll need from the store cupboard:

None

Instructions

1. Layer each glass with cream, nuts, and applesauce. Repeat the layers twice.
2. Top with applesauce and nutmeg.
3. Place in the fridge to cool before serving.

Nutrition Facts Per Serving

Calories: 270; Fat: 26g; Carbs: 7g; Protein:4g

Basic Poached Eggs

Prep time: 5 minutes, cook time: 3 minutes; Serves 4

5 Ingredients:

4 eggs, cold

3 tablespoons vinegar

Salt and pepper to taste

Chopped green onions for garnish

What you'll need from the store cupboard:

Water

Instructions

1. Put water in a saucepan.
2. Bring to a boil and add vinegar.
3. Crack eggs into separate bowls.

4. Give the boiling water a swirl and pour the eggs gently into the mixture.
5. Allow cooking for 3 minutes.
6. Take the eggs out and season with salt and pepper to taste.

7. Garnish with green onions.

Nutrition Facts Per Serving
Calories: 163; Fat: 10g; Carbs: 6g; Protein:8g

Keto Crustless Breakfast Pizza

Prep time: 5 minutes, cook time: 12 minutes; Serves 4

5 Ingredients:
4 large sausage links, removed from casing
4 eggs, beaten
1/3 cup tomato puree
½ cup shredded Italian cheese
Dried oregano leaves

What you'll need from the store cupboard:
Cooking spray
Salt and pepper to taste

Instructions
1. Preheat the oven to 400⁰F.
2. Coat a skillet with cooking spray and heat over medium flame.
3. Saute the sausage meat for 2 minutes until golden. Set aside.

4. Season the eggs with salt and pepper to taste.
5. Pour the eggs in a baking dish.
6. Place in the oven for 5 minutes to set.
7. Spread the tomato puree on the surface of the egg and spread the cooked sausage links. Sprinkle cheese and oregano on top.
8. Place on a baking sheet and bake for another 5 minutes.

Nutrition Facts Per Serving
Calories: 335; Fat: 27g; Carbs: 6g; Protein:18g

Keto Microwaved Egg and Cheese

Prep time: 2 minutes, cook time: 1 minute; Serves 1

5 Ingredients:
1 egg, beaten
1 tablespoon Mexican cheese blend, shredded
1 red tomato, chopped
1 tablespoon coriander leaves, chopped

What you'll need from the store cupboard:
Salt and pepper to taste

Instructions
1. Place the egg in a microwave mug and season with salt and pepper to taste.

2. Add in the Mexican cheese blend.
3. Place in the microwave oven.
4. Microwave for 1 minute with 30-second increment.
5. Top with chopped tomato and coriander leaves.

Nutrition Facts Per Serving
Calories: 172; Fat: 12g; Carbs: 5g; Protein:10g

Easy Egg, Bacon, and Mexican Cheese Breakfast

Prep time: 5 minutes, cook time: 5 minutes; Serves 2

5 Ingredients:
½ cup Mexican cheese blend, shredded
4 slices bacon, cooked
4 eggs, beaten
½ cup chopped tomatoes for garnish

What you'll need from the store cupboard:
Cooking spray
Salt and pepper to taste

Instructions

1. Coat a non-stick skillet with cooking spray and heat over medium flame.
2. Beat the eggs and season with salt and pepper.
3. Pour in the eggs and allow them to set. Gently pull the eggs across the pan using a turner and continue folding until cooked.
4. Spoon bacon on top of eggs.

18

5. Top with cheese.
6. Fold the eggs over the filling and press gently.
7. Cut into wedges and serve with chopped tomatoes.

Nutrition Facts Per Serving
Calories: 587; Fat: 48g; Carbs: 5g; Protein:23g

Broccoli Cheddar Omelet

Prep time: 5 minutes, cook time: 5 minutes; Serves 2
5 Ingredients:
2 eggs, beaten
2 tablespoons milk
1/3 cup cooked broccoli florets
2 tablespoons shredded cheddar cheese
Parsley for garnish
What you'll need from the store cupboard:
Cooking spray
Salt and pepper to taste
Instructions
1. Beat the eggs and milk in a bowl until well-combined. Season with salt and pepper to taste.
2. Coat an omelet pan with cooking spray and heat over medium flames.
3. Pour in the egg mixture. While the eggs are setting, push the cooked portion to the center using an inverted turner. Continue cooking the eggs.
4. Place the omelet and cheese on one side of the egg then fold.
5. Slide on to a plate.
6. Garnish with parsley last.
Nutrition Facts Per Serving
Calories: 177; Fat: 14g; Carbs: 4g; Protein:13g

Breakfast Pudding

Prep time: 5 minutes, cook time: 7 minutes; Serves 6
5 Ingredients:
½ packet of stevia
¼ cup arrowroot powder
3 cups coconut milk
4 egg yolks
2 tablespoons butter
What you'll need from the store cupboard:
¼ teaspoon salt
2 teaspoon vanilla
Fresh fruit for garnish
Instructions
1. In a bowl, mix stevia, arrowroot powder, and salt.
2. Place in a saucepan and pour in coconut milk and eggs until smooth.
3. Turn on the heat and allow it to simmer over medium flame until the sauce thickens. Remove from the heat and stir in butter and vanilla.
4. Pour into custard cups and refrigerate.
5. Garnish with fresh fruits of your choice before serving.
Nutrition Facts Per Serving
Calories: 148; Fat: 11g; Carbs: 4g; Protein:6g

Sausage Cheddar Breakfast Bowl

Prep time: 5 minutes, cook time: 5 minutes; Serves 1
5 Ingredients:
2 eggs, beaten
2 tablespoons milk
2 tablespoons breakfast sausage, cooked and crumbled
1 tablespoon cheddar cheese, shredded
1 red tomato, chopped
What you'll need from the store cupboard:
Cooking spray
Cooking oil
Salt and pepper to taste
Instructions

1. Whisk the egg and milk in a bowl. Season with salt and pepper to taste.
2. Heat skillet sprayed with cooking oil over medium flame and cook the eggs.
3. Stir the eggs until fluffy.
4. Place in a bowl and add in breakfast sausages, cheddar cheese, and tomatoes.
5. Serve immediately.

Nutrition Facts Per Serving
Calories: 365; Fat: 25g; Carbs: 9g; Protein:24g

Broccoli Cheese Soup

Prep time: 5 minutes, cook time: 15 minutes; Serves 4

5 Ingredients:
2 cloves of garlic, minced
1 head broccoli, cut into florets
26 ounces cream of chicken soup
1 can heavy cream
2 cups shredded cheddar cheese

What you' ll need from the store cupboard:
Cooking oil

Instructions
1. Heat oil in a large saucepan over medium flame and sauté the garlic until fragrant.
2. Add in the broccoli and sauté for 1 minute.
3. Stir in the cream of chicken soup and allow boiling for 8 minutes.
4. Reduce the heat and simmer.
5. Pour in the cheese and continue cooking for another 5 minutes.
6. Serve warm.

Nutrition Facts Per Serving
Calories: 536; Fat: 47g; Carbs:8g; Protein:17g

Crispy Baked Zucchini Fries with Parmensan

Prep time:15 mins; Cook time: 30 mins; Serves 2

5 Ingredients:
2 eggs
3/4 cup grated Parmesan cheese
2 pounds zucchinis, cut into 1/2-inch French fry strips
1 teaspoon paprika
1/2 teaspoon. ground black pepper

What you'll need from the store cupboard:
Cooking spray
1 tablespoon. dried mixed herbs
1 1/2 teaspoons. garlic powder

Instructions
1. Preheat oven to 425 degrees F and use cooking spray to a baking sheet lined with aluminum foil.
2. Add Parmesan cheese, paprika, garlic powder, paprika, and pepper in a bowl, well combined. In an another bowl, stir in eggs.
3. Dip zucchini fries into beaten eggs, shaking off excess. Dredge in Parmesan mixture to coat and spread coated fries on the baking sheet.
4. Place in oven and bake for 30 to 35 minutes or until golden brown. Serve.

Nutrition Facts Per Serving
Per Serving: 356 calories; 23 g fat; 10.4 g carbohydrates; 18.6 g protein

Keto Paleo Scotch Eggs

Prep time: 5 mins; Cook time: 15 mins; Serves 6

5 Ingredients:

1 egg, lightly beaten
1 lb. sausage; divided into 6 parts; keto-friendly
5 hard-boiled eggs, peeled
Mustard with hot sauce and oil spray
1 cup. almond flour/coconut flour; for coating

Instructions

1. Flatten each sausage into a thin patty, 4 inches wide.
2. Place 1 boiled egg in the center of the sausage patty and wrap it completely around the egg; Repeat this process.
3. Coat each wrapped egg-sausage with flour, shaking off excess. Then dip into the beaten egg; spray with oil spray on both sides.
4. Cook for 12-16 minutes at 400 degrees F in the Air Fryer basket, flipping halfway through cooking.
5. Once done, cut in halves and serve with mustard along with hot sauce. Serve.

Nutrition Facts Per Serving

Per Serving: Calories 407 ; Fat 29 g; Carbohydrates 10 g; Protein 24 g

Poached Egg with Artichokes

Prep time: 10 mins; Cook time: 40 mins; Serves 6

5 Ingredients:

4 artichokes, uncooked and trimmed to the heart
4 eggs
1 recipe hollandaise sauce, keto-friendly
1 cup black olives, sliced
1/2 cup chopped fresh chives

What you'll need from the store cupboard:

1 tablespoon olive oil
2 tablespoons white vinegar
1 quart water

Directions

1. In a large pot, bring water and 1 tbsp. vinegar to a boil. Add in artichokes hearts and cook for 30 minutes. Drain well.
2. Prepare hollandaise sauce according to recipe Directions.
3. Pour 3 inches. water into a large saucepan, simmer for a few minutes. Stir in 1 tbsp. vinegar. Break the eggs into the water and cook for 3 to 5 minutes. Yolks should still be soft in center. Transfer simmered eggs with a slotted spoon to a warm dish.
4. Place artichoke hearts on a serving platter and keep a poached egg over top. Drizzle with hollandaise sauce. Then sprinkle olive slices on top of sauce. Garnish with chopped chives.

Nutrition Facts Per Serving

Per Serving: 204 calories; 28 g fat; 12.5 g carbohydrates; 18 g protein

Cocktail Kielbasa with Mustard Sauce

Prep time: 10 minutes, cook time: 6 hours; Serves 8

5 Ingredients:

2 pounds kielbasa (Polish sausage)

1 jar prepared mustard

1 bay leaf

What you'll need from the store cupboard:

Pepper to taste

Instructions

1. Slice kielbasa into bite-sized pieces.
2. Place all ingredients in the slow cooker.
3. Give a good stir to combine everything.
4. Close the lid and cook on low for 6 hours.
5. Remove the bay leaf.
6. Serve on toothpicks.

Nutrition Facts Per Serving

Calories: 256; Fat: 20g; Carbs:4g; Protein: 14g

Cajun Spiced Pecans

Prep time: 5 minutes, cook time: 10 minutes; Serves 10

5 Ingredients:

1-pound pecan halves

¼ cup butter

1 packet Cajun seasoning mix

¼ teaspoon ground cayenne pepper

What you'll need from the store cupboard:

Salt and pepper to taste

Instructions

1. Place a nonstick saucepan on medium fire and melt butter.
2. Add pecans and remaining ingredients.
3. Sauté for 5 minutes.
4. Remove from fire and let it cool completely.
5. Serve and enjoy.

Nutrition Facts Per Serving

Calories: 356.5; Fat: 37.3g; Carbs: 6.8g; Protein: 4.2g

Cheesy Cheddar Cauliflower

Prep time: 15 minutes, cook time: 20 minutes; Serves 6

5 Ingredients:

½ cup butter

2 cups half and half cream

4 cups cheddar cheese, grated

3 cups cauliflower florets

What you'll need from the store cupboard:

½ cup water

Pepper and salt to taste

Instructions

1. In a heavy-bottomed pot on medium-high fire, melt butter.
2. Stir in cream and cheddar cheese. Add in water. Mix well and cook for 5 minutes.
3. Add cauliflower florets and cook for 6 minutes. Season with pepper.
4. Serve and enjoy.

Nutrition Facts Per Serving

Calories: 500; Fat: 42g; Carbs: 9g; Protein: 21g

Balsamic Zucchini

Prep time: 0 minutes, cook time: 20 minutes; Serves 4

5 Ingredients:

3 medium zucchinis, cut into thin slices

1/2 cup chopped sweet onion

1/2 teaspoon dried rosemary, crushed

2 tablespoons balsamic vinegar

1/3 cup crumbled feta cheese

What you'll need from the store cupboard:

1/2 teaspoon salt
1/4 teaspoon pepper
4 tablespoon olive oil
Instructions
1. In a large skillet, heat oil over medium-high heat; sauté zucchini and onion until crisp-tender, 6-8 minutes. Stir in seasonings. Add vinegar; cook and stir 2 minutes. Top with cheese.

Nutrition Facts Per Serving
Calories: 175; Fat: 16g; Carbs: 5g; Protein: 4g

Zesty Balsamic Chard

Prep time: 5 minutes, cook time: 20 minutes; Serves 6
5 Ingredients:
2 medium onions, chopped
6 garlic cloves, sliced
1/2 cup white balsamic vinegar
2 bunches Swiss chard, coarsely chopped (about 16 cups)
1/2 cup walnut halves, toasted
What you' ll need from the store cupboard:
1/4 teaspoon salt
1/4 teaspoon pepper
3 tablespoons olive oil

Instructions
1. In a 6-qt. Stockpot, heat oil over medium-high heat. Add onions; cook and stir until tender. Add garlic; cook 1 minute longer.
2. Add vinegar, stirring to loosen any browned bits from pot. Add remaining ingredients; cook 4-6 minutes or until chard is tender, stirring occasionally.

Nutrition Facts Per Serving
Calories: 144; Fat: 13g; Carbs: 4g; Protein: 4g

Simple Tender Crisp Cauli-Bites

Prep time: 10 minutes, cook time: 10 minutes; Serves 3
5 Ingredients:
2 cups cauliflower florets
2 clove garlic minced
4 tablespoons olive oil
¼ tsp salt
½ tsp pepper
What you' ll need from the store cupboard:
Instructions
1. In a small bowl, mix well olive oil salt, pepper, and garlic.

2. Place cauliflower florets on a baking pan. Drizzle with seasoned oil and toss well to coat.
3. Evenly spread in a single layer and place a pan on the top rack of the oven.
4. Broil on low for 5 minutes. Turnover florets and return to the oven.
5. Continue cooking for another 5 minutes.
6. Serve and enjoy.

Nutrition Facts Per Serving
Calories: 183; Fat:18g; Carbs: 4.9g; Protein: 1.7g

French Fried Butternut Squash

Prep time: 15 minutes, cook time: 20 minutes; Serves 6
5 Ingredients:
1 medium butternut squash
1 tablespoon chopped fresh thyme
1 tablespoon chopped fresh rosemary
4 tablespoons olive oil
1/2 teaspoon salt
What you' ll need from the store cupboard:
Cooking spray
Instructions

1. Heat oven to 425°F. Lightly coat a baking sheet with cooking spray.
2. Peel skin from butternut squash and cut into even sticks, about 1/2-inch-wide and 3 inches long.
3. In a medium bowl, combine the squash, oil, thyme, rosemary, and salt; mix until the squash is evenly coated.

4. Spread onto the baking sheet and roast for 10 minutes.
5. Remove the baking sheet from the oven and shake to loosen the squash.
6. Return to oven and continue to roast for 10 minutes or until golden brown.
7. Serve and enjoy.

Nutrition Facts Per Serving
Calories: 86; Fat: 9g; Carbs: 1g; Protein: 1g

Garlic Flavored Kale Taters

Prep time: 15 minutes, cook time: 20 minutes; Serves 4

5 Ingredients:
4 cups kale, rinsed and chopped
2 cups cauliflower florets, finely chopped
2 tbsp almond milk
1 clove of garlic, minced
3 tablespoons oil

What you'll need from the store cupboard:
1/8 teaspoon black pepper
cooking spray

Instructions
1. Heat oil in a large skillet and sauté the garlic for 2 minutes. Add the kale until it wilts. Transfer to a large bowl.
2. Add the almond milk. Season with pepper to taste.
3. Evenly divide into 4 and form patties.
4. Lightly grease a baking pan with cooking spray. Place patties on pan. Place pan on the top rack of the oven and broil on low for 6 minutes. Turnover patties and cook for another 4 minutes.
5. Serve and enjoy.

Nutrition Facts Per Serving
Calories: 117; Fat: 11g; Carbs: 5g; Protein: 2g

Tuna Topped Pickles

Prep time: 20 minutes, cook time: 0 minutes; Serves 5

5 Ingredients:
1 tbsp fresh dill, and more for garnish
¼ cup full-fat mayonnaise
1 can light flaked tuna, drained
5 dill pickles

What you'll need from the store cupboard:
¼ tsp pepper

Instructions
1. Slice pickles in half, lengthwise. With a spoon, deseed the pickles and discard seeds.
2. In a small bowl, mix well the mayo, dill, and tuna using a fork.
3. Evenly divide them into 10 and spread over deseeded pickles.
4. Garnish with more dill on top and sprinkle black pepper.
5. Evenly divide into suggested servings and enjoy.

Nutrition Facts Per Serving
Calories: 180; Fat: 14g; Carbs: 4g; Protein: 11g

Pesto Stuffed Mushrooms

Prep time: 20 minutes, cook time: 25 minutes; Serves 6

5 Ingredients:
6 large cremini mushrooms
6 bacon slices
2 tablespoons basil pesto
5 tablespoons low-fat cream cheese softened

What you'll need from the store cupboard:
None

Instructions
1. Line a cookie sheet with foil and preheat oven to 375°F.
2. In a small bowl mix well, pesto and cream cheese.
3. Remove stems of mushrooms and discard. Evenly fill mushroom caps with pesto-cream cheese filling.
4. Get one stuffed mushroom and a slice of bacon. Wrap the bacon all over the mushrooms. Repeat process on remaining mushrooms and bacon.

5. Place bacon-wrapped mushrooms on prepared pan and bake for 25 minutes or until bacon is crispy.
6. Let it cool, evenly divide into suggested servings, and enjoy.

Nutrition Facts Per Serving
Calories: 137.8; Fat: 12.2g; Carbs: 2.0g; Protein: 5.0g

Keto "Cornbread"

Prep time: 10 minutes, cook time: 30 minutes; Serves 8
5 Ingredients:
1 ¼ cups coconut milk
4 eggs, beaten
4 tbsp baking powder
½ cup almond meal
What you'll need from the store cupboard:
3 tablespoons olive oil
Instructions
1. Prepare 8 x 8-inch baking dish or a black iron skillet then add shortening.
2. Put the baking dish or skillet inside the oven on 425ºF and leave there for 10 minutes.
3. In a bowl, add coconut milk and eggs then mix well. Stir in the rest of the ingredients.
4. Once all ingredients are mixed, pour the mixture into the heated skillet.
5. Then cook for 15 to 20 minutes in the oven until golden brown.

Nutrition Facts Per Serving
Calories: 196; Fat: 18.9g; Carbs: 2.6g; Protein: 5.4g

Ricotta and Pomegranate

Prep time: 15 minutes, cook time: 12 minutes; Serves 3
5 Ingredients:
1 cup Ricotta cheese
3 tablespoons olive oil
1/2 cup pomegranate Arils
2 tsp thyme, fresh
2 cups arugula leaves
What you'll need from the store cupboard:
Pepper and salt to taste
1/2 tsp grated lemon zest

Instructions
1. Mix all ingredients in a bowl.
2. Toss until well combined.
3. Season with pepper and salt.
4. Serve and enjoy.

Nutrition Facts Per Serving
Calories: 312; Fat: 25g; Carbs: 9g; Protein: 11g

Middle Eastern Style Tuna Salad

Prep time: 20 minutes, cook time: 0 minutes; Serves 6
5 Ingredients:
¼ cup chopped pitted ripe olives
¼ cup drained and chopped roasted red peppers
2 green onions, sliced
2 pcs of 6-oz cans of tuna in water, drained and flaked
6 cups salad greens like lettuce
What you'll need from the store cupboard:
¼ cup Mayonnaise
Instructions
1. Except for salad greens, mix all the ingredients in a bowl.
2. Arrange salad greens on the bottom of the bowl and top with tuna mixture.
3. Serve and enjoy.

Nutrition Facts Per Serving
Calories: 92; Fat: 8g; Carbs: 3g; Protein: 3g

Crab Stuffed Mushrooms

Prep time: 15 minutes, cook time: 25 minutes; Serves 3

5 Ingredients:

2 tbsp minced green onion

1 cup cooked crabmeat, chopped finely

¼ cup Monterey Jack cheese, shredded

1 tsp lemon juice

¼ lb, fresh button mushrooms

What you'll need from the store cupboard:

Pepper and salt to taste

3 tablespoons olive oil

Instructions

1. Destem mushrooms, wash, and drain well.
2. Chop mushroom stems.
3. Preheat oven to 400ºF and lightly grease a baking pan with cooking spray.
4. In a small bowl, whisk well green onion, crabmeat, lemon juice, dill, and chopped mushroom stems.
5. Evenly spread mushrooms on prepared pan with cap sides up. Evenly spoon crabmeat mixture on top of mushroom caps.
6. Pop in the oven and bake for 20 minutes.
7. Remove from oven and sprinkle cheese on top.
8. Return to oven and broil for 3 minutes.
9. Serve and enjoy.

Nutrition Facts Per Serving

Calories: 286; Fat: 17.3g; Carbs:10g; Protein: 7.9g

Sour Cream and Onion Dip Carrot Sticks

Prep time: 15 minutes, cook time: 0 minutes; Serves 3

5 Ingredients:

1 sweet onion, peeled and minced

½ cup sour cream

2 tbsp mayonnaise

4 tablespoons olive oil

4 stalks celery, cut into 3-inch lengths

What you'll need from the store cupboard:

Pepper and salt to taste

Instructions

1. In a bowl, whisk well sour cream and mayonnaise until thoroughly combined.
2. Stir in onion and mix well.
3. Let it sit for an hour in the fridge and serve with celery sticks on the side.

Nutrition Facts Per Serving

Calories: 143; Fat: 13g; Carbs: 7g; Protein: 3g

Keto Caprese Salad

Prep time: 10 minutes, cook time: 0 minutes; Serves 2

5 Ingredients:

2 roma tomatoes, sliced thinly

8 large fresh basil leaves

2 oz fresh mozzarella part-skim, sliced into ½-inch cubes

2 tsp balsamic vinegar

4 tsp extra virgin olive oil

What you'll need from the store cupboard:

Pepper to taste

Instructions

1. Place tomatoes on a plate.
2. Season with pepper. Sprinkle with basil and mozzarella,
3. Drizzle balsamic vinegar and olive oil before serving.

Nutrition Facts Per Serving

Calories: 130; Fat: 9g; Carbs: 4g; Protein: 7g

Stuffed Jalapeno

Prep time: 20 minutes, cook time: 20 minutes; Serves 4

5 Ingredients:

12 jalapeno peppers, halved lengthwise and seeded

2-oz cream cheese softened

2-oz shredded cheddar cheese

¼ cup almond meal

What you'll need from the store cupboard:

Salt and pepper to taste

Instructions

1. Spray a cookie sheet with cooking spray and preheat oven to 400ºF.

2. Equally fill each jalapeno with cheddar cheese, cream cheese, and sprinkle almond meal on top. Place on a prepped baking sheet.

3. Pop in oven and bake for 20 minutes.

4. Serve and enjoy.

Nutrition Facts Per Serving

Calories: 187; Fat: 13.2g; Carbs: 7.7g; Protein: 5.9g

Easy Garlic Keto Bread

Prep time:5 minutes, cook time: 1 minute 30 seconds; Serves 1

5 Ingredients:

1 large egg

1 tbsp milk

1 tbsp coconut flour

1 tbsp almond flour

¼ tsp baking powder

What you'll need from the store cupboard:

Salt to taste

Instructions

1. Mix all ingredients in a bowl until well combined.

2. Pour into a mug and place in the microwave oven.

3. Cook for 1 minute and 30 seconds.

4. Once cooked, invert the mug.

5. Allow to cool before slicing.

Nutrition Facts Per Serving

Calories: 75; Fat:7g; Carbs: 3g; Protein: 4g

Jalapeno Popper Spread

Prep time:10 mins; Cook time: 3 mins; Serves 8

5 Ingredients:

2 (8 ounce) packages cream cheese, softened; low-carb

1 cup. mayonnaise

1 (4 ounce) can chopped green chilies, drained

2 ounces canned diced jalapeno peppers, drained

1 cup. grated Parmesan cheese

Instructions

1. Combine cream cheese and mayonnaise in a bowl until incorporated. Add in jalapeno peppers and green chilies. In a microwave safe bowl, spread jalapeno peppers mixture and sprinkle with Parmesan cheese.

2. Microwave jalapeno peppers mixture on High about 3 minutes or until warm.

Nutrition Facts

Per Serving: 110 calories; 11.1 g fat; 1 g carbohydrates; 2.1 g protein

Cheese-jalapeno Mushrooms

Prep time: 15 minutes, cook time: 20 minutes; Serves 8

5 Ingredients:

2 slices bacon

1 (3 ounce) package cream cheese, softened; low-carb

3 tablespoons shredded Cheddar cheese

1 jalapeno pepper, ribs and seeds removed, finely chopped

8 mushrooms, stems removed and chopped and caps reserved; keto-friendly

What you'll need from the store cupboard:

Salt and pepper to taste

Cooking spray

Instructions

1. Preheat the oven to 400 degrees F.

2. In a large bowl, combine bacon, cream cheese, cheese, jalapenos, salt and pepper. Mix well.

3. Spoon the bacon filling into each mushroom cap. Then transfer the stuffed mushroom caps to a baking dish or sheet sprayed with cooking spray.

4. Bake until the mushroom caps are cooked, about 15-20 minutes.

5. Serve and enjoy.

Nutrition Facts Per Serving

Per Serving: 151 calories; 13.4 g fat; 2.5 g carbohydrates; 6.1 g protein

Tasty Cream Cheese Stuffed Mushrooms

Prep time: 10 minutes, cook time: 20 minutes; Serves 2

5 Ingredients:

12 mushrooms, keto-friendly

1 (8 ounce) package cream cheese, softened; low-carb

1/4 cup grated Parmesan cheese

1/4 teaspoon ground black pepper

1/4 teaspoon ground cayenne pepper

What you'll need from the store cupboard:

1 tablespoon olive oil

1 tablespoon minced garlic

1/4 teaspoon onion powder

Instructions

1. Preheat oven to 350 degrees F.

2. Clean mushrooms; chop stems and discard the cut ends.

3. Heat oil in a large skillet over medium heat, sauté garlic and chopped stems until crispy. Set aside.

4. In a bowl, combine mushroom mixture with cream cheese, Parmensan cheese, black pepper, onion powder and cayenne pepper, stir well.

5. Scoop the filling into each mushroom cap and transfer to a greased baking sheet.

6. Bake for 20 minutes or until liquid has formed under caps.

Nutrition Facts Per Serving

Per Serving: 88 calories; 8.2 g fat; 1.5 g carbohydrates; 2.7 g protein

Grilled Cheese Bacon Jalapeno

Prep time: 10 minutes, cook time: 40 minutes; Serves 2

5 Ingredients:

8 ounces cream cheese

2 tablespoons grated Parmesan cheese

1 1/2 cups shredded Cheddar cheese

16 whole jalapeno peppers with stems

8 slices bacon, cut in half crosswise

What you'll need from the store cupboard:

Oil spray

1 1/2 teaspoons garlic powder

Instructions

1. Preheat a grill over medium heat and brush grill grates with oil.

2. Combine cream cheese, Parmesan cheese, cheddar cheese and garlic powder in a small bowl, toss well.

3. Cut the jalapeños in half lengthwise. Using a small spoon, scrape out seeds & membranes.

4. Stuff the cheese mixture into the jalapeno halves. Wrap each jalapeno completely with bacon. Secure with toothpicks.

5. Place jalapenos on the grill and grill until cheese mixture is hot and bubbling around the edges, about 30 to 40 minutes.

Nutrition Facts Per Serving

Per Serving: 164 calories; 15 g fat; 1.6 g carbohydrates; 5.8 g protein

Cranberry Sauce Meatballs

Prep time: 10 minutes, cook time: 25 minutes; Serves 2

5 Ingredients:

1 pound lean ground beef

1 egg

2 tablespoons water

1/2 cup cauliflower rice

3 tablespoons minced onion

What you'll need from the store cupboard:

1 (8 ounce) can jellied cranberry sauce, keto-friendly

3/4 cup chili sauce

Instructions

1. Preheat oven to 350 degrees F.

2. Mix the ground beef, egg, water, cauliflower rice and minced onions together until well combined. Form into small meatballs and place on a rack over a foil-lined baking sheet.

3. Bake the meatballs for 20 to 25 minutes, turning halfway through.

4. Combine sauce ingredients in a large saucepan over low heat, toss with meatballs and allow to simmer on low for 1 hour.

5. Serve and garnish with parsley if desired.

Nutrition Facts Per Serving

Per Serving: 193 calories; 10.2 g fat; 8.6 g carbohydrates; 9.8 g protein

Cauliflower Mash

Prep time: 10 minutes, cook time: 10 minutes; Serves 4

5 Ingredients:

1 head of cauliflower

¼ tsp, garlic powder

1 handful of chives, chopped

What you'll need from the store cupboard:

¼ tsp, salt

¼ tsp, ground black pepper

Instructions

1. Bring a pot of water to boil.
2. Chop cauliflower into florets. Place in a pot of boiling water and boil for 5 minutes.
3. Drain well.
4. Place florets in a blender. Add remaining ingredients except for chives and pulse to desired consistency.
5. Transfer to a bowl and toss in chives.
6. Serve and enjoy.

Nutrition Facts Per Serving

Calories: 18; Fat: 0.2g; Carbs: 3.7g; Protein: 1.3g

Coconut Cauliflower Rice

Prep time: 5 minutes, cook time: 15 minutes; Serves 3

5 Ingredients:

1 head cauliflower, grated

½ cup heavy cream

¼ cup butter, melted

3 cloves of garlic, minced

1 onion, chopped

What you'll need from the store cupboard:

Salt and pepper to taste

Instructions

1. Place a nonstick saucepan on high fire and heat cream and butter.
2. Saute onion and garlic for 3 minutes.
3. Stir in grated cauliflower. Season with pepper and salt.
4. Cook until cauliflower is tender, around 5 minutes.
5. Turn off fire and let it set for 5 minutes.
6. Serve and enjoy.

Nutrition Facts Per Serving

Calories: 246; Fat: 23g; Carbs: 9g; Protein: 3g

Keto Enchilada Bake

Prep time: 10 minutes, cook time: 20 minutes; Serves 6

5 Ingredients:

1 package House Foods Organic Extra Firm Tofu

1 cup roma tomatoes, chopped

1 cup shredded cheddar cheese

1 small avocado, pitted and sliced

½ cup sour cream

What you'll need from the store cupboard:

5 tablespoons olive oil

Salt and pepper to taste

Instructions

1. Preheat oven to 350⁰F.
2. Cut tofu into small cubes and sauté with oil and seasoning. Set aside and reserve the oil.
3. Place the tofu in the bottom of a casserole dish.
4. Mix the reserved oil and tomatoes and pour over the tofu.
5. Sprinkle with cheese on top.
6. Bake for 20 minutes.
7. Top with avocado and sour cream toppings.
8. Serve and enjoy.

Nutrition Facts Per Serving

Calories: 568; Fat: 40g; Carbs: 6g; Protein: 38g

Sausage Roll

Prep time: 20 minutes, cook time: 1 hour and 15 minutes; Serves 6

5 Ingredients:

6 vegan sausages (defrosted)

1 cup mushrooms

1 onion

2 fresh sage leaves

1 package tofu skin sheet

What you'll need from the store cupboard:

Salt and pepper to taste

5 tablespoons olive oil

Instructions

1. Preheat the oven to 180°F/356°F assisted.
2. Defrost the vegan sausages.
3. Roughly chop the mushrooms and add them to a food processor. Process until mostly broken down. Peel and roughly chop the onions, then add them to the processor along with the defrosted vegan sausages, sage leaves, and a pinch of salt and pepper. Pour in the oil. Process until all the ingredients have mostly broken down, and only a few larger pieces remain.
4. Heat a frying pan on a medium heat. Once hot, transfer the mushroom mixture to the pan and fry for 20 minutes or until almost all of the moisture has evaporated, frequently stirring to prevent the mixture sticking to the pan.
5. Remove the mushroom mixture from the heat and transfer to a plate. Leave to cool completely. Tip: if it's cold outside, we leave the mushroom mixture outdoors, so it cools quicker.
6. Meanwhile, either line a large baking tray with baking paper or (if the pastry already comes wrapped in a sheet of baking paper) roll out the tofu skin onto the tray and cut it in half both lengthways and widthways to create 4 equal-sized pieces of tofu skin.
7. Spoon a quarter of the mushroom mixture along the length of each rectangle of tofu skin and shape the mixture into a log. Add one vegan sausage and roll into a log.
8. Seal the roll by securing the edged with a toothpick.
9. Brush the sausage rolls with olive oil and bake for 40-45 minutes until golden brown. Enjoy!

Nutrition Facts Per Serving

Calories:113; Fat: 11g; Carbs: 3g; Protein: 0.9g

Grilled Cauliflower

Prep time: 10 minutes, cook time: 20 minutes; Serves 8

5 Ingredients:

1 large head cauliflower

1 teaspoon ground turmeric

1/2 teaspoon crushed red pepper flakes

Lemon juice, additional olive oil, and pomegranate seeds, optional

What you'll need from the store cupboard:

2 tablespoons olive oil

2 tablespoons melted butter

Instructions

1. Remove leaves and trim stem from cauliflower. Cut cauliflower into eight wedges. Mix turmeric and pepper flakes. Brush wedges with oil; sprinkle with turmeric mixture.
2. Grill, covered, over medium-high heat or broil 4 minutes from heat until cauliflower is tender, 8-10 minutes on each side. If desired, drizzle with lemon juice and additional oil. Brush with melted butter and serve with pomegranate seeds.

Nutrition Facts Per Serving

Calories:66; Fat: 6.3g; Carbs: 2.3g; Protein: 0.7g

Garlic and Greens

Prep time: 30 minutes, cook time: 20 minutes; Serves 4

5 Ingredients:

1-pound kale, trimmed and torn (about 20 cups)

1/4 cup chopped oil-packed sun-dried tomatoes

5 garlic cloves, minced

2 tablespoons minced fresh parsley

What you'll need from the store cupboard:

1/4 teaspoon salt

3 tablespoons olive oil

Instructions

1. In a 6-qt. stockpot, bring 1 inch. of water to a boil. Add kale; cook, covered, 10-15 minutes or until tender. Remove with a slotted spoon; discard cooking liquid.
2. In the same pot, heat oil over medium heat. Add tomatoes and garlic; cook and stir 1 minute. Add kale, parsley and salt; heat through, stirring occasionally.

Nutrition Facts Per Serving

Calories: 160; Fat: 13g; Carbs: 9g; Protein: 6g

Garlic Lemon Mushrooms

Prep time: 15 minutes, cook time: 20 minutes Serves 4

5 Ingredients:

1/4 cup lemon juice

3 tablespoons minced fresh parsley

3 garlic cloves, minced

1-pound large fresh mushrooms

4 tablespoons olive oil

What you'll need from the store cupboard:

Pepper to taste

Instructions

1. For the dressing, whisk together the first 5 ingredients. Toss mushrooms with 2 tablespoons dressing.
2. Grill mushrooms, covered, over medium-high heat until tender, 5-7 minutes per side. Toss with remaining dressing before serving.

Nutrition Facts Per Serving

Calories: 160; Fat: 14g; Carbs: 6.8g; Protein: 4g

Roasted Leeks and Asparagus

Prep time: 15 mins, cook time: 25 minutes; Serves 12

5 Ingredients:

3 pounds fresh asparagus, trimmed

2 medium leeks (white portion only), halved lengthwise

1-1/2 teaspoons dill weed

1/2 teaspoon crushed red pepper flakes

3 tablespoons melted butter

What you'll need from the store cupboard:

1/4 teaspoon pepper

1/2 teaspoon salt

4 ½ tablespoons olive oil

Instructions

1. Place asparagus and leeks on an ungreased 15x10x1-inch baking pan. Combine the remaining ingredients; pour over vegetables.
2. Bake at 400⁰F for 20-25 minutes or until tender, stirring occasionally.

Nutrition Facts Per Serving

Calories: 98; Fat: 8g; Carbs: 6g; Protein: 3g

Grilled Spicy Eggplant

Prep time: 20 minutes, cook time: 20 minutes; Serves 2

5 Ingredients:

2 small eggplants, cut into 1/2-inch slices

1/4 cup olive oil

2 tablespoons lime juice

3 teaspoons Cajun seasoning

What you'll need from the store cupboard:

Salt and pepper to taste

Instructions

1. Brush eggplant slices with oil. Drizzle with lime juice; sprinkle with Cajun seasoning. Let stand for 5 minutes.
2. Grill eggplant, covered, over medium heat or broil 4 minutes. from heat until tender, 4-5 minutes per side.
3. Season with pepper and salt to taste.
4. Serve and enjoy.

Nutrition Facts Per Serving
Calories: 350 Fat: 28g; Carbs: 7g; Protein: 5g

Guacamole

Prep time: 10 minutes, cook time: 0 minutes; Serves 2

5 Ingredients:
2 medium ripe avocados
1 tablespoon lemon juice
1/4 cup chopped tomatoes
4 tablespoons olive oil

What you' ll need from the store cupboard:
1/4 teaspoon salt
Pepper to taste

Instructions

1. Peel and chop avocados; place them in a small bowl. Sprinkle with lemon juice.
2. Add tomatoes and salt.
3. Season with pepper to taste and mash coarsely with a fork. Refrigerate until serving.

Nutrition Facts Per Serving
Calories: 565; Fat: 56g; Carbs: 10g; Protein: 6g

Zucchini Garlic Fries

Prep time: 10 minutes, cook time: 25 minutes; Serves 6

5 Ingredients:
¼ teaspoon garlic powder
½ cup almond flour
2 large egg, beaten
3 medium zucchinis, sliced into fry sticks
3 tablespoons olive oil

What you' ll need from the store cupboard:
Salt and pepper to taste

Instructions

1. Preheat oven to 400ºF.
2. Mix all ingredients in a bowl until the zucchini fries are well coated.
3. Place fries on a cookie sheet and spread evenly.
4. Put in the oven and cook for 15 minutes.
5. Stir fries, continue baking for an additional 10 minutes.

Nutrition Facts Per Serving
Calories: 80; Fat: 8g; Carbs: 0.5g; Protein: 2g

Keto Cauliflower Hash Browns

Prep time: 10 mins; Cook time: 30 mins; Serves 4

5 Ingredients:
1 lb cauliflower
3 eggs
½ yellow onion, grated
2 pinches pepper
4 oz. butter, for frying

What you'll need from the store cupboard:
1 tsp salt

Instructions

1. Rinse, trim and grate the cauliflower using a food processor or grater.
2. In a large bowl, add the cauliflower onion and pepper, tossing evenly. Set aside for 5 to 10 minutes.
3. In a large skillet over medium heat, heat a generous amount of butter on medium heat. The cooking process will go quicker if you plan to have room for 3 – 4 pancakes (about 3 to 4 inches each) at a time. Use the oven on low heat to keep the first batches of pancakes warm while you make the others.

4. Place scoops of the grated cauliflower mixture in the frying pan and flatten them carefully until they measure about 3 to 4 inches in diameter.

5. Fry for 4 to 5 minutes on each side. Adjust the heat to make sure they don't burn. Serve.

Nutrition Facts Per Serving

Per Serving: 282 calories; 26 g fat; 5 g carbohydrates; 7 g protein

Herb Butter with Parsley

Prep time: 15 mins; Cook time: 0 minutes; Serves 1

5 Ingredients:

5 oz. butter, at room temperature
1 garlic clove, pressed
½ tbsp garlic powder
4 tbsp fresh parsley, finely chopped
1 tsp lemon juice

What you'll need from the store cupboard:

½ tsp salt

Instructions

1. In a bowl, stir all ingredients until completely combined. Set aside for 15 minutes or refrigerate it before serving.

Nutrition Facts Per Serving

Per Serving: 258 calories; 28 g fat; 1 g carbohydrates; 1g protein

Lemon Grilled Veggie

Prep time: 10 mins; Cook time: 20 minutes; Serves 4

5 Ingredients:

2/3 eggplant
1 zucchini
10 oz. cheddar cheese
20 black olives
2 oz. leafy greens

What you'll need from the store cupboard:

½ cup olive oil
1 lemon, the juice
1 cup mayonnaise
4 tbsp almonds
Salt and pepper

Instructions

1. Cut eggplant and zucchini lengthwise into half inch-thick slices. Season with salt to coat evenly. Set aside for 5-10 minutes.

2. Preheat the oven to 450 degrees F.

3. Pat zucchini and eggplant slices' surface dry with a kitchen towel.

4. Line a baking sheet with parchment paper and place slices on it. Spray with olive oil on top and season with pepper.

5. Bake for 15-20 minutes or until cooked through, flipping halfway.

6. Once done, transfer to a serving platter. Drizzle olive oil and lemon juice on top.

7. Serve with cheese cubes, almonds, olives, mayonnaise and leafy greens.

Nutrition Facts Per Serving

Per Serving: 1013 calories; 99 g fat; 9 g carbohydrates; 21 g protein

Chapter-8 | 5-Ingredient Salad Recipes

Green Salad

Prep time: 15 minutes, cook time: 30 minutes; Serves 4

5 Ingredients:
2 cups green beans, chopped
2 cups shredded spinach
½ cup parmesan cheese
3 cups basil leaves
3 cloves of garlic

What you'll need from the store cupboard:
Salt to taste
¼ cup olive oil

Instructions
1. Heat a little olive oil in a skillet over medium heat and add the green beans and season with salt to taste. Sauté for 3 to 5 minutes.
2. Place the green beans in a bowl and add in the spinach.
3. In a food processor, combine half of the parmesan cheese, basil, and garlic. Add in the rest of the oil and season with salt and pepper to taste.
4. Pour into the green beans and toss to coat the ingredients.

Nutrition Facts Per Serving
Calories: 196; Fat: 17g; Carbs: 6g; Protein: 5g

Watermelon and Cucumber Salad

Prep time: 10 minutes, cook time: 0 minutes; Serves 10

5 Ingredients:
½ large watermelon, diced
1 cucumber, peeled and diced
1 red onion, chopped
¼ cup feta cheese
½ cup heavy cream

What you'll need from the store cupboard:
Salt to taste

5 tbsp MCT or coconut oil

Instructions
1. Place all ingredients in a bowl.
2. Toss everything to coat.
3. Place in the fridge to cool before serving.

Nutrition Facts Per Serving
Calories: 910; Fat:100g; Carbs: 2.5g; Protein: 0.9g

Pesto Arugula Salad

Prep time: 5 minutes, cook time: 10 minutes; Serves 4

5 Ingredients:
¾ cup red peppers, seeded and chopped
¾ cup commercial basil pesto
1 small mozzarella cheese ball, diced
3 handfuls of arugulas, washed

What you'll need from the store cupboard:
Salt and pepper to taste
5 tablespoons olive oil

Instructions
1. Mix all ingredients in a salad bowl and toss to coat.
2. Season with salt and pepper to taste.

Nutrition Facts Per Serving
Calories: 214; Fat: 20g; Carbs: 2.8g; Protein: 6.7g

Strawberry, Cucumber, And Mozzarella Salad

Prep time: 10 minutes, cook time: 10 minutes; Serves 3

5 Ingredients:
5 ounces organic salad greens of your choice
2 medium cucumber, spiralized
2 cups strawberries, hulled and chopped
8 ounces mini mozzarella cheese balls

½ cup balsamic vinegar

What you'll need from the store cupboard:
5 tablespoons olive oil
Salt to taste

Instructions
1. Toss all ingredients in a salad bowl.
2. Allow chilling in the fridge for at least 10 minutes before serving.

Nutrition Facts Per Serving
Calories: 351; Fat: 31g; Carbs: 10g; Protein: 7g

Citrusy Brussels Sprouts Salad

Prep time: 15 minutes, cook time: 3 minutes; Serves 6
5 Ingredients:
2 tablespoons olive oil
¾ pound Brussels sprouts
1 cup walnuts
Juice from 1 lemon
½ cup grated parmesan cheese
What you'll need from the store cupboard:
Salt and pepper to taste
Instructions

1. Heat oil in a skillet over medium flame and sauté the Brussels sprouts for 3 minutes until slightly wilted. Removed from heat and allow to cool.
2. In a bowl, toss together the cooled Brussels sprouts and the rest of the ingredients.
3. Toss to coat.

Nutrition Facts Per Serving
Calories: 259; Fat: 23g; Carbs: 8g; Protein: 6g

Crunchy and Salty Cucumber Salad

Prep time: 10 minutes, cook time: 0 minutes; Serves 4
5 Ingredients:
2 Persian cucumbers, sliced thinly
1 medium radish, trimmed and sliced thinly
Juice from 1 lemon
½ cup parmesan cheese, shredded
What you'll need from the store cupboard:
A dash of flaky sea salt
A dash of ground black pepper
5 tablespoons olive oil
Instructions

1. Place all vegetables in a bowl.
2. Stir in the lemon juice and parmesan cheese.
3. Season with salt and pepper to taste
4. Add olive oil or salad oil.
5. Toss to mix everything.

Nutrition Facts Per Serving
Calories: 209; Fat:20. 4g; Carbs: 3.7g; Protein: 3.8g

Celery Salad

Prep time: 5 minutes, cook time: 0 minutes; Serves 4
5 Ingredients:
3 cups celery, thinly sliced
½ cup parmigiana cheese, shaved
1/3 cup toasted walnuts
4 tablespoons extra virgin olive oil
1 tablespoon red wine vinegar
What you'll need from the store cupboard:
Salt and pepper to taste
Instructions

1. Place the celery, cheese, and walnuts in a bowl.
2. In a smaller bowl, combine the olive oil and vinegar. Season with salt and pepper to taste. Whisk to combine everything.
3. Drizzle over the celery, cheese, and walnuts. Toss to coat.

Nutrition Facts Per Serving
Calories: 156; Fat: 14g; Carbs: 3.6g; Protein: 4.3

Easy Tomato Salad

Prep time: 5 minutes, cook time: 0 minutes; Serves 4

5 Ingredients:

1 ½ cups cherry tomatoes, sliced
¼ cup white wine vinegar
1/8 cup chives
3 tablespoons olive oil

What you'll need from the store cupboard:

Salt and pepper to taste

Instructions

1. Put all ingredients in a bowl.
2. Toss to combine.
3. Serve immediately.

Nutrition Facts Per Serving

Calories: 95; Fat: 10.1g; Carbs: 0.6g; Protein: 0.03g

Asparagus Niçoise Salad

Prep time: 20 minutes, cook time: 0 minutes; Serves 4

5 Ingredients:

1-pound fresh asparagus, trimmed and blanched
2 ½ ounces white tuna in oil
½ cup pitted Greek olives, halved
½ cup zesty Italian salad dressing

What you'll need from the store cupboard:

Salt and pepper to taste

3 tablespoons olive oil

Instructions

1. Place all ingredients in a bowl.
2. Toss to mix all ingredients.
3. Serve.

Nutrition Facts Per Serving

Calories: 239; Fat:20g; Carbs: 10g; Protein: 8g

Bacon and Pea Salad

Prep time: 10 minutes, cook time: 5 minutes; Serves 6

5 Ingredients:

4 bacon strips
2 cups fresh peas
½ cup shredded cheddar cheese
½ cup ranch salad dressing
1/3 cup chopped red onions

What you'll need from the store cupboard:

Salt and pepper to taste
3 tablespoons olive oil

Instructions

1. Heat skillet over medium flame and fry the bacon until crispy or until the fat has rendered. Transfer into a plate lined with a paper towel and crumble.
2. In a bowl, combine the rest of the ingredients and toss to coat.
3. Add in the bacon bits last.

Nutrition Facts Per Serving

Calories: 205; Fat: 20.4g; Carbs: 2.9g; Protein:3.5g

Insalata Caprese

Prep time: 10 minutes, cook time: 0 minutes; Serves 8

5 Ingredients:

2 ½ pounds tomatoes, cut into 1-in pieces
8 ounces mozzarella cheese pearls
½ cup ripe olives, pitted
¼ cup fresh basil, sliced thinly
Balsamic vinegar (optional)

What you'll need from the store cupboard:

Salt and pepper to taste
3 tablespoons olive oil

Instructions

1. Place all ingredients in a bowl.
2. Season with salt and pepper to taste. Drizzle with balsamic vinegar if available.
3. Toss to coat.
4. Serve immediately.

Nutrition Facts Per Serving

Calories: 160; Fat: 12g; Carbs: 7g; Protein: 6g

Salmon Salad with Walnuts

Prep time: 10 minutes, cook time: 10 minutes; Serves 2

5 Ingredients:

2 salmon fillets

2 tablespoons balsamic vinaigrette, divided

1/8 teaspoon pepper

2 cups mixed salad greens

1/4 cup walnuts

What you'll need from the store cupboard:

2 tablespoons crumbled cheese

Salt and pepper to taste

3 tablespoons olive oil

Instructions

1. Brush the salmon with half of the balsamic vinaigrette and sprinkle with pepper.
2. Grill the salmon over medium heat for 5 minutes on each side.
3. Crumble the salmon and place in a mixing bowl. Add the rest of the ingredients and season with salt and pepper to taste.

Nutrition Facts Per Serving

Calories: 313; Fat: 30g; Carbs: 8g; Protein: 5g

Balsamic Cucumber Salad

Prep time: 10 minutes, cook time: 0 minutes; Serves 6

5 Ingredients:

1 large English cucumber, halved and sliced

1 cup grape tomatoes, halved

1 medium red onion, sliced thinly

¼ cup balsamic vinaigrette

¾ cup feta cheese

What you'll need from the store cupboard:

Salt and pepper to taste

¼ cup olive oil

Instructions

1. Place all ingredients in a bowl.
2. Toss to coat everything with the dressing.
3. Allow chilling before serving.

Nutrition Facts Per Serving

Calories: 253; Fat: 16.7g; Carbs:9g; Protein: 4.8g

Kale And Brussels Sprouts Salad

Prep time: 10 minutes, cook time: 0 minutes; Serves 6

5 Ingredients:

1 small bunch kale, thinly sliced

½ pound fresh Brussels sprouts, thinly sliced

½ cup pistachios, chopped coarsely

½ cup honey mustard salad dressing

¼ cup parmesan cheese, shredded

What you'll need from the store cupboard:

Salt and pepper to taste

Instructions

1. Place all ingredients in a salad bowl.
2. Toss to coat everything.
3. Serve.

Nutrition Facts Per Serving

Calories: 198; Fat:15g; Carbs: 9g; Protein: 5g

Sour Cream and Cucumbers

Prep time: 15 minutes, cook time: 0 minutes; Serves 8

5 Ingredients:

½ cup sour cream

3 tablespoons white vinegar

4 medium cucumbers, sliced thinly

1 small sweet onion, sliced thinly

What you'll need from the store cupboard:

Salt and pepper to taste

3 tablespoons olive oil

Instructions

1. In a bowl, whisk the sour cream and vinegar. Season with salt and pepper to taste. Whisk until well-combined.
2. Add in the cucumber and the rest of the ingredients.
3. Toss to coat.
4. Allow chilling before serving.

Nutrition Facts Per Serving

Calories: 96; Fat: 8.3g; Carbs: 4.8g; Protein:0.9g

Minty Watermelon Cucumber Salad

Prep time: 10 minutes, cook time: 0 minutes; Serves 12

5 Ingredients:

8 cups cubed seedless watermelon
2 English cucumbers, halved and sliced
¼ cup minced fresh mint
¼ cup balsamic vinegar
¼ cup olive oil

What you' ll need from the store cupboard:

Salt and pepper to taste

Instructions

1. Place everything in a bowl and toss to coat everything.
2. Allow chilling before serving.

Nutrition Facts Per Serving

Calories: 95; Fat: 8.1g; Carbs: 4g; Protein: 0.5g

Pesto Tomato Cucumber Salad

Prep time: 10 minutes, cook time: 0 minutes; Serves 8

5 Ingredients:

½ cup Italian salad dressing
¼ cup prepared pesto
3 large tomatoes, sliced
2 medium cucumbers, halved and sliced
1 small red onion, sliced

What you' ll need from the store cupboard:

Salt and pepper to taste
3 tablespoons olive oil

Instructions

1. In a bowl, whisk the salad dressing and pesto. Season with salt and pepper to taste.
2. Toss gently to incorporate everything.
3. Refrigerate before serving.

Nutrition Facts Per Serving

Calories:128; Fat: 12g; Carbs: 3.7g; Protein: 1.08g

Bacon Tomato Salad

Prep time: 15 minutes, cook time: 0 minutes; Serves 6

5 Ingredients:

6 ounces iceberg lettuce blend
2 cups grape tomatoes, halved
¾ cup coleslaw salad dressing
¾ cup cheddar cheese, shredded
12 bacon strips, cooked and crumbled

What you' ll need from the store cupboard:

Salt and pepper to taste

Instructions

1. Put the lettuce and tomatoes in a salad bowl.
2. Drizzle with the dressing and sprinkle with cheese. Season with salt and pepper to taste then mix.
3. Garnish with bacon bits on top.

Nutrition Facts Per Serving

Calories: 268; Fat: 20g; Carbs: 8g; Protein: 10g

Strawberry Lemon Salad

Prep time: 20 mins; Cook time: 0 mins; Serves 6

5 Ingredients:

1 cup lemon yogurt
1 tablespoon stevia
2 cups halved fresh strawberries

What you'll need from the store cupboard:

1 teaspoon lemon juice

Instructions

1. In a medium bowl, toss together the lemon yogurt, stevia, and lemon juice until well combined; add in strawberries, stir until coat evenly. Serve and enjoy.

Nutrition Facts Per Serving

Per Serving: 112 calories; 13 g fat; 6 g carbohydrates; 8 g protein

Fruit Salad with Lemon Poppy seeds

Prep time: 25 mins; Cook time: 25 mins; Serves 5

5 Ingredients:

1 tablespoon poppy seeds

1 head romaine lettuce, torn into bite-size pieces

4 ounces shredded Swiss cheese

1 avocado- peeled, cored and diced

2 teaspoons diced onion

What you'll need from the store cupboard:

1/2 cup lemon juice

1/2 cup stevia

1/2 teaspoon salt

2/3 cup olive oil

1 teaspoon Dijon style prepared mustard

Instructions

1. Combine stevia, lemon juice, onion, mustard, and salt in a blender. Process until well blended.

2. Add oil until mixture is thick and smooth. Add poppy seeds, stir just a few seconds or more to mix.

3. In a large serving bowl, toss together the remaining ingredients.

4. Pour dressing over salad just before serving, and toss to coat.

Nutrition Facts Per Serving

Per Serving: 277 calories; 20.6 g fat; 6 g carbohydrates; 4.9 g protein

Mayo Bacon Broccoli Salad

Prep time: 15mins; Cook time: 15 mins; Serves 6

5 Ingredients

10 slices bacon

1 head fresh broccoli, cut into bite size pieces

1/2 cup red onion, chopped

1/2 cup almond, chopped

1 cup sunflower seeds

What you'll need from the store cupboard:

1 cup mayonnaise

2 tablespoons stevia

3 tablespoons white wine vinegar

Instructions

1. In a heavy-bottomed skillet over medium-high heat, brown the bacon evenly.

Drain, crumble and place on a plate.

2. Mix the broccoli, onion and almond in a bowl, stir together the vinegar, stevia and mayonnaise in an another bowl. Combine with broccoli mixture until mixed thoroughly. Refrigerate for at least 2 hours to marinate.

3. Sprinkle crumbled bacon and seeds over salad before you serve.

Nutrition Facts Per Serving

Per Serving: 395 calories; 24 g total fat; 7 g carbohydrates; 12.9 g protein

Spinach Fruit Salad with Seeds

Prep time: 10 mins; Cook time: 1 hour 10 minutes; Serves 4

5 Ingredients:

2 tablespoons sesame seeds

1 tablespoon poppy seeds

1 tablespoon minced onion

10 ounces fresh spinach - rinsed, dried and torn into bite-size pieces

1 quart strawberries - cleaned, hulled and sliced

What you'll need from the store cupboard:

1/2 cup stevia

1/2 cup olive oil

1/4 cup distilled white vinegar

1/4 teaspoon Worcestershire sauce

1/4 teaspoon paprika

Instructions

1. Mix together the spinach and strawberry in a large bowl, stir in the sesame seeds, poppy seeds, stevia, olive oil, vinegar, paprika, Worcestershire sauce and onion in a medium bowl. Cover and cool for 1 hour.

2. Pour dressing over salad to combine well. Serve immediately or refrigerate for 15 minutes.

Nutrition Facts Per Serving

Per Serving: 220 calories; 18 g fat; 8.6 g carbohydrates; 6 g protein

Butternut Squash and Cauliflower Stew

Prep time:5 minutes, cook time:10 minutes; Serves 4

5 Ingredients:

3 cloves of garlic, minced
1 cup cauliflower florets
1 ½ cups butternut squash, cubed
2 ½ cups heavy cream

What you'll need from the store cupboard:

Pepper and salt to taste
3 tbsp coconut oil

Instructions

1. Heat the oil in a pan and saute the garlic until fragrant.
2. Stir in the rest of the ingredients and season with salt and pepper to taste.
3. Close the lid and bring to a boil for 10 minutes.
4. Serve and enjoy.

Nutrition Facts Per Serving

Calories: 385; Fat: 38.1g; Carbs: 10g; Protein:2g

Provolone Over Herbed Portobello Mushrooms

Prep time: 10 minutes, cook time: 10 minutes; Serves 2

5 Ingredients:

2 Portobello mushrooms, stemmed and wiped clean
1 tsp minced garlic
¼ tsp dried rosemary
1 tablespoon balsamic vinegar
¼ cup grated provolone cheese

What you'll need from the store cupboard:

4 tablespoons olive oil
Salt and pepper to taste

Instructions

1. In an oven, position rack 4-inches away from the top and preheat broiler.
2. Prepare a baking dish by spraying with cooking spray lightly.
3. Stemless, place mushroom gill side up.
4. Mix well garlic, rosemary, balsamic vinegar, and olive oil in a small bowl. Season with salt and pepper to taste.
5. Drizzle over mushrooms equally.
6. Marinate for at least 5 minutes before popping into the oven and broiling for 4 minutes per side or until tender.
7. Once cooked, remove from oven, sprinkle cheese, return to broiler and broil for a minute or two or until cheese melts.
8. Remove from oven and serve right away.

Nutrition Facts Per Serving

Calories: 168; Fat: 5.1g; Carbs: 21.5g; Protein: 8.6g

Greek Styled Veggie-Rice

Prep time: 15 minutes, cook time: 20 minutes; Serves 3

5 Ingredients:

3 tbsp chopped fresh mint
1 small tomato, chopped
1 head cauliflower, cut into large florets
¼ cup fresh lemon juice
½ yellow onion, minced

What you'll need from the store cupboard:

pepper and salt to taste
¼ cup extra virgin olive oil

Instructions

1. In a bowl, mix lemon juice and onion and leave for 30 minutes. Then drain onion and reserve the juice and onion bits.
2. In a blender, shred cauliflower until the size of a grain of rice.
3. On medium fire, place a medium nonstick skillet and for 8-10 minutes cook cauliflower while covered.
4. Add grape tomatoes and cook for 3 minutes while stirring occasionally.

5. Add mint and onion bits. Cook for another three minutes.
6. Meanwhile, in a small bowl whisk pepper, salt, 3 tbsp reserved lemon juice, and olive oil until well blended.
7. Remove cooked cauliflower, transfer to a serving bowl, pour lemon juice mixture, and toss to mix.
8. Before serving, if needed season with pepper and salt to taste.

Nutrition Facts Per Serving
Calories: 120; Fat: 9.5g; Carbs: 4.0g; Protein: 2.3g

Garlic 'n Sour Cream Zucchini Bake

Prep time: 10 minutes, cook time: 35 minutes; Serves 3
5 Ingredients:
1 ½ cups zucchini slices
5 tablespoons olive oil
1 tablespoon minced garlic
1/4 cup grated Parmesan cheese
1 (8 ounces) package cream cheese, softened
What you'll need from the store cupboard:
Salt and pepper to taste
Instructions
1. Lightly grease a baking sheet with cooking spray.
2. Place zucchini in a bowl and put in olive oil and garlic.
3. Place zucchini slices in a single layer in dish.
4. Bake for 35 minutes at 390°F until crispy.
5. In a bowl, whisk well, remaining ingredients.
6. Serve with zucchini

Nutrition Facts Per Serving
Calories: 385; Fat: 32.4g; Carbs: 9.5g; Protein: 11.9g

Paprika 'n Cajun Seasoned Onion Rings

Prep time: 15 minutes, cook time: 25 minutes; Serves 6
5 Ingredients:
1 large white onion
2 large eggs, beaten
½ teaspoon Cajun seasoning
¾ cup almond flour
1 ½ teaspoon paprika
What you'll need from the store cupboard:
½ cups coconut oil for frying
¼ cup water
Salt and pepper to taste
Instructions
1. Preheat a pot with oil for 8 minutes.
2. Peel the onion, cut off the top and slice into circles.
3. In a mixing bowl, combine the water and the eggs. Season with pepper and salt.
4. Soak the onion in the egg mixture.
5. In another bowl, combine the almond flour, paprika powder, Cajun seasoning, salt and pepper.
6. Dredge the onion in the almond flour mixture.
7. Place in the pot and cook in batches until golden brown, around 8 minutes per batch.

Nutrition Facts Per Serving
Calories: 262; Fat: 24.1g; Carbs: 3.9g; Protein: 2.8g

Creamy Kale and Mushrooms

Prep time: 10 minutes, cook time: 15 minutes; Serves 3
5 Ingredients:
3 cloves of garlic, minced
1 onion, chopped
1 bunch kale, stems removed and leaves chopped
3 white button mushrooms, chopped
1 cup heavy cream
What you'll need from the store cupboard:
5 tablespoons oil

Salt and pepper to taste

Instructions

1. Heat oil in a pot.
2. Sauté the garlic and onion until fragrant for 2 minutes.
3. Stir in mushrooms. Season with pepper and salt. Cook for 8 minutes.
4. Stir in kale and coconut milk. Simmer for 5 minutes.
5. Adjust seasoning to taste.

Nutrition Facts Per Serving

Calories: 365; Fat: 35.5g; Carbs: 7.9g; Protein: 6.0g

Stir-Fried Buttery Mushrooms

Prep time: 15 minutes, cook time: 15 minutes; Serves 4

5 Ingredients:

4 tablespoons butter
3 cloves of garlic, minced
6 ounces fresh brown mushrooms, sliced
7 ounces fresh shiitake mushrooms, sliced
A dash of thyme

What you'll need from the store cupboard:

2 tablespoons olive oil
Salt and pepper to taste

Instructions

1. Heat the butter and oil in a pot.
2. Sauté the garlic until fragrant, around 2 minutes.
3. Stir in the rest of the ingredients and cook until soft, around 13 minutes.

Nutrition Facts Per Serving

Calories: 231; Fat: 17.5g; Carbs: 8.7g; Protein: 3.8g

Stir Fried Bok Choy

Prep time: 10 minutes, cook time: 15 minutes; Serves 4

5 Ingredients:

4 cloves of garlic, minced
1 onion, chopped
2 heads bok choy, rinsed and chopped
2 tablespoons sesame oil
2 tablespoons sesame seeds, toasted

What you'll need from the store cupboard:

3 tablespoons oil
Salt and pepper to taste

Instructions

1. Heat the oil in a pot for 2 minutes.
2. Sauté the garlic and onions until fragrant, around 3 minutes.
3. Stir in the bok choy, salt, and pepper.
4. Cover pan and cook for 5 minutes.
5. Stir and continue cooking for another 3 minutes.
6. Drizzle with sesame oil and sesame seeds on top before serving.

Nutrition Facts Per Serving

Calories: 358; Fat: 28.4g; Carbs: 5.2g; Protein: 21.5g

Cauliflower Fritters

Prep time: 20 minutes, cook time: 15 minutes; Serves 6

5 Ingredients:

1 large cauliflower head, cut into florets
2 eggs, beaten
½ teaspoon turmeric
1 large onion, peeled and chopped

What you'll need from the store cupboard:

½ teaspoon salt
¼ teaspoon black pepper
6 tablespoons oil

Instructions

1. Place the cauliflower florets in a pot with water.
2. Bring to a boil and drain once cooked.
3. Place the cauliflower, eggs, onion, turmeric, salt, and pepper into the food processor.
4. Pulse until the mixture becomes coarse.
5. Transfer into a bowl. Using your hands, form six small flattened balls and place

in the fridge for at least 1 hour until the mixture hardens.
6. Heat the oil in a skillet and fry the cauliflower patties for 3 minutes on each side.

7. Serve and enjoy.
Nutrition Facts Per Serving
Calories: 157; Fat: 15.3g; Carbs: 2.28g; Protein: 3.9g

Scrambled Eggs with Mushrooms and Spinach

Prep time: 3 minutes, cook time: 15 minutes; Serves 2
5 Ingredients:
2 large eggs
1 teaspoon butter
1/2 cup thinly sliced fresh mushrooms
1/2 cup fresh baby spinach, chopped
2 tablespoons shredded provolone cheese
What you' ll need from the store cupboard:
1/8 teaspoon salt
1/8 teaspoon pepper
Instructions
1. In a small bowl, whisk eggs, salt, and pepper until blended. In a small nonstick

skillet, heat butter over medium-high heat. Add mushrooms; cook and stir 3-4 minutes or until tender. Add spinach; cook and stir until wilted. Reduce heat to medium.
2. Add egg mixture; cook and stir just until eggs are thickened and no liquid egg remains. Stir in cheese.
Nutrition Facts Per Serving
Calories: 162; Fat: 11g; Carbs: 2g; Protein: 14g

Endives Mix with Lemon Dressing

Prep time: 15 minutes, cook time: 0 minutes; Serves 8
5 Ingredients:
1 bunch watercress (4 ounces)
2 heads endive, halved lengthwise and thinly sliced
1 cup pomegranate seeds (about 1 pomegranate)
1 shallot, thinly sliced
2 lemons, juiced and zested
What you' ll need from the store cupboard:
1/4 teaspoon salt

1/8 teaspoon pepper
1/4 cup olive oil
Instructions
1. In a large bowl, combine watercress, endive, pomegranate seeds, and shallot.
2. In a small bowl, whisk the lemon juice, zest, salt, pepper, and olive oil. Drizzle over salad; toss to coat.
Nutrition Facts Per Serving
Calories: 151; Fat:13g; Carbs: 6g; Protein: 2g

Egg and Tomato Salad

Prep time: 20 minutes, cook time: 1 minute; Serves 2
5 Ingredients:
4 hard-boiled eggs, peeled and sliced
2 red tomatoes, chopped
1 small red onion, chopped
2 tablespoons lemon juice, freshly squeezed
What you' ll need from the store cupboard:
Salt and pepper to taste
4 tablespoons olive oil

Instructions
1. Place all ingredients in a mixing bowl.
2. Toss to coat all ingredients.
3. Garnish with parsley if desired.
4. Serve over toasted whole wheat bread.
Nutrition Facts Per Serving
Calories: 189; Fat: 15.9g; Carbs: 9.1g; Protein: 14.7g

Grilled Parmesan Eggplant

Prep time: 5 minutes, cook time: 15 minutes; Serves 4

5 Ingredients:

1 medium-sized eggplant

1 log (1 pound) fresh mozzarella cheese, cut into sixteen slices

1 small tomato, cut into eight slices

1/2 cup shredded Parmesan cheese

Chopped fresh basil or parsley

What you'll need from the store cupboard:

1/2 teaspoon salt

1 tablespoon olive oil

1/2 teaspoon pepper

Instructions

1. Trim ends of the eggplant; cut eggplant crosswise into eight slices. Sprinkle with salt; let stand 5 minutes.

2. Blot eggplant dry with paper towels; brush both sides with oil and sprinkle with pepper. Grill, covered, over medium heat 4-6 minutes on each side or until tender. Remove from grill.

3. Top eggplant with mozzarella cheese, tomato, and Parmesan cheese. Grill, covered, 1-2 minutes longer or until cheese begins to melt. Top with basil.

Nutrition Facts Per Serving

Calories: 449; Fat: 31g; Carbs: 10g; Protein: 26g

Creamy Artichoke and Spinach

Prep time: 5 minutes, cook time: 15 minutes; Serves 4

5 Ingredients:

5 tablespoons olive oil

1 can (8 ounces) water-packed artichoke hearts quartered

1 package (3 ounces) frozen spinach

1 cup shredded part-skim mozzarella cheese, divided

1/4 cup grated Parmesan cheese

What you'll need from the store cupboard:

1/2 teaspoon salt

1/4 teaspoon pepper

Instructions

1. Heat oil in a pan over medium flame. Add artichoke hearts and season with salt and pepper to taste. Cook for 5 minutes. Stir in the spinach until wilted.

2. Place in a bowl and stir in mozzarella cheese, Parmesan cheese, salt, and pepper. Toss to combine.

3. Transfer to a greased 2-qt. Broiler-safe baking dish; sprinkle with remaining mozzarella cheese. Broil 4-6 in. from heat 2-3 minutes or until cheese is melted.

Nutrition Facts Per Serving

Calories: 283; Fat: 23.9g; Carbs: 7.3g; Protein: 11.5g

Curried Tofu

Prep time: 5 minutes, cook time: 15 minutes; Serves 6

5 Ingredients:

2 cloves of garlic, minced

1 onion, cubed

12-ounce firm tofu, drained and cubed

1 teaspoon curry powder

1 tablespoon soy sauce

What you'll need from the store cupboard:

¼ teaspoon pepper

5 tablespoons olive oil

Instructions

1. Heat the oil in a skillet over medium flame.

2. Sauté the garlic and onion until fragrant.

3. Stir in the tofu and stir for 3 minutes.

4. Add the rest of the ingredients and adjust the water.

5. Close the lid and allow simmering for 10 minutes.

6. Serve and enjoy.

Nutrition Facts Per Serving

Calories: 148; Fat: 14.1g; Carbs: 4.4g; Protein: 6.2g

Strawberry Mug Cake

Prep time: 5 mins; Cook time: 3 mins; Serves 8

5 Ingredients:

2 slices fresh strawberry

1 teaspoon chia seeds

1 teaspoon poppy seeds

What you'll need from the store cupboard:

1/4 teaspoon baking powder

3 leaves fresh mint

2 tablespoons cream of coconut

Instructions

1. Add all the ingredients together in a mug, stir until finely combined.

2. Cook in microwave at full power for 3 minutes then allow to cool before you serve.

Nutrition Facts

Per Serving: 196 calories; 12 g fat; 4.7 g carbohydrates; 2.4 g protein

Zucchini Noodles

Prep time: 10 mins; Cook time: 15 mins; Serves 6

5 Ingredients:

2 cloves garlic, minced

2 medium zucchini, cut into noodles with a spiralizer

12 zucchini blossoms, pistils removed; cut into strips

6 fresh basil leaves, cut into strips, or to taste

What you'll need from the store cupboard:

4 tablespoons olive oil

Salt to taste

Instructions

1. In a large skillet over low heat, cook garlic in olive oil for 10 minutes until slightly browned. Add in zucchini and zucchini blossoms, stir well.

2. Toss in green beans and season with salt to taste; sprinkle with basil and serve.

Nutrition Facts Per Serving

Per Serving: 348 calories; 28.1 g fat; 13.5 g carbohydrates; 5.7 g protein

Grated Cauliflower with Seasoned Mayo

Prep time: 10 mins; Cook time: 15 mins; Serves 2

5 Ingredients:

1 lb grated cauliflower
3 oz. butter
4 eggs
3 oz. pimientos de padron or poblano peppers
½ cup mayonnaise

What you'll need from the store cupboard:

1 tsp olive oil
Salt and pepper
1 tsp garlic powder (optional)

Instructions

1. In a bowl, whisk together the mayonnaise and garlic and set aside.

2. Rinse, trim and grate the cauliflower using a food processor or grater.

3. Melt a generous amount of butter and fry grated cauliflower for about 5 minutes. Season salt and pepper to taste.

4. Fry poblanos with oil until lightly crispy. Then fry eggs as you want and sprinkle salt and pepper over them.

5. Serve with poblanos and cauliflower. Drizzle some mayo mixture on top.

Nutrition Facts Per Serving

Per Serving: 898 calories; 87g fat; 9g g carbohydrates; 17g protein

Cilantro-lime Guacamole

Prep time: 10 mins; Cook time: 10 minutes; Serves 4

5 Ingredients:

3 avocados, peeled, pitted, and mashed
1 lime, juiced
1/2 cup diced onion
3 tablespoons chopped fresh cilantro
2 Roma (plum) tomatoes, diced

What you'll need from the store cupboard:

1 teaspoon salt
1 teaspoon minced garlic
1 pinch ground cayenne pepper (optional)
1 teaspoon minced garlic

Instructions

1. In a mixing bowl, mash the avocados with a fork. Sprinkle with salt and lime juice.

2. Stir together diced onion, tomatoes, cilantro, pepper and garlic.

3. Serve immediately, or refrigerate until ready to serve.

Nutrition Facts Per Serving

Per Serving: 362 calories; 22.2 g fat; 8 g carbohydrates; 19 g protein

Chili Cheese Taco Dip

Prep time: 10 minutes, cook time: 45 minutes; Serves 16

5 Ingredients:

1-pound ground beef
1-pound mild Mexican cheese, grated
1 can tomato salsa
1 packet Mexican spice blend
1 can tomato sauce

What you' ll need from the store cupboard:

Salt and pepper to taste
1 cup water

Instructions

1. Heat a heavy-bottomed pot on medium heat and sauté the ground beef until browned, around 10 minutes. Season with pepper and salt.

2. Add tomato salsa, Mexican spice blend, and tomato sauce. Bring to a boil, lower fire to a simmer, and simmer for 25 minutes.

3. Stir in half of the cheese and mix well. Continue simmering until well-combined, around 10 minutes more.

4. Sprinkle remaining cheese on top and serve.

Nutrition Facts Per Serving

Calories: 160; Fat: 11.3g; Carbs: 1.6g; Protein: 12.4g

Buffalo Sauce

Prep time: 10 minutes, cook time: 30 minutes; Serves 8

5 Ingredients:

8 ounces Cream Cheese (softened)
½ cup Buffalo Wing Sauce
½ cup Blue Cheese Dressing
1 ½ cups Cheddar Cheese (Shredded)
1 ¼ cups Chicken Breast (Cooked)

What you' ll need from the store cupboard:

None

Instructions

1. Preheat oven to 350ºF.

2. Blend together buffalo sauce, white salad dressing, cream cheese, chicken, and shredded cheese.

3. Top with any other optional ingredients like blue cheese chunks.

4. Bake for 25-30 minutes

Nutrition Facts Per Serving

Calories: 325; Fat: 28g; Carbs: 2.2g; Protein: 16g

Artichoke Pesto Dip

Prep time: 15 minutes, cook time: 20 minutes; Serves 1

5 Ingredients:

1 (15oz) jar marinated artichoke hearts
8 ounces cream cheese (at room temperature)
4 ounces parmesan cheese (grated)
2 tablespoons basil pesto
¼ cup shelled pistachio (chopped, optional)

What you' ll need from the store cupboard:

None

Instructions

1. Preheat oven to 375ºF.
2. Drain and chop artichoke hearts.
3. Mix artichokes, cream cheese, parmesan, and pesto.
4. Pour into 4 ramekins evenly.
5. Bake for 15-20 minutes.

Nutrition Facts Per Serving

Calories: 214; Fat: 19g; Carbs: 5g; Protein: 8g

Feta Avocado Dip

Prep time: 10 minutes, cook time: 0 minutes; Serves 4

5 Ingredients:

2 avocadoes (mashed)

½ cup feta cheese (crumbled)

1 plum tomatoes (diced)

1 teaspoon garlic (minced)

½ lemon (juiced)

What you'll need from the store cupboard:

Salt

Pepper

4 tablespoons olive oil

Instructions

1. Fold ingredients together. Do not stir too much to leave chunks of feta and avocado.
2. Serve and enjoy.

Nutrition Facts Per Serving

Calories: 220; Fat: 19g; Carbs: 8.1g; Protein: 5g

Green Jalapeno Sauce

Prep time: 5 minutes, cook time: 0 minutes; Serves 1

5 Ingredients:

½ avocado

1 large jalapeno

1 cup fresh cilantro

2 tablespoons extra virgin olive oil

3 tablespoons water

What you'll need from the store cupboard:

Water

½ teaspoon salt

Instructions

1. Add all ingredients in a blender.
2. Blend until smooth and creamy.
3. Serve and enjoy.

Nutrition Facts Per Serving

Calories: 407; Fat: 42g; Carbs: 10g; Protein: 2.4g

Vegetarian Fish Sauce

Prep time: 5 minutes, cook time: 20 minutes; Serves 16

5 Ingredients:

1/4 cup dried shiitake mushrooms

1-2 tbsp tamari (for a depth of flavor)

3 tbsp coconut aminos

What you'll need from the store cupboard:

1 ¼ cup water

2 tsp sea salt

Instructions

1. To a small saucepan, add water, coconut aminos, dried shiitake mushrooms, and sea salt. Bring to a boil, then cover, reduce heat, and simmer for 15-20 minutes.
2. Remove from heat and let cool slightly. Pour liquid through a fine-mesh strainer into a bowl, pressing on the mushroom mixture with a spoon to squeeze out any remaining liquid.
3. To the bowl, add tamari. Taste and adjust as needed, adding more sea salt for saltiness.
4. Store in a sealed container in the refrigerator for up to 1 month and shake well before use. Or pour into an ice cube tray, freeze, and store in a freezer-safe container for up to 2 months.

Nutrition Facts Per Serving

Calories: 39.1; Fat: 2g; Carbs: 5g; Protein: 0.3g

Simple Tomato Sauce

Prep time: 5 minutes, cook time: 20 minutes; Serves 4

5 Ingredients:

1 (28-ounce) can whole peeled tomatoes
3 garlic cloves, smashed
5 tablespoons olive oil
Kosher salt
2 tablespoons unsalted butter

What you'll need from the store cupboard:

Salt

Instructions

1. Purée tomatoes in a food processor until they're as smooth or chunky as you like.
2. Transfer tomatoes to a large Dutch oven or other heavy pot. (Or, use an immersion blender and blend directly in the pot.)
3. Add garlic, oil, and a 5-finger pinch of salt.
4. Bring to a boil and cook, occasionally stirring, until sauce is reduced by about one-third, about 20 minutes. Stir in butter.

Nutrition Facts Per Serving

Calories: 219; Fat: 21.3g; Carbs: 7.6g; Protein: 1.9g

Buttery Dijon Sauce

Prep time: 5 minutes, cook time: 0 minutes; Serves 2

5 Ingredients:

3 parts brown butter
1-part vinegar or citrus juice or a combo
1-part strong Dijon mustard
A small handful of flat-leaf parsley (optional)
3/4 teaspoon freshly ground pepper

What you'll need from the store cupboard:

1 teaspoon salt

Instructions

1. Add everything to a food processor and blitz until just smooth.
2. You can also mix this up with an immersion blender. Use immediately or store in the refrigerator for up to one day. Blend again before use.

Nutrition Facts Per Serving

Calories: 306; Fat: 34.4g; Carbs: 0.7g; Protein: 0.4g

Roasted Garlic Lemon Dip

Prep time: 10 minutes, cook time: 30 minutes; Serves 3

5 Ingredients:

3 medium lemons
3 cloves garlic, peeled and smashed
5 tablespoons olive oil, divided
1/2 teaspoon kosher salt
Pepper to taste

What you'll need from the store cupboard:

Salt
Pepper

Instructions

1. Arrange a rack in the middle of the oven and heat to 400°F.
2. Cut the lemons in half crosswise and remove the seeds. Place the lemons cut-side up in a small baking dish. Add the garlic and drizzle with 2 tablespoons of the oil.
3. Roast until the lemons are tender and lightly browned, about 30 minutes. Remove the baking dish to a wire rack.
4. When the lemons are cool enough to handle, squeeze the juice into the baking dish. Discard the lemon pieces and any remaining seeds. Pour the contents of the baking dish, including the garlic, into a blender or mini food processor. Add the remaining 3 tablespoons oil and salt. Process until the garlic is completely puréed, and the sauce is emulsified and slightly thickened. Serve warm or at room temperature.

Nutrition Facts Per Serving

Calories: 165; Fat: 17g; Carbs: 4.8g; Protein: 0.6g

Cheesy Avocado Dip

Prep time: 15 minutes, cook time: 20 minutes; Serves

5 Ingredients:
1/2 medium ripe avocado (about 4 ounces), peeled and pitted
2 crumbled blue cheese
1 freshly squeezed lemon juice
1/2 kosher salt
1/2 cup water

What you'll need from the store cupboard:
None

Instructions

1. Scoop the flesh of the avocado into the bowl of a food processor fitted with the blade attachment or blender.
2. Add the blue cheese, lemon juice, and salt. Blend until smooth and creamy, 30 to 40 seconds.
3. With the motor running, add the water and blend until the sauce is thinned and well-combined.

Nutrition Facts Per Serving
Calories: 86; Fat: 7.2g; Carbs: 2.9g; Protein: 3.5g

Lemon Tahini Sauce

Prep time: 5 minutes, cook time: 5 minutes; Serves 2

5 Ingredients:
1/2 cup packed fresh herbs, such as parsley, basil, mint, cilantro, dill, or chives
1/4 cup tahini
Juice of 1 lemon (about 1/4 cup)
1/2 teaspoon kosher salt

What you'll need from the store cupboard:
1 tablespoon water

Instructions
1. Place all the ingredients in the bowl of a food processor fitted with the blade attachment or a blender. Process continuously until the herbs are finely minced, and the sauce is well-blended, 3 to 4 minutes.
2. Serve immediately or store in a covered container in the refrigerator until ready to serve.

Nutrition Facts Per Serving
Calories: 94; Fat: 8.1g; Carbs: 4.3g; Protein: 2.8g

Greek Yogurt Dressing

Prep time: 15 minutes, cook time: 0 minutes; Serves 2

5 Ingredients:
¼ tsp ground ginger
½ tsp prepared mustard
2 tbsp low-fat mayonnaise
½ cup plain Greek yogurt

What you'll need from the store cupboard:
Salt and pepper to taste

Instructions

1. In a bowl, whisk well all ingredients.
2. Adjust seasoning to taste.
3. Serve and enjoy with your favorite salad greens.

Nutrition Facts Per Serving
Calories: 51; Fat: 2.8g; Carbs: 3.5g; Protein: 3.0g

Celery-Onion Vinaigrette

Prep time: 15 minutes, cook time: 0 minutes; Serves 4

5 Ingredients:
1 tbsp finely chopped celery
1 tbsp finely chopped red onion
4 garlic cloves, minced
½ cup red wine vinegar

What you'll need from the store cupboard:
1 tbsp extra virgin olive oil

Instructions

1. Prepare the dressing by mixing pepper, celery, onion, olive oil, garlic, and vinegar in a small bowl. Whisk well to combine.
2. Let it sit for at least 30 minutes to let flavors blend.

3. Serve and enjoy with your favorite salad greens.

Nutrition Facts Per Serving
Calories: 41; Fat: 3.4g; Carbs: 1.4g; Protein: 0.2g

Fat-Burning Dressing

Prep time: 5 minutes, cook time: 3 minutes; Serves 6

5 Ingredients:
2 tablespoons coconut oil
¼ cup olive oil
2 cloves of garlic, minced
2 tablespoons freshly chopped herbs of your choice
¼ cup mayonnaise

What you'll need from the store cupboard:
Salt and pepper to taste

Instructions

1. Heat the coconut oil and olive oil and sauté the garlic until fragrant in a saucepan.
2. Allow cooling slightly before adding the mayonnaise.
3. Season with salt and pepper to taste.

Nutrition Facts Per Serving
Calories: 262; Fat: 22.5g; Carbs: 0.6g; Protein: 14.1g

Cowboy Sauce

Prep time: 10 minutes, cook time: 10 minutes; Serves 6

5 Ingredients:
1 stick butter
2 cloves of garlic, minced
1 tablespoon fresh horseradish, grated
1 teaspoon dried thyme
1 teaspoon paprika powder

What you'll need from the store cupboard:
Salt and pepper to taste
¼ cup water

Instructions
1. Add all ingredients to a pot and bring to a simmer.
2. Simmer for 10 minutes.
3. Adjust seasoning to taste.

Nutrition Facts Per Serving
Calories: 194; Fat: 20.6g; Carbs: 0.9g; Protein: 1.3g

Ketogenic Caesar Salad Dressing

Prep time: 5 minutes, cook time: 10 minutes; Serves 6

5 Ingredients:
½ cup olive oil
1 tablespoon Dijon mustard
½ cup parmesan cheese, grated
2/3-ounce anchovies, chopped
½ lemon juice, freshly squeezed

What you'll need from the store cupboard:
Salt and pepper to taste

Instructions
1. Add all ingredients to a pot and bring to a simmer. Stir frequently.
2. Simmer for 10 minutes.
3. Adjust seasoning to taste.

Nutrition Facts Per Serving
Calories: 203; Fat: 20.7g; Carbs: 1.5g; Protein: 3.4g

Keto Thousand Island Dressing

Prep time: 5 minutes, cook time: 10 minutes; Serves 10

5 Ingredients:

1 cup mayonnaise

1 tablespoon lemon juice, freshly squeezed

4 tablespoons dill pickles, chopped

1 teaspoon Tabasco

1 shallot chopped finely

What you'll need from the store cupboard:

Salt and pepper to taste

Instructions

1. Add all ingredients to a pot and bring to a simmer. Stir frequently.
2. Simmer for 10 minutes.
3. Adjust seasoning to taste.

Nutrition Facts Per Serving

Calories: 85; Fat: 7.8g; Carbs: 2.3g; Protein: 1.7g

Ketogenic-Friendly Gravy

Prep time: 5 minutes, cook time: 10 minutes; Serves 6

5 Ingredients:

2 tablespoons butter

1 white onion, chopped

¼ cup coconut milk

2 cups bone broth

1 tablespoon balsamic vinegar

What you'll need from the store cupboard:

Salt and pepper to taste

Instructions

1. Add all ingredients to a pot and bring to a simmer. Stir frequently.
2. Simmer for 10 minutes.
3. Adjust seasoning to taste.

Nutrition Facts Per Serving

Calories: 59; Fat: 6.3g; Carbs: 1.1g; Protein: 0.2g

Keto Ranch Dip

Prep time: 5 minutes, cook time: 10 minutes; Serves 8

5 Ingredients:

1 cup egg white, beaten

1 lemon juice, freshly squeezed

Salt and pepper to taste

1 teaspoon mustard paste

1 cup olive oil

What you'll need from the store cupboard:

Salt and pepper to taste

Instructions

1. Add all ingredients to a pot and bring to a simmer. Stir frequently.
2. Simmer for 10 minutes.
3. Adjust seasoning to taste.

Nutrition Facts Per Serving

Calories: 258; Fat: 27.1g; Carbs: 1.2g; Protein: 3.4g

Chapter-11 | 5-Ingredient Smoothie Recipes

High Protein, Green and Fruity Smoothie

Prep time: 10 minutes, cook time: 0 minutes; Serves 2

5 Ingredients:

1 cup spinach, packed

½ cup strawberries, chopped

½ avocado, peeled, pitted, and frozen

1 tbsp almond butter

¼ cup packed kale, stem discarded, and leaves chopped

What you'll need from the store cupboard:

1 cup ice-cold water

5 tablespoons MCT oil or coconut oil

Instructions

1. Blend all ingredients in a blender until smooth and creamy.
2. Serve and enjoy.

Nutrition Facts Per Serving

Calories: 459; Fat: 47.3g; Carbs: 10g; Protein: 1.6g

Nutritiously Green Milk Shake

Prep time: 10 minutes, cook time: 5 minutes; Serves 1

5 Ingredients:

1 cup coconut cream

1 packet Stevia, or more to taste

1 tbsp coconut flakes, unsweetened

2 cups spring mix salad

3 tbsps coconut oil

What you'll need from the store cupboard:

1 cup water

Instructions

1. Add all ingredients in a blender.
2. Blend until smooth and creamy.
3. Serve and enjoy.

Nutrition Facts Per Serving

Calories: 887; Fat: 95.3g; Carbs: 10g; Protein: 10.5g

Coconut-Mocha Shake

Prep time: 5 minutes, cook time: 0 minutes; Serves 1

5 Ingredients:

2 tbsp cocoa powder

1 tbsp coconut flakes, unsweetened

2 packet Stevia, or more to taste

1 cup brewed coffee, chilled

What you'll need from the store cupboard:

3 tbsps coconut oil

Instructions

1. Add all ingredients in a blender.
2. Blend until smooth and creamy.
3. Serve and enjoy.

Nutrition Facts Per Serving

Calories: 402; Fat: 43.7g; Carbs: 9g; Protein: 2.4g

Mocha Milk Shake

Prep time: 5 minutes, cook time: 0 minutes; Serves 1

5 Ingredients:

1 cup almond milk

2 tbsp cocoa powder

2 packet Stevia, or more to taste

1 cup brewed coffee, chilled

What you'll need from the store cupboard:

3   tbsps coconut oil

Instructions

1. Add all ingredients in a blender.
2. Blend until smooth and creamy.
3. Serve and enjoy.

Nutrition Facts Per Serving

Calories: 527; Fat: 50.2g; Carbs: 9.9g; Protein: 13.1g

Cinnamon Choco Coffee Milk Shake

Prep time: 5 minutes, cook time: 0 minutes; Serves 1

5 Ingredients:
½ cup coconut milk
1 tbsp cocoa powder
1 cup brewed coffee, chilled
1 packet Stevia, or more to taste
½ tsp cinnamon
What you' ll need from the store cupboard:
5 tbsps coconut oil

Instructions
1. Add all ingredients in a blender.
2. Blend until smooth and creamy.
3. Serve and enjoy.
Nutrition Facts Per Serving
Calories: 880; Fat: 97.4g; Carbs: 10g; Protein: 4.1g

Raspberry and Greens Shake

Prep time: 5 minutes, cook time: 0 minutes; Serves 1

5 Ingredients:
½ cup half and half
1 packet Stevia, or more to taste
4 raspberries, fresh
1 tbsp macadamia oil
1 cup Spinach
What you' ll need from the store cupboard:
1 cup water

Instructions
1. Add all ingredients in a blender.
2. Blend until smooth and creamy.
3. Serve and enjoy.
Nutrition Facts Per Serving
Calories: 151; Fat: 15.5g; Carbs: 2.7g; Protein: 1.4g

Nutty Greens Shake

Prep time: 5 minutes, cook time: 0 minutes; Serves 1

5 Ingredients:
½ cup half and half, liquid
1 packet Stevia, or more to taste
3 pecan nuts
3 macadamia nuts
1 cup spring mix salad greens
What you' ll need from the store cupboard:
1 ½ cups water

3 tablespoons coconut oil
Instructions
1. Add all ingredients in a blender.
2. Blend until smooth and creamy.
3. Serve and enjoy.
Nutrition Facts Per Serving
Calories: 628; Fat: 65.6g; Carbs: 10.5g; Protein: 7.0g

Almond Choco Shake

Prep time: 5 minutes, cook time: 0 minutes; Serves 1

5 Ingredients:
½ cup heavy cream, liquid
1 tbsp cocoa powder
1 packet Stevia, or more to taste
5 almonds, chopped
What you' ll need from the store cupboard:
1 ½ cups water
3 tbsp coconut oil

Instructions
1. Add all ingredients in a blender.
2. Blend until smooth and creamy.
3. Serve and enjoy.
Nutrition Facts Per Serving
Calories: 485; Fat: 45.9g; Carbs: 9.7g; Protein: 11.9g

Strawberry-Choco Shake

Prep time: 5 minutes, cook time: 0 minutes; Serves 1

5 Ingredients:

½ cup heavy cream, liquid
1 tbsp cocoa powder
1 packet Stevia, or more to taste
4 strawberries, sliced
1 tbsp coconut flakes, unsweetened

What you'll need from the store cupboard:

1 ½ cups water

3 tbsps coconut oil

Instructions

1. Add all ingredients in a blender.
2. Blend until smooth and creamy.
3. Serve and enjoy.

Nutrition Facts Per Serving

Calories: 610; Fat:65.3g; Carbs: 10.1g; Protein: 2.6g

Raspberry-Choco Shake

Prep time: 5 minutes, cook time: 0 minutes; Serves 1

5 Ingredients:

¼ cup heavy cream, liquid
1 tbsp cocoa powder
1 packet Stevia, or more to taste
¼ cup raspberries

What you'll need from the store cupboard:

1 ½ cups water

Instructions

1. Add all ingredients in a blender.
2. Blend until smooth and creamy.
3. Serve and enjoy.

Nutrition Facts Per Serving

Calories: 438; Fat: 45.0g; Carbs: 11.1g; Protein: 3.8g

Creamy Choco Shake

Prep time: 5 minutes, cook time: 0 minutes; Serves 1

5 Ingredients:

½ cup heavy cream
2 tbsp cocoa powder
1 packet Stevia, or more to taste
1 cup water

What you'll need from the store cupboard:

3 tbsps coconut oil

Instructions

1. Add all ingredients in a blender.
2. Blend until smooth and creamy.
3. Serve and enjoy.

Nutrition Facts Per Serving

Calories: 582; Fat: 64.6g; Carbs: 7.9g; Protein:3.2g

Nutty Choco Milk Shake

Prep time: 5 minutes, cook time: 0 minutes; Serves 1

5 Ingredients:

¼ cup half and half
1 tbsp cocoa powder
1 packet Stevia, or more to taste
4 pecans
1 tbsp macadamia oil

What you'll need from the store cupboard:

1 ½ cups water

3 tbsp coconut oil

Instructions

1. Add all ingredients in a blender.
2. Blend until smooth and creamy.
3. Serve and enjoy.

Nutrition Facts Per Serving

Calories: 689; Fat: 73g; Carbs: 9.4g; Protein: 4.8g

Strawberry-chocolate Yogurt Shake

Prep time: 5 minutes, cook time: 0 minutes; Serves 1

5 Ingredients:

½ cup whole milk yogurt
4 strawberries, chopped
1 tbsp cocoa powder
3 tbsp coconut oil
1 tbsp pepitas

What you'll need from the store cupboard:

1 ½ cups water

1 packet Stevia, or more to taste

Instructions

1. Add all ingredients in a blender.
2. Blend until smooth and creamy.
3. Serve and enjoy.

Nutrition Facts Per Serving

Calories: 496; Fat: 49.3g; Carbs: 10.5g; Protein: 7.7g

Lemony-Avocado Cilantro Shake

Prep time: 5 minutes, cook time: 0 minutes; Serves 1

5 Ingredients:

½ cup half and half
1 packet Stevia, or more to taste
¼ avocado, meat scooped
1 tbsp chopped cilantro
3 tbsps coconut oil

What you'll need from the store cupboard:

1 ½ cups water

Instructions

1. Add all ingredients in a blender.
2. Blend until smooth and creamy.
3. Serve and enjoy.

Nutrition Facts Per Serving

Calories: 501; Fat: 49g; Carbs: 8.4g; Protein: 4.04g

Berry-choco Goodness Shake

Prep time: 5 minutes, cook time: 0 minutes; Serves 1

5 Ingredients:

½ cup half and half
¼ cup raspberries
¼ cup blackberry
¼ cup strawberries, chopped
3 tbsps avocado oil

What you'll need from the store cupboard:

1 packet Stevia, or more to taste
1 tbsp cocoa powder

1 ½ cups water

Instructions

1. Add all ingredients in a blender.
2. Blend until smooth and creamy.
3. Serve and enjoy.

Nutrition Facts Per Serving

Calories: 450; Fat: 43.3g; Carbs: 7g; Protein: 4.4g

Coconut-melon Yogurt Shake

Prep time: 5 minutes, cook time: 0 minutes; Serves 1

5 Ingredients:

¼ cup half and half
3 tbsp coconut oil
½ cup melon, slices
1 tbsp coconut flakes, unsweetened
1 tbsp chia seeds

What you'll need from the store cupboard:

1 ½ cups water

1 packet Stevia, or more to taste

Instructions

1. Add all ingredients in a blender.
2. Blend until smooth and creamy.
3. Serve and enjoy.

Nutrition Facts Per Serving

Calories: 440; Fat: 43g; Carbs: 8g; Protein: 2.4g

Strawberry-coconut Shake

Prep time: 5 minutes, cook time: 0 minutes; Serves 1

5 Ingredients:

½ cup whole milk yogurt
3 tbsp MCT oil
¼ cup strawberries, chopped
1 tbsp coconut flakes, unsweetened
1 tbsp hemp seeds

What you'll need from the store cupboard:

1 ½ cups water

1 packet Stevia, or more to taste

Instructions

1. Add all ingredients in a blender.
2. Blend until smooth and creamy.
3. Serve and enjoy.

Nutrition Facts Per Serving

Calories: 511; Fat:50.9g; Carbs: 10.2g; Protein: 6.4g

Blackberry-Chocolate Shake

Prep time: 5 minutes, cook time: 0 minutes; Serves 1

5 Ingredients:

½ cup half and half
1 tbsp blackberries
3 tbsps MCT oil
1 tbsp Dutch-processed cocoa powder
2 tbsp Macadamia nuts, chopped

What you'll need from the store cupboard:

1 ½ cups water

1 packet Stevia, or more to taste

Instructions

1. Add all ingredients in a blender.
2. Blend until smooth and creamy.
3. Serve and enjoy.

Nutrition Facts Per Serving

Calories: 463; Fat: 43.9g; Carbs: 10.1g; Protein: 2.7g

Lettuce Green Shake

Prep time: 5 minutes, cook time: 0 minutes; Serves 1

5 Ingredients:

¾ cup whole milk yogurt
2 cups 5-lettuce mix salad greens
3 tbsp MCT oil
1 tbsp chia seeds

What you'll need from the store cupboard:

1 ½ cups water
1 packet Stevia, or more to taste

Instructions

1. Add all ingredients in a blender.
2. Blend until smooth and creamy.
3. Serve and enjoy.

Nutrition Facts Per Serving

Calories: 483; Fat: 47g; Carbs: 6.1g; Protein: 8.1g

Italian Greens and Yogurt Shake

Prep time: 5 minutes, cook time: 0 minutes; Serves 1

5 Ingredients:

½ cup half and half
½ cup Italian greens
1 packet Stevia, or more to taste
1 tbsp hemp seeds

What you'll need from the store cupboard:

3 tbsp coconut oil
1 cup water

Instructions

1. Add all ingredients in a blender.
2. Blend until smooth and creamy.
3. Serve and enjoy.

Nutrition Facts Per Serving

Calories: 476; Fat: 46.9g; Carbs: 10.3g; Protein: 5.2g

Garden Greens & Yogurt Shake

Prep time: 5 minutes, cook time: 0 minutes; Serves 1

5 Ingredients:
1 cup whole milk yogurt
1 cup Garden greens
3 tbsp MCT oil
1 tbsp flaxseed, ground
What you'll need from the store cupboard:
1 cup water
1 packet Stevia, or more to taste

Instructions
1. Add all ingredients in a blender.
2. Blend until smooth and creamy.
3. Serve and enjoy.

Nutrition Facts Per Serving
Calories: 581; Fat: 53g; Carbs: 7.2g; Protein: 11.7g

Hazelnut-Lettuce Yogurt Shake

Prep time: 5 minutes, cook time: 0 minutes; Serves 1

5 Ingredients:
1 cup whole milk yogurt
1 cup lettuce chopped
1 tbsp Hazelnut chopped
1 packet Stevia, or more to taste
1 tbsp olive oil
What you'll need from the store cupboard:
1 cup water

Instructions
1. Add all ingredients in a blender.
2. Blend until smooth and creamy.
3. Serve and enjoy.

Nutrition Facts Per Serving
Calories: 282; Fat: 22.2g; Carbs: 8.8g; Protein: 9.4g

Nutty Arugula Yogurt Smoothie

Prep time: 5 minutes, cook time: 0 minutes; Serves 1

5 Ingredients:
1 cup whole milk yogurt
1 cup baby arugula
3 tbsps avocado oil
2 tbsps macadamia nuts
1 packet Stevia, or more to taste
What you'll need from the store cupboard:
1 cup water

Instructions
1. Add all ingredients in a blender.
2. Blend until smooth and creamy.
3. Serve and enjoy.

Nutrition Facts Per Serving
Calories: 540; Fat: 51.5g; Carbs: 9.4g; Protein: 9.3g

Baby Kale and Yogurt Smoothie

Prep time: 5 minutes, cook time: 0 minutes; Serves 1

5 Ingredients:
½ cup whole milk yogurt
½ cup baby kale greens
1 packet Stevia, or more to taste
3 tbsps MCT oil
½ tbsp sunflower seeds
What you'll need from the store cupboard:
1 cup water

Instructions
1. Add all ingredients in a blender.
2. Blend until smooth and creamy.
3. Serve and enjoy.

Nutrition Facts Per Serving
Calories: 329; Fat: 26.2g; Carbs: 2.6g; Protein: 11.0g

Minty-Coco and Greens Shake

Prep time: 5 minutes, cook time: 0 minutes; Serves 1

5 Ingredients:

½ cup coconut milk

2 peppermint leaves

2 packets Stevia, or as needed

1 cup 50/50 salad mix

1 tbsp coconut oil

What you'll need from the store cupboard:

1 ½ cups water

Instructions

1. Add all ingredients in a blender.
2. Blend until smooth and creamy.
3. Serve and enjoy.

Nutrition Facts Per Serving

Calories: 344; Fat: 37.8g; Carbs: 5.8g; Protein: 2.7g

Avocado and Greens Smoothie

Prep time: 5 minutes, cook time: 0 minutes; Serves 1

5 Ingredients:

½ cup coconut milk

¼ avocado fruit

½ cup spring mix greens

3 tbsps avocado oil

What you'll need from the store cupboard:

1 ½ cups water

2 packets Stevia, or as needed

Instructions

1. Add all ingredients in a blender.
2. Blend until smooth and creamy.
3. Serve and enjoy.

Nutrition Facts Per Serving

Calories: 764; Fat: 77.4g; Carbs: 10.3g; Protein: 3.8g

Blueberry and Greens Smoothie

Prep time: 5 minutes, cook time: 0 minutes; Serves 1

5 Ingredients:

¼ cup coconut milk

2 tbsps blueberries

½ cup arugula

1 tbsp hemp seeds

2 packets Stevia, or as needed

What you'll need from the store cupboard:

1 ½ cups water

3 tbsps coconut oil

Instructions

1. Add all ingredients in a blender.
2. Blend until smooth and creamy.
3. Serve and enjoy.

Nutrition Facts Per Serving

Calories: 572; Fat:59.8g; Carbs: 10.4g; Protein:3.6g

Boysenberry and Greens Shake

Prep time: 5 minutes, cook time: 0 minutes; Serves 1

5 Ingredients:

¼ cup coconut milk

2 tbsps Boysenberry

2 packets Stevia, or as needed

¼ cup Baby Kale salad mix

3 tbsps MCT oil

What you'll need from the store cupboard:

1 ½ cups water

Instructions

1. Add all ingredients in a blender.
2. Blend until smooth and creamy.
3. Serve and enjoy.

Nutrition Facts Per Serving

Calories: 502; Fat: 55.1g; Carbs: 3.9g; Protein: 1.7g

Raspberry-coffee Creamy Smoothie

Prep time: 5 minutes, cook time: 0 minutes; Serves 1

5 Ingredients:

¼ cup coconut milk

1 ½ cups brewed coffee, chilled

2 tbsps raspberries

2 tbsps avocado meat

1 tsp chia seeds

What you'll need from the store cupboard:

2 packets Stevia or more to taste

3 tbsps coconut oil

Instructions

1. Add all ingredients in a blender.
2. Blend until smooth and creamy.

3. Serve and enjoy.

Nutrition Facts Per Serving

Calories:350; Fat: 33.2g; Carbs: 8.2g; Protein: 4.9g

Coco-loco Creamy Shake

Prep time: 5 minutes, cook time: 0 minutes; Serves 1

5 Ingredients:

½ cup coconut milk

2 tbsp Dutch-processed cocoa powder, unsweetened

1 cup brewed coffee, chilled

1 tbsp hemp seeds

1-2 packets Stevia

What you'll need from the store cupboard:

3 tbsps MCT oil or coconut oil

Instructions

1. Add all ingredients in a blender.
2. Blend until smooth and creamy.
3. Serve and enjoy.

Nutrition Facts Per Serving

Calories:567; Fat: 61.1g; Carbs: 10.2g; Protein:5.4g

Cardamom-cinnamon Spiced Coco-latte

Prep time: 5 minutes, cook time: 0 minutes; Serves 1

5 Ingredients:

½ cup coconut milk

¼ tsp cardamom powder

1 tbsp chocolate powder

1 ½ cups brewed coffee, chilled

1 tbsp coconut oil

What you'll need from the store cupboard:

¼ tsp cinnamon

¼ tsp nutmeg

Instructions

1. Add all ingredients in a blender.
2. Blend until smooth and creamy.
3. Serve and enjoy.

Nutrition Facts Per Serving

Calories: 362; Fat: 38.7g; Carbs: 7.5g; Protein: 3.8g

Hazelnut and Coconut Shake

Prep time: 5 minutes, cook time: 0 minutes; Serves 1

5 Ingredients:

¼ coconut milk

¼ cup hazelnut, chopped

2 tbsps MCT oil or coconut oil

What you'll need from the store cupboard:

1 ½ cups water

1 packet Stevia, optional

Instructions

1. Add all ingredients in a blender.
2. Blend until smooth and creamy.
3. Serve and enjoy.

Nutrition Facts Per Serving

Calories: 591; Fat: 62.1g; Carbs: 8.9g; Protein: 6.5g

Hazelnut and Coconut Shake

Prep time: 5 minutes, cook time: 0 minutes; Serves 1

5 Ingredients:

¼ coconut milk

¼ cup hazelnut, chopped

2 tbsps MCT oil or coconut oil

What you'll need from the store cupboard:

1 ½ cups water

1 packet Stevia, optional

Instructions
1. Add all ingredients in a blender.
2. Blend until smooth and creamy.
3. Serve and enjoy.

Nutrition Facts Per Serving
Calories: 591; Fat: 62.1g; Carbs: 8.9g; Protein: 6.5g

Ice Blueberry Milk Smoothie

Prep time:5 mins; Cook time: 5 mins; Serves 3
5 Ingredients:
2 blueberries
2 cups almond milk
1/2 cup butter
2 tablespoons stevia, or to taste
2 cups ice cubes
Instructions

1. Combine all ingredients in a blender; process until well blended, about 30 seconds.
Nutrition Facts Per Serving
Per Serving: 228 calories; 17g fat; 6g carbohydrates; 12.8 g protein;

Strawberry Vanilla Extract Smoothie

Prep time:5 mins; Cook time: 5 mins; Serves 3
5 Ingredients
1 cup almond milk
14 frozen strawberries
1 1/2 teaspoons stevia
What you'll need from the store cupboard:
1/2 teaspoon vanilla extract
Instructions

1. Place almond milk and strawberries in a blender, blend until creamy. Add vanilla and stevia if desired, blend again and serve.
Nutrition Facts Per Serving
Per Serving: 240.4 calories; 18.8 g fat; 5 g carbohydrates; 12.8 g protein

Lime Strawberry Smoothie

Prep time: 3 mins; Cook time: 3 mins; Serves 3
5 Ingredients:
4 ice cubes
1/4 fresh strawberry
1 large avocado, diced
1 cup lime juice
Instructions
1. In a food processor, combine all

ingredients and puree on High until a smooth smoothie is formed. Serve and enjoy.
Nutrition Facts Per Serving
Per Serving: 127 calories; 11 g fat; 4 g carbohydrates; 3 g protein

Strawberry and Yogurt Smoothie

Prep time: 5 mins; Cook time: 5 minutes; Serves 3
5 Ingredients:
1/2 cup yogurt
1 cup strawberries
1 teaspoon almond milk
1 teaspoon lime juice
What you'll need from the store cupboard:
1 1/2 teaspoons stevia

Instructions
1. Place all ingredients in a blender, blender until finely smooth. Serve and enjoy.
Nutrition Facts Per Serving
Per Serving: 155.2 calories; 12.4 g fat; 6.3g carbohydrates; 4.6 g protein

Chapter-12 | 5-Ingredient Side Dishes & Snack Recipes

Sweet and Hot Nuts

Prep time: 5 minutes, cook time: 4 hours; Serves 12
5 Ingredients:
½ pound assorted nuts, raw
1/3 cup butter, melted
1 teaspoon cayenne pepper or to taste
1 tablespoon MCT oil or coconut oil
What you'll need from the store cupboard:
1 packet stevia powder
¼ tsp salt

Instructions
1. Place all ingredients in the crockpot.
2. Give it a good stir to combine everything.
3. Close the lid and cook on low for 4 hours.

Nutrition Facts Per Serving
Calories: 271; Fat: 21.6g; Carbs: 2.9g; Protein: 7.0g

Chicken Enchilada Dip

Prep time: 5 minutes, cook time:240 minutes; Serves 16
5 Ingredients:
2 pounds cooked rotisserie chicken, shredded
1 cup enchilada sauce
½ cup cheddar cheese
2 stalk green onions, sliced
3 tbsp olive oil
What you'll need from the store cupboard:
Salt and pepper to taste
Instructions

1. Place all ingredients in the crockpot except for the green onions.
2. Give a good stir to combine everything.
3. Close the lid and cook on low for 4 hours. Mix well and adjust seasoning to taste.
4. Garnish with green onions.

Nutrition Facts Per Serving
Calories: 178; Fat:13.6g; Carbs: 1.5g; Protein: 16.2g

Teriyaki Chicken Wings

Prep time: 10 minutes, cook time: 50 minutes; Serves 9
5 Ingredients:
3 pounds chicken wings
1 onion, chopped
2 cups commercial teriyaki sauce
1 tablespoon chili garlic paste
2 teaspoons ginger paste
What you'll need from the store cupboard:
Salt and pepper to taste
Instructions
1. In a heavy-bottomed pot, place on medium-high fire and lightly grease with cooking spray.

2. Pan fry chicken for 4 minutes per side. Cook in two batches.
3. Stir in remaining ingredients in a pot, along with the chicken.
4. Cover and cook on low fire for 30 minutes, stirring every now and then. Continue cooking until desired sauce thickness is achieved.
5. Serve and enjoy.

Nutrition Facts Per Serving
Calories: 214; Fat: 5.4g; Carbs: 5.4g; Protein: 34.3g

Asian Glazed Meatballs

Prep time: 10 minutes, cook time: 35 minutes; Serves 4
5 Ingredients:
1-pound frozen meatballs, thawed to room temperature
½ cup hoisin sauce

1 tablespoon apricot jam, keto-friendly
2 tablespoons soy sauce
½ teaspoon sesame oil

What you'll need from the store cupboard:
5 tbsp MCT oil or coconut oil
2 tbsp water

Instructions
1. Place a heavy-bottomed pot on medium-high fire and heat coconut oil.
2. Sauté meatballs until lightly browned, around 10 minutes.
3. Stir in remaining ingredients and mix well.
4. Cover and cook for 25 minutes on low fire, mixing now and then.
5. Serve and enjoy.

Nutrition Facts Per Serving
Calories: 536; Fat: 51.6g; Carbs: 6.5g; Protein: 16.3g

Cajun Spiced Pecans

Prep time: 5 minutes, cook time: 10 minutes; Serves 12

5 Ingredients:
1-pound pecan halves
¼ cup melted butter
1 packet Cajun seasoning mix
¼ teaspoon ground cayenne pepper

What you'll need from the store cupboard:
Salt and pepper to taste

Instructions
1. Preheat oven to 400ºF.
2. In a small bowl, whisk well-melted butter, Cajun seasoning, cayenne, salt, and pepper.
3. Place pecan halves on a cookie sheet. Drizzle with sauce. Toss well to coat.
4. Pop in the oven and roast for 10 minutes.
5. Let it cool completely, serve, and enjoy.

Nutrition Facts Per Serving
Calories: 297.1; Fat: 31.1g; Carbs: 5.7g; Protein: 3.5g

Basil Keto Crackers

Prep time: 30 minutes, cook time: 15 minutes; Serves 6

5 Ingredients:
1 ¼ cups almond flour
½ teaspoon baking powder
¼ teaspoon dried basil powder
A pinch of cayenne pepper powder
1 clove of garlic, minced

What you'll need from the store cupboard:
Salt and pepper to taste
3 tablespoons oil

Instructions
1. Preheat oven to 350ºF and lightly grease a cookie sheet with cooking spray.
2. Mix everything in a mixing bowl to create a dough.
3. Transfer the dough on a clean and flat working surface and spread out until 2mm thick. Cut into squares.
4. Place gently in an even layer on the prepped cookie sheet. Cook for 10 minutes.
5. Cook in batches.
6. Serve and enjoy.

Nutrition Facts Per Serving
Calories: 205; Fat: 19.3g; Carbs: 2.9g; Protein: 5.3g

Walnut Butter on Cracker

Prep time: 5 minutes, cook time: 0 minutes; Serves 1

5 Ingredients:
1 tablespoon walnut butter
2 pieces Mary's gone crackers

What you'll need from the store cupboard:
none

Instructions
1. Spread ½ tablespoon of walnut butter per cracker and enjoy.

Nutrition Facts Per Serving
Calories: 134; Fat: 14.0g; Carbs: 4.0g; Protein: 1.0g

Homemade Apricot and Soy Nut Trail Mix

Prep time: 15 minutes, cook time: 10 minutes; Serves 20

5 Ingredients:

¼ cup dried apricots, chopped

1 cup pumpkin seeds

½ cup roasted cashew nuts

1 cup roasted, shelled pistachios

What you'll need from the store cupboard:

Salt to taste

3 tbsp MCT oil or coconut oil

Instructions

1. In a medium mixing bowl, place all ingredients.
2. Thoroughly combine.
3. Bake in the oven for 10 minutes at 375⁰F.
4. In 20 small zip-top bags, get ¼ cup of the mixture and place in each bag.
5. One zip-top bag is equal to one serving.
6. If properly stored, this can last up to two weeks.

Nutrition Facts Per Serving

Calories: 129; Fat: 10.75g; Carbs: 4.6g; Protein: 5.2g

Baba Ganoush Eggplant Dip

Prep time: 15 minutes, cook time: 80 minutes; Serves 4

5 Ingredients:

1 head of garlic, unpeeled

1 large eggplant, cut in half lengthwise

5 tablespoons olive oil

Lemon juice to taste

2 minced garlic cloves

What you'll need from the store cupboard:

Pepper and salt to taste

Instructions

1. With the rack in the middle position, preheat oven to 350°F.
2. Line a baking sheet with parchment paper. Place the eggplant cut side down on the baking sheet.
3. Roast until the flesh is very tender and pulls away easily from the skin, about 1 hour depending on the eggplant's size. Let it cool.
4. Meanwhile, cut the tips off the garlic cloves. Place the cloves in a square of aluminum foil. Fold up the edges of the foil and crimp together to form a tightly sealed packet. Roast alongside the eggplant until tender, about 20 minutes. Let cool.
5. Mash the cloves by pressing with a fork.
6. With a spoon, scoop the flesh from the eggplant and place it in the bowl of a food processor. Add the mashed garlic, oil and lemon juice. Process until smooth. Season with pepper.

Nutrition Facts Per Serving

Calories: 192; Fat: 17.8g; Carbs: 10.2g; Protein: 1.6g

No Cook Choco and Coconut Bars

Prep time: 10 minutes, cook time: 30 minutes; Serves 9

5 Ingredients:

1 tbsp Stevia

¾ cup shredded coconut, unsweetened

½ cup ground nuts (almonds, pecans, or walnuts)

¼ cup unsweetened cocoa powder

4 tbsp coconut oil

What you'll need from the store cupboard:

Instructions

1. In a medium bowl, mix shredded coconut, nuts, and cocoa powder.
2. Add Stevia and coconut oil.
3. Mix batter thoroughly.
4. In a 9x9 square inch pan or dish, press the batter and for a 30-minutes place in the freezer.
5. Evenly divide into suggested servings and enjoy.

Nutrition Facts Per Serving

Calories: 99.7; Fat: 9.3g; Carbs: 2.7g; Protein: 1.3g

Easy Baked Parmesan Chips

Prep time: 5 minutes, cook time: 10 minutes; Serves 10

5 Ingredients:

1 cup grated Parmesan cheese, low fat

1 tablespoon olive oil

What you'll need from the store cupboard:

Instructions

1. Lightly grease a cookie sheet and preheat oven to 400°F.

2. Evenly sprinkle parmesan cheese on a cookie sheet into 10 circles. Place them about ½-inch apart.

3. Drizzle with oil

4. Bake until lightly browned and crisped.

5. Let it cool, evenly divide into suggested servings and enjoy.

Nutrition Facts Per Serving

Calories: 142; Fat:12.8g; Carbs: 1.4g; Protein: 2.8g

Baked Vegetable Side

Prep time:10 minutes, cook time: 15 minutes; Serves 4

5 Ingredients:

1 large zucchini, sliced

1 bell pepper, sliced

½ cup peeled garlic cloves, sliced

A dash of oregano

What you'll need from the store cupboard:

4 tablespoons olive oil

Salt and pepper to taste

Instructions

1. Place all ingredients in a mixing bowl. Stir to coat everything.

2. Place in a baking sheet.

3. Bake in a 350°F preheated oven for 15 minutes.

4. Serve and enjoy.

Nutrition Facts Per Serving

Calories: 191; Fat: 23.0g; Carbs: 10.0g; Protein: 3.0g

Shrimp Fra Diavolo

Prep time: 15 minutes, cook time: 5 minutes; Serves 3

5 Ingredients:

3 tablespoons butter

1 onion, diced

5 cloves of garlic, minced

1 teaspoon red pepper flakes

¼ pound shrimps, shelled

What you'll need from the store cupboard:

2 tablespoons olive oil

Salt and pepper to taste

Instructions

1. Heat the butter and the olive oil in a skillet and sauté the onion and garlic until fragrant.

2. Stir in the red pepper flakes and shrimps. Season with salt and pepper to taste.

3. Stir for 3 minutes.

4. Serve and enjoy.

Nutrition Facts Per Serving

Calories: 388; Fat: 32.1g; Carbs: 4.5g; Protein: 21.0g

Tart Raspberry Crumble Bar

Prep time: 10 minutes, cook time: 55 minutes; Serves 9

5 Ingredients:

1/2 cup whole toasted almonds

1 cup almond flour

1 cup cold, unsalted butter, cut into cubes

2 eggs, beaten

3-ounce dried raspberries

What you'll need from the store cupboard:

1/4 teaspoon salt

3 tbsp MCT or coconut oil.

Instructions

1. In a food processor, pulse almonds until chopped coarsely. Transfer to a bowl.

2. Add almond flour and salt into the food processor and pulse until a bit combined. Add butter, eggs, and MCT oil. Pulse until you have a coarse batter. Evenly divide batter into two bowls.
3. In the first bowl of batter, knead well until it forms a ball. Wrap in cling wrap, flatten a bit and chill for an hour for easy handling.
4. In the second bowl of batter, add the raspberries. In a pinching motion, pinch batter to form clusters of streusel. Set aside.
5. When ready to bake, preheat oven to 375ºF and lightly grease an 8x8-inch baking pan with cooking spray.
6. Discard cling wrap and evenly press dough on the bottom of the pan, up to 1-inch up the sides of the pan, making sure that everything is covered in dough.
7. Top with streusel.
8. Pop in the oven and bake until golden brown and berries are bubbly around 45 minutes.
9. Remove from oven and cool for 20 minutes before slicing into 9 equal bars.
10. Serve and enjoy or store in a lidded container for 10-days in the fridge.

Nutrition Facts Per Serving
Calories: 229; Fat: 22.9g; Carbs: 3.9g; Protein: 2.8g

Chocolate Mousse

Prep time: 15 minutes, cook time: 0 minutes; Serves 4
5 Ingredients:
1 large, ripe avocado
1/4 cup sweetened almond milk
1 tbsp coconut oil
1/4 cup cocoa or cacao powder
1 tsp vanilla extract
What you'll need from the store cupboard:
none
Instructions

1. In a food processor, process all ingredients until smooth and creamy.
2. Transfer to a lidded container and chill for at least 4 hours.
3. Serve and enjoy.

Nutrition Facts Per Serving
Calories: 125; Fat: 11.0g; Carbs: 6.9g; Protein: 1.2g

Zucchini and Cheese Gratin

Prep time: 15 minutes, cook time: 15 minutes; Serves 8
5 Ingredients:
5 tablespoons butter
1 onion, sliced
½ cup heavy cream
4 cups raw zucchini, sliced
1 ½ cups shredded pepper Jack cheese
What you'll need from the store cupboard:
Salt and pepper to taste
Instructions

1. Place all ingredients in a mixing bowl and give a good stir to incorporate everything.
2. Pour the mixture in a heat-proof baking dish.
3. Place in a 350ºF preheated oven and bake for 15 minutes.
4. Serve and enjoy.

Nutrition Facts Per Serving
Calories: 280; Fat: 20.0g; Carbs: 5.0g; Protein: 8.0g

Soy Garlic Mushrooms

Prep time: 20 minutes, cook time: 10 minutes; Serves 8
5 Ingredients:
2 pounds mushrooms, sliced
3 tablespoons olive oil
2 cloves of garlic, minced
¼ cup coconut aminos
4 tablespoons butter
What you'll need from the store cupboard:
Salt and pepper to taste
Instructions

1. Place all ingredients in a dish except for the butter and mix until well-combined.
2. Allow marinating for 2 hours in the fridge.
3. In a large saucepan on medium fire, melt the butter and add mushrooms and sauté for 8 minutes. Season with pepper and salt to taste.
4. Serve and enjoy.

Nutrition Facts Per Serving
Calories: 152; Fat: 11.9g; Carbs: 4.7g; Protein: 3.8g

Old Bay Chicken Wings

Prep time: 5 minutes, cook time: 30 minutes; Serves 4

5 Ingredients:
3 pounds chicken wings
¾ cup almond flour
1 tablespoon old bay spices
1 teaspoon lemon juice, freshly squeezed
½ cup butter

What you'll need from the store cupboard:
Salt and pepper to taste

Instructions
1. Preheat oven to 400°F.
2. In a mixing bowl, combine all ingredients except for the butter.
3. Place in an even layer in a baking sheet.
4. Bake for 30 minutes. Halfway through the cooking time, shake the fryer basket for even cooking.
5. Once cooked, drizzle with melted butter.

Nutrition Facts Per Serving
Calories: 700; Fat: 59.2g; Carbs: 1.6g; Protein: 52.5g

Tofu Stuffed Peppers

Prep time: 5 minutes, cook time: 10 minutes; Serves 8

5 Ingredients:
1 package firm tofu, crumbled
1 onion, finely chopped
½ teaspoon turmeric powder
1 teaspoon coriander powder
8 banana peppers, top-end sliced and seeded

What you'll need from the store cupboard:
Salt and pepper to taste
3 tablespoons oil

Instructions
1. Preheat oven to 400°F.
2. In a mixing bowl, combine the tofu, onion, coconut oil, turmeric powder, red chili powder, coriander powder, and salt. Mix until well-combined.
3. Scoop the tofu mixture into the hollows of the banana peppers.
4. Place the stuffed peppers in one layer in a lightly greased baking sheet.
5. Cook for 10 minutes.
6. Serve and enjoy.

Nutrition Facts Per Serving
Calories: 187; Fat: 15.6g; Carbs: 4.1g; Protein: 1.2g

No Cook Coconut and Chocolate Bars

Prep time: 15 minutes, cook time: 30 minutes; Serves 6

5 Ingredients:
1 tbsp Stevia
¾ cup shredded coconut, unsweetened
½ cup ground nuts (almonds, pecans, or walnuts)
¼ cup unsweetened cocoa powder
4 tbsp coconut oil

What you'll need from the store cupboard:
Done

Instructions
1. In a medium bowl, mix shredded coconut, nuts, and cocoa powder.
2. Add Stevia and coconut oil.
3. Mix batter thoroughly.
4. In a 9x9 square inch pan or dish, press the batter and for a 30-minutes place in the freezer.
5. Serve and enjoy.

Nutrition Facts Per Serving
Calories: 200; Fat: 17.8g; Carbs: 2.3g; Protein: 1.6g

Air Fryer Garlic Chicken Wings

Prep time: 5 minutes, cook time: 25 minutes; Serves 4

5 Ingredients:

16 pieces chicken wings

¾ cup almond flour

4 tablespoons minced garlic

¼ cup butter, melted

2 tablespoons Stevia powder

What you'll need from the store cupboard:

Salt and pepper to taste**Instructions**

1. Preheat oven to 400°F.
2. In a mixing bowl, combine the chicken wings, almond flour, Stevia powder, and garlic. Season with salt and pepper to taste.
3. Place in a lightly greased cookie sheet in an even layer and cook for 25 minutes.
4. Halfway through the cooking time, turnover chicken.
5. Once cooked, place in a bowl and drizzle with melted butter. Toss to coat.
6. Serve and enjoy.

Nutrition Facts Per Serving

Calories: 365; Fat: 26.9g; Carbs: 7.8g; Protein: 23.7g

Sautéed Brussels Sprouts

Prep time: 5 minutes, cook time: 8 minutes; Serves 4

5 Ingredients:

2 cups Brussels sprouts, halved

1 tablespoon balsamic vinegar

4 tablespoons olive oil

What you'll need from the store cupboard:

Salt and pepper to taste

Instructions

1. Place a saucepan on medium-high fire and heat oil for a minute.
2. Add all ingredients and sauté for 7 minutes.
3. Season with pepper and salt.
4. Serve and enjoy.

Nutrition Facts Per Serving

Calories:162; Fat: 16.8g; Carbs: 4.6g; Protein: 1.5g

Bacon Jalapeno Poppers

Prep time: 15 minutes, cook time: 10 minutes; Serves 8

5 Ingredients:

4-ounce cream cheese

¼ cup cheddar cheese, shredded

1 teaspoon paprika

16 fresh jalapenos, sliced lengthwise and seeded

16 strips of uncured bacon, cut into half

What you'll need from the store cupboard:

Salt and pepper to taste

Instructions

1. Preheat oven to 400°F.
2. In a mixing bowl, mix the cream cheese, cheddar cheese, salt, and paprika until well-combined.
3. Scoop half a teaspoon onto each half of jalapeno peppers.
4. Use a thin strip of bacon and wrap it around the cheese-filled jalapeno half.
5. Place in a single layer in a lightly greased baking sheet and roast for 10 minutes.
6. Serve and enjoy.

Nutrition Facts Per Serving

Calories: 225; Fat: 18.9g; Carbs: 3.2g; Protein: 10.6g

Crispy Keto Pork Bites

Prep time: 20 minutes, cook time: 30 minutes; Serves 3

5 Ingredients:

½ pork belly, sliced to thin strips
1 tablespoon butter
1 onion, diced
4 tablespoons coconut cream

What you'll need from the store cupboard:

Salt and pepper to taste

Instructions

1. Place all ingredients in a mixing bowl and allow to marinate in the fridge for 2 hours.
2. When 2 hours is nearly up, preheat oven to 400ºF and lightly grease a cookie sheet with cooking spray.
3. Place the pork strips in an even layer on the cookie sheet.
4. Roast for 30 minutes and turnover halfway through cooking.

Nutrition Facts Per Serving

Calories: 448; Fat: 40.6g; Carbs: 1.9g; Protein: 19.1g

Fat Burger Bombs

Prep time: 30 minutes, cook time: 20 minutes; Serves 6

5 Ingredients:

12 slices uncured bacon, chopped
1 cup almond flour
2 eggs, beaten
½ pound ground beef
3 tablespoons olive oil

What you'll need from the store cupboard:

Salt and pepper to taste

Instructions

1. In a mixing bowl, combine all ingredients except for the olive oil.
2. Use your hands to form small balls with the mixture. Place in a baking sheet and allow it to set in the fridge for at least 2 hours.
3. Once 2 hours is nearly up, preheat oven to 400ºF.
4. Place meatballs in a single layer in a baking sheet and brush the meatballs with olive oil on all sides.
5. Cook for 20 minutes.

Nutrition Facts Per Serving

Calories: 448; Fat: 40.6g; Carbs: 1.9g; Protein: 19.1g

Onion Cheese Muffins

Prep time: 20 minutes, cook time: 20 minutes; Serves 6

5 Ingredients:

¼ cup Colby jack cheese, shredded
¼ cup shallots, minced
1 cup almond flour
1 egg
3 tbsp sour cream

What you'll need from the store cupboard:

½ tsp salt
3 tbsp melted butter or oil

Instructions

1. Line 6 muffin tins with 6 muffin liners. Set aside and preheat oven to 350ºF.
2. In a bowl, stir the dry and wet ingredients alternately. Mix well using a spatula until the consistency of the mixture becomes even.
3. Scoop a spoonful of the batter to the prepared muffin tins.
4. Bake for 20 minutes in the oven until golden brown.
5. Serve and enjoy.

Nutrition Facts Per Serving

Calories: 193; Fat: 17.4g; Carbs: 4.6g; Protein: 6.3g

Bacon-Flavored Kale Chips

Prep time: 20 minutes, cook time: 25 minutes; Serves 6

5 Ingredients:

2 tbsp butter

¼ cup bacon grease

1-lb kale, around 1 bunch

What you'll need from the store cupboard:

1 to 2 tsp salt

Instructions

1. Remove the rib from kale leaves and tear it into 2-inch pieces.
2. Clean the kale leaves thoroughly and dry them inside a salad spinner.
3. In a skillet, add the butter to the bacon grease and warm the two fats under low heat. Add salt and stir constantly.
4. Set aside and let it cool.
5. Put the dried kale in a Ziploc back and add the cool liquid bacon grease and butter mixture.
6. Seal the Ziploc back and gently shake the kale leaves with the butter mixture. The leaves should have this shiny consistency, which means that they are coated evenly with the fat.
7. Pour the kale leaves on a cookie sheet and sprinkle more salt if necessary.
8. Bake for 25 minutes inside a preheated 350°F oven or until the leaves start to turn brown as well as crispy.
9. Serve and enjoy.

Nutrition Facts Per Serving

Calories: 148; Fat: 13.1g; Carbs: 6.6g; Protein: 3.3g

Keto-Approved Trail Mix

Prep time: 10 minutes, cook time: 3 minutes; Serves 8

5 Ingredients:

¼ cup salted pumpkin seeds

½ cup slivered almonds

¾ cup roasted pecan halves

¼ cup unsweetened cranberries

¾ cup toasted coconut flakes

What you'll need from the store cupboard:

None

Instructions

1. In a skillet, place almonds and pecans. Heat for 2-3 minutes and let it cool.
2. Once cooled, in a large resealable plastic bag, combine all ingredients.
3. Seal and shake vigorously to mix.
4. Serve and enjoy.

Nutrition Facts Per Serving

Calories: 184; Fat: 14.4g; Carbs: 8.0g; Protein: 4.4g

Reese Cups

Prep time: 15 minutes, cook time: 1 minute; Serves 12

5 Ingredients:

¼ cup unsweetened shredded coconut

1 cup almond butter

½ cup dark chocolate chips

1 tablespoon Stevia

What you'll need from the store cupboard:

1 tablespoon coconut oil

Instructions

1. Line 12 muffin tins with 12 muffin liners.
2. Place the almond butter, honey, and oil in a glass bowl and microwave for 30 seconds or until melted. Divide the mixture into 12 muffin tins. Let it cool for 30 minutes in the fridge.
3. Add the shredded coconuts and mix until evenly distributed.
4. Pour the remaining melted chocolate on top of the coconuts. Freeze for an hour.
5. Carefully remove the chocolates from the muffin tins to create perfect Reese cups.
6. Serve and enjoy.

Nutrition Facts Per Serving

Calories: 214; Fat: 17.1g; Carbs: 10.7g; Protein: 5.0g

Curry ' n Poppy Devilled Eggs

Prep time: 20 minutes, cook time: 8 minutes; Serves 6

5 Ingredients:

½ cup mayonnaise
½ tbsp poppy seeds
1 tbsp red curry paste
6 eggs

What you'll need from the store cupboard:

¼ tsp salt

Instructions

1. Place eggs in a small pot and add enough water to cover it. Bring to a boil without a cover, lower fire to a simmer and simmer for 8 minutes.

2. Immediately dunk in ice-cold water once done the cooking. Peel eggshells and slice eggs in half lengthwise.

3. Remove yolks and place them in a medium bowl. Add the rest of the ingredients in the bowl except for the egg whites. Mix well.

4. Evenly return the yolk mixture into the middle of the egg whites.

5. Serve and enjoy.

Nutrition Facts Per Serving

Calories: 200; Fat: 19.0g; Carbs: 1.0g; Protein: 6.0g

Cheddar Cheese Chips

Prep time: 5 minutes, cook time: 8 minutes; Serves 4

5 Ingredients:

8 oz cheddar cheese or provolone cheese or Edam cheese, in slices
½ tsp paprika powder

What you'll need from the store cupboard:

None

Instructions

1. Line baking sheet with foil and preheat oven to 400⁰F.

2. Place cheese slices on a baking sheet and sprinkle the paprika powder on top.

3. Pop in the oven and bake for 8 to 10 minutes.

4. Pay an attention when the timer reaches 6 to 7 minutes as a burnt cheese tastes bitter.

5. Serve and enjoy.

Nutrition Facts Per Serving

Calories: 228; Fat: 19.0g; Carbs: 2.0g; Protein: 13.0g

Cardamom and Cinnamon Fat Bombs

Prep time: 5 minutes, cook time: 3 minutes; Serves 10

5 Ingredients:

¼ tsp ground cardamom (green)
¼ tsp ground cinnamon
½ cup unsweetened shredded coconut
½ tsp vanilla extract
3-oz unsalted butter, room temperature

What you'll need from the store cupboard:

None

Instructions

1. Place a nonstick pan on medium fire and toast coconut until lightly browned.

2. In a bowl, mix all ingredients.

3. Evenly roll into 10 equal balls.

4. Let it cool in the fridge.

5. Serve and enjoy.

Nutrition Facts Per Serving

Calories: 90; Fat: 10.0g; Carbs: 0.4g; Protein: 0.4g

Chapter-13 | 5-Ingredient Fish and Seafood Recipes

Boiled Garlic Clams

Prep time: 3 minutes, cook time: 10 minutes; Serves 6

5 Ingredients:
3 tbsp butter
6 cloves of garlic
50 small clams in the shell, scrubbed
½ cup fresh parsley, chopped
4 tbsp. extra virgin olive oil

What you'll need from the store cupboard:
1 cup water
Salt and pepper to taste

Instructions
1. Heat the olive oil and butter in a large pot placed on medium-high fire for a minute.
2. Stir in the garlic and cook until fragrant and slightly browned.
3. Stir in the clams, water, and parsley. Season with salt and pepper to taste.
4. Cover and cook for 5 minutes or until clams have opened.
5. Discard unopened clams and serve.

Nutrition Facts Per Serving
Calories: 159; Fat: 12.8g; Carbs: 0.9g; Protein: 11.3g

Rosemary-Lemon Shrimps

Prep time: 3 minutes, cook time: 8 minutes; Serves 4

5 Ingredients:
5 tablespoons butter
½ cup lemon juice, freshly squeezed
1 ½ lb. shrimps, peeled and deveined
¼ cup coconut aminos
1 tsp rosemary

What you'll need from the store cupboard:
Pepper to taste

Instructions
1. Place all ingredients in a large pan on a high fire.
2. Boil for 8 minutes or until shrimps are pink.
3. Serve and enjoy.

Nutrition Facts Per Serving
Calories: 315; Fat: 17.9g; Carbs: 3.7g; Protein: 35.8g

Mustard-crusted Salmon

Prep time: 15 minutes, cook time: 15 minutes; Serves 4

5 Ingredients:
1 ¼ lb. salmon fillets, cut into 4 portions
2 tsp. lemon juice
2 tbsp. stone-ground mustard
Lemon wedges, for garnish

What you'll need from the store cupboard:
4 tbsp olive oil
Salt and pepper to taste

Instructions
1. Place a trivet in a large saucepan and pour a cup of water into the pan. Bring to a boil.
2. Place salmon in a heatproof dish that fits inside saucepan and drizzle with olive oil. Season the salmon fillets with salt, pepper, and lemon juice. Sprinkle with mustard on top and garnish with lemon wedges on top. Seal dish with foil.
3. Place the dish on the trivet inside the saucepan. Cover and steam for 15 minutes.
4. Serve and enjoy.

Nutrition Facts Per Serving
Calories: 360; Fat: 24.8g; Carbs: 2.9g; Protein: 29g

Five-Spice Steamed Tilapia

Prep time: 15 minutes, cook time: 15 minutes; Serves 4

5 Ingredients:

1 lb. Tilapia fillets,
1 tsp. Chinese five-spice powder
3 tablespoons coconut oil
3 scallions, sliced thinly

What you'll need from the store cupboard:

Salt and pepper to taste

Instructions

1. Place a trivet in a large saucepan and pour a cup of water into the pan. Bring to a boil.

2. Place tilapia in a heatproof dish that fits inside a saucepan. Drizzle oil on tilapia. Season with salt, pepper, and Chinese five-spice powder. Garnish with scallions.

3. Seal dish with foil. Place the dish on the trivet inside the saucepan. Cover and steam for 15 minutes.

4. Serve and enjoy.

Nutrition Facts Per Serving

Calories: 201; Fat: 12.3g; Carbs:0.9g; Protein: 24g

Express Shrimp and Cauliflower Jambalaya

Prep time: 20 minutes, cook time: 15 minutes; Serves 4

5 Ingredients:

2 cloves garlic, peeled and minced
1 head cauliflower, grated
1 cup chopped tomatoes
8 oz. raw shrimp, peeled and deveined
1 tbsp Cajun seasoning

What you'll need from the store cupboard:

Salt and pepper
4 tbsp coconut oil
1 tbsp water

Instructions

1. On medium-high fire, heat a nonstick saucepan for 2 minutes. Add oil to a pan and swirl to coat bottom and sides. Heat oil for a minute.

2. Add garlic and sauté for a minute. Stir in tomatoes and stir fry for 5 minutes. Add water and deglaze the pan.

3. Add remaining ingredients. Season generously with pepper.

4. Increase fire to high and stir fry for 3 minutes.

5. Lower fire to low, cover, and cook for 5 minutes.

6. Serve and enjoy.

Nutrition Facts Per Serving

Calories: 314; Fat: 22.25g; Carbs: 7.8g; Protein: 21.4g

Salmon with Pepita And Lime

Prep time: 15 minutes, cook time: 15 minutes; Serves 4

5 Ingredients:

2 tbsp. Pepitas, ground
¼ tsp. chili powder
1 lb. salmon fillet, cut into 4 portions
2 tbsp. lime juice

What you'll need from the store cupboard:

Salt and pepper to taste

Instructions

1. Place a trivet in a large saucepan and pour a cup of water into the pan. Bring it to a boil.

2. Place salmon in a heatproof dish that fits inside a saucepan. Drizzle lime juice on the fillet. Season with salt, pepper, and chili powder. Garnish with ground pepitas.

3. Seal dish with foil. Place the dish on the trivet inside the saucepan. Cover and steam for 15 minutes.

4. Serve and enjoy.

Nutrition Facts Per Serving

Calories: 185; Fat: 9g; Carbs: 1g; Protein: 24g

Steamed Chili-Rubbed Tilapia

Prep time: 15 minutes, cook time: 15 minutes; Serves 4

5 Ingredients:
1 lb. tilapia fillet, skin removed
2 tbsp. chili powder
3 cloves garlic, peeled and minced
2 tbsp. extra virgin olive oil
2 tbsp soy sauce

What you'll need from the store cupboard:
none

Instructions

1. Place a trivet in a large saucepan and pour a cup or two of water into the pan. Bring it to a boil.
2. Place tilapia in a heatproof dish that fits inside a saucepan. Drizzle soy sauce and oil on the filet. Season with chili powder and garlic.
3. Seal dish with foil. Place the dish on the trivet inside the saucepan. Cover and steam for 15 minutes.
4. Serve and enjoy.

Nutrition Facts Per Serving
Calories: 211; Fat: 10g; Carbs: 2g; Protein: 26g

Thyme-Sesame Crusted Halibut

Prep time: 20 minutes, cook time: 15 minutes; Serves 2

5 Ingredients:
8 oz. halibut, cut into 2 portions
1 tbsp. lemon juice, freshly squeezed
1 tsp. dried thyme leaves
1 tbsp. sesame seeds, toasted

What you'll need from the store cupboard:
Salt and pepper to taste

Instructions

1. Place a trivet in a large saucepan and pour a cup or two of water into the pan. Bring it to a boil.
2. Place halibut in a heatproof dish that fits inside a saucepan. Season with lemon juice, salt, and pepper. Sprinkle with dried thyme leaves and sesame seeds.
3. Seal dish with foil. Place the dish on the trivet inside the saucepan. Cover and steam for 15 minutes.
4. Serve and enjoy.

Nutrition Facts Per Serving
Calories: 246; Fat: 17.7g; Carbs: 4.2g; Protein: 17.5g

Steamed Lemon Mustard Salmon

Prep time: 15 minutes, cook time: 15 minutes; Serves 4

5 Ingredients:
2 tbsp Dijon mustard
1 whole lemon
2 cloves of garlic, minced
4 salmon fillets, skin removed
1 tbsp dill weed

What you'll need from the store cupboard:
Salt and pepper to taste

Instructions

1. Slice lemon in half. Slice one lemon in circles and juice the other half in a small bowl.
2. Whisk in mustard, garlic, and dill weed in a bowl of lemon. Season with pepper and salt.
3. Place a trivet in a large saucepan and pour a cup or two of water into the pan. Bring to a boil.
4. Place lemon slices in a heatproof dish that fits inside a saucepan. Season salmon with pepper and salt. Slather mustard mixture on top of salmon.
5. Seal dish with foil. Place the dish on the trivet inside the saucepan. Cover and steam for 15 minutes.
6. Serve and enjoy.

Nutrition Facts Per Serving
Calories: 402; Fat: 14.8g; Carbs: 2.2g; Protein: 65.3g

Steamed Cod with Ginger and Scallions

Prep time: 15 minutes, cook time: 15 minutes; Serves 4

5 Ingredients:

4 cod fillets, skin removed
3 tbsp. lemon juice, freshly squeezed
2 tbsp. coconut aminos
2 tbsp. grated ginger
6 scallions, chopped

What you'll need from the store cupboard:

5 tbsp coconut oil
Pepper and salt to taste

Instructions

1. Place a trivet in a large saucepan and pour a cup or two of water into the pan. Bring to a boil.
2. In a small bowl, whisk well lemon juice, coconut aminos, coconut oil, and grated ginger.
3. Place scallions in a heatproof dish that fits inside a saucepan. Season scallions mon with pepper and salt. Drizzle with ginger mixture. Sprinkle scallions on top.
4. Seal dish with foil. Place the dish on the trivet inside the saucepan. Cover and steam for 15 minutes.
5. Serve and enjoy.

Nutrition Facts Per Serving

Calories: 514; Fat: 40g; Carbs: 10g; Protein: 28.3g

Steamed Greek Snapper

Prep time: 10 minutes, cook time: 15 minutes; Serves 12

5 Ingredients:

6 tbsp. olive oil
1 clove of garlic, minced
2 tbsp. Greek yogurt
12 snapper fillets

What you'll need from the store cupboard:

Salt and pepper to taste

Instructions

1. In a small bowl, combine the olive oil, garlic, and Greek yogurt. Season with salt and pepper to taste.
2. Place a trivet in a large saucepan and pour a cup or two of water into the pan. Bring to a boil.
3. Place snapper in a heatproof dish that fits inside a saucepan. If needed, cook in batches. Season snapper with pepper and salt and drizzle with olive oil. Slather with yogurt mixture.
4. Seal dish with foil. Place the dish on the trivet inside the saucepan. Cover and steam for 15 minutes.
5. Serve and enjoy.

Nutrition Facts Per Serving

Calories: 280; Fat: 9.8g; Carbs: 0.4g; Protein: 44.8g

Flounder with Dill and Capers

Prep time: 10 minutes, cook time: 15 minutes; Serves 4

5 Ingredients:

4 flounder fillets
1 tbsp. chopped fresh dill
2 tbsp. capers, chopped
4 lemon wedges

What you'll need from the store cupboard:

6 tbsp olive oil
Salt and pepper to taste

Instructions

1. Place a trivet in a large saucepan and pour a cup or two of water into the pan. Bring to a boil.
2. Place flounder in a heatproof dish that fits inside a saucepan. Season snapper with pepper and salt. Drizzle with olive oil on all sides. Sprinkle dill and capers on top of the filet.
3. Seal dish with foil. Place the dish on the trivet inside the saucepan. Cover and steam for 15 minutes.
4. Serve and enjoy with lemon wedges.

Nutrition Facts Per Serving

Calories: 447; Fat: 35.9g; Carbs: 8.6g; Protein: 20.3g

Halibut En Papillote

Prep time: 10 minutes, cook time: 15 minutes; Serves 4

5 Ingredients:

4 halibut fillets

½ tbsp. grated ginger

1 cup chopped tomatoes

1 shallot, thinly sliced

1 lemon

What you'll need from the store cupboard:

5 tbsp olive oil

Salt and pepper to taste

Instructions

1. Slice lemon in half. Slice one lemon in circles.
2. Juice the other half of the lemon in a small bowl. Mix in grated ginger and season with pepper and salt.
3. Place a trivet in a large saucepan and pour a cup or two of water into the pan. Bring to a boil.
4. Get 4 large foil and place one fillet in the middle of each foil. Season with fillet salt and pepper. Drizzle with olive oil. Add the grated ginger, tomatoes, and shallots equally. Fold the foil to create a pouch and crimp the edges.
5. Place the foil containing the fish on the trivet. Cover saucepan and steam for 15 minutes.
6. Serve and enjoy in pouches.

Nutrition Facts Per Serving

Calories: 410; Fat: 32.3g; Carbs: 2.7g; Protein: 20.3g

Chili-Garlic Salmon

Prep time: 10 minutes, cook time: 15 minutes; Serves 4

5 Ingredients:

5 tbsp. sweet chili sauce

¼ cup coconut aminos

4 salmon fillets

3 tbsp. green onions, chopped

3 cloves garlic, peeled and minced

What you'll need from the store cupboard:

Pepper to taste

Instructions

1. Place a trivet in a large saucepan and pour a cup or two of water into the pan. Bring to a boil.
2. In a small bowl, whisk well sweet chili sauce, garlic, and coconut aminos.
3. Place salmon in a heatproof dish that fits inside a saucepan. Season salmon with pepper. Drizzle with sweet chili sauce mixture. Sprinkle green onions on top of the filet.
4. Seal dish with foil. Place the dish on the trivet inside the saucepan. Cover and steam for 15 minutes.
5. Serve and enjoy.

Nutrition Facts Per Serving

Calories: 409; Fat: 14.4g; Carbs: 0.9g; Protein: 65.4g

Halibut with Pesto

Prep time: 15 minutes, cook time: 15 minutes; Serves 4

5 Ingredients:

4 halibut fillets

1 cup basil leaves

2 cloves of garlic, minced

1 tbsp. lemon juice, freshly squeezed

2 tbsp pine nuts

What you'll need from the store cupboard:

2 tbsp. oil, preferably extra virgin olive oil

Salt and pepper to taste

Instructions

1. In a food processor, pulse the basil, olive oil, pine nuts, garlic, and lemon juice until coarse. Season with salt and pepper to taste.
2. Place a trivet in a large saucepan and pour a cup or two of water into the pan. Bring to a boil.

3. Place salmon in a heatproof dish that fits inside a saucepan. Season salmon with pepper and salt. Drizzle with pesto sauce.
4. Seal dish with foil. Place the dish on the trivet inside the saucepan. Cover and steam for 15 minutes.
5. Serve and enjoy.

Nutrition Facts Per Serving
Calories: 401; Fat: 8.4g; Carbs: 0.8g; Protein: 75.8g

Chili-Lime Shrimps

Prep time: 5 minutes, cook time: 10 minutes; Serves 4

5 Ingredients:
1 ½ lb. raw shrimp, peeled and deveined
1 tbsp. chili flakes
5 tbsp sweet chili sauce
2 tbsp. lime juice, freshly squeezed
1 tsp cayenne pepper

What you'll need from the store cupboard:
Salt and pepper to taste
5 tbsp oil
3 tbsp water

Instructions
1. In a small bowl, whisk well chili flakes, sweet chili sauce, cayenne pepper, and water.
2. On medium-high fire, heat a nonstick saucepan for 2 minutes. Add oil to a pan and swirl to coat bottom and sides. Heat oil for a minute.
3. Stir fry shrimp, around 5 minutes. Season lightly with salt and pepper.
4. Stir in sweet chili mixture and toss well shrimp to coat.
5. Turn off fire, drizzle lime juice and toss well to coat.
6. Serve and enjoy.

Nutrition Facts Per Serving
Calories: 306; Fat: 19.8g; Carbs: 1.7g; Protein: 34.9.g

Steamed Herbed Red Snapper

Prep time: 3 minutes, cook time: 15 minutes; Serves 4

5 Ingredients:
4 red snapper fillets
¼ tsp. paprika
3 tbsp. lemon juice, freshly squeezed
1 ½ tsp chopped fresh herbs of your choice (rosemary, thyme, basil, or parsley)

What you'll need from the store cupboard:
6 tbsp olive oil
Salt and pepper to taste

Instructions
1. In a small bowl, whisk well paprika, lemon juice, olive oil, and herbs. Season with pepper and salt.
2. Place a trivet in a large saucepan and pour a cup or two of water into the pan. Bring to a boil.
3. Place snapper in a heatproof dish that fits inside a saucepan. Season snapper with pepper and salt. Drizzle with lemon mixture.
4. Seal dish with foil. Place the dish on the trivet inside the saucepan. Cover and steam for 15 minutes.
5. Serve and enjoy.

Nutrition Facts Per Serving
Calories: 374; Fat: 20.3g; Carbs: 2.1g; Protein: 45.6g

Simple Steamed Salmon Fillets

Prep time: 10 minutes, cook time: 15 minutes; Serves 3

5 Ingredients:
10 oz. salmon fillets
2 tbsp. coconut aminos
2 tbsp. lemon juice, freshly squeezed
1 tsp. sesame seeds, toasted
3 tbsp sesame oil

What you'll need from the store cupboard:

Salt and pepper to taste

Instructions

1. Place a trivet in a large saucepan and pour a cup or two of water into the pan. Bring to a boil.
2. Place salmon in a heatproof dish that fits inside the saucepan. Season salmon with pepper and salt. Drizzle with coconut aminos, lemon juice, sesame oil, and sesame seeds.
3. Seal dish with foil. Place the dish on the trivet inside the saucepan. Cover and steam for 15 minutes.
4. Serve and enjoy.

Nutrition Facts Per Serving

Calories: 210; Fat: 17.4g; Carbs: 2.6g; Protein: 20.1g

Red Curry Halibut

Prep time: 3 minutes, cook time: 15 minutes; Serves 4

5 Ingredients:

4 halibut fillets, skin removed

1 cup chopped tomatoes

3 green curry leaves

2 tbsp. chopped cilantro

1 tbsp. lime juice, freshly squeezed

What you' ll need from the store cupboard:

3 tbsp olive oil

Pepper and salt to taste

Instructions

1. Place a trivet in a large saucepan and pour a cup or two of water into the pan. Bring to a boil.
2. Place halibut in a heatproof dish that fits inside the saucepan. Season halibut with pepper and salt. Drizzle with olive oil. Sprinkle chopped tomatoes, curry leaves, chopped cilantro, and lime juice.
3. Seal dish with foil. Place the dish on the trivet inside the saucepan. Cover and steam for 15 minutes.
4. Serve and enjoy.

Nutrition Facts Per Serving

Calories: 429; Fat: 15.5g; Carbs: 1.8g; Protein: 76.1g

Coconut Curry Cod

Prep time: 15 minutes, cook time: 17 minutes; Serves 4

5 Ingredients:

4 cod fillets

1 ½ cups coconut milk, freshly squeezed if possible

2 tsp. grated ginger

2 tsp. curry powder

1 sprig cilantro, chopped

What you' ll need from the store cupboard:

Salt and pepper to taste

Instructions

1. Add all ingredients in a nonstick saucepan. Cover and cook for 10 minutes on a high fire.
2. Lower fire to a simmer and simmer for 7 minutes.
3. Season with pepper and salt.
4. Serve and enjoy.

Nutrition Facts Per Serving

Calories: 291; Fat: 22.1g; Carbs: 5.7g; Protein: 19.7g

Lemon-Rosemary Shrimps

Prep time: 3 minutes, cook time: 12 minutes; Serves 4

5 Ingredients:

½ cup lemon juice, freshly squeezed

1 ½ lb. shrimps, peeled and deveined

2 tbsp fresh rosemary

¼ cup coconut aminos

2 tbsp butter

What you' ll need from the store cupboard:

Pepper to taste

4 tbsp olive oil

Instructions

1. Place a nonstick saucepan on medium-high fire and heat oil and butter for 2 minutes.

2. Stir in shrimps and coconut aminos. Season with pepper. Sauté for 5 minutes.
3. Add remaining ingredients and cook for another 5 minutes while stirring frequently.

4. Serve and enjoy.

Nutrition Facts Per Serving

Calories: 359; Fat: 22.4g; Carbs: 3.7g; Protein: 35.8g

Golden Pompano in Microwave

Prep time: 20 minutes, cook time: 11 minutes; Serves 2

5 Ingredients:

½-lb pompano
1 tbsp soy sauce, low sodium
1-inch thumb ginger, diced
1 lemon, halved
1 stalk green onions, chopped

What you'll need from the store cupboard:

¼ cup water
1 tsp pepper
4 tbsp olive oil

Instructions

1. In a microwavable casserole dish, mix well all ingredients except for pompano, green onions, and lemon.
2. Squeeze half of the lemon in dish and slice into thin circles the other half.
3. Place pompano in the dish and add lemon circles on top of the fish. Drizzle with pepper and olive oil.
4. Cover top of a casserole dish with a microwave-safe plate.
5. Microwave for 5 minutes.
6. Remove from microwave, turn over fish, sprinkle green onions, top with a microwavable plate.
7. Return to microwave and cook for another 3 minutes.
8. Let it rest for 3 minutes more.
9. Serve and enjoy.

Nutrition Facts Per Serving

Calories: 464; Fat: 39.5g; Carbs: 6.3g; Protein: 22.2g

Salmon and Cauliflower Rice Pilaf

Prep time: 5 minutes, cook time: 25 minutes; Serves 4

5 Ingredients:

1 cauliflower head, shredded
¼ cup dried vegetable soup mix
1 cup chicken broth
1 pinch saffron
1-lb wild salmon fillets

What you'll need from the store cupboard:

6 tbsp olive oil
Pepper and salt to taste

Instructions

1. Place a heavy-bottomed pot on medium-high fire and add all ingredients and mix well.
2. Bring to a boil, lower fire to a simmer, and simmer for 10 minutes.
3. Turn off fire, shred salmon, adjust seasoning to taste.
4. Let it rest for 5 minutes.
5. Fluff again, serve, and enjoy.

Nutrition Facts Per Serving

Calories: 429; Fat: 31.5g; Carbs: 4.7g; Protein: 31.8g

Lemon Chili Halibut

Prep time: 5 minutes, cook time: 15 minutes; Serves 2

5 Ingredients:

1-lb halibut fillets
1 lemon, sliced
1 tablespoon chili pepper flakes

What you'll need from the store cupboard:

Pepper and salt to taste
4 tbsp olive oil

Instructions

1. In a heat-proof dish that fits inside saucepan, place fish. Top fish with chili flakes, lemon slices, salt, and pepper. Drizzle with olive oil. Cover dish with foil
2. Place a large saucepan on the medium-high fire. Place a trivet inside the saucepan and fill the pan halfway with water. Cover and bring to a boil.
3. Place dish on the trivet.
4. Cover pan and steam for 10 minutes. Let it rest in pan for another 5 minutes.
5. Serve and enjoy topped with pepper.

Nutrition Facts Per Serving
Calories: 675; Fat: 58.4g; Carbs: 4.2g; Protein: 42.7g

Chipotle Salmon Asparagus

Prep time: 25 minutes, cook time: 15 minutes; Serves 2
5 Ingredients:
1-lb salmon fillet, skin on
2 teaspoon chipotle paste
A handful of asparagus spears, trimmed
1 lemon, sliced thinly
A pinch of rosemary
What you'll need from the store cupboard:
Salt to taste
5 tbsp olive oil
Instructions
1. In a heat-proof dish that fits inside the saucepan, add asparagus spears on the bottom of the dish. Place fish, top with rosemary, and lemon slices. Season with chipotle paste and salt. Drizzle with olive oil. Cover dish with foil.
2. Place a large saucepan on the medium-high fire. Place a trivet inside the saucepan and fill the pan halfway with water. Cover and bring to a boil.
3. Place dish on the trivet.
4. Cover pan and steam for 10 minutes. Let it rest in pan for another 5 minutes.
5. Serve and enjoy topped with pepper.

Nutrition Facts Per Serving
Calories: 651; Fat: 50.7g; Carbs: 2.8g; Protein: 35.0g

Enchilada Sauce on Mahi Mahi

Prep time: 5 minutes, cook time: 15 minutes; Serves 2
5 Ingredients:
2 Mahi fillets, fresh
¼ cup commercial enchilada sauce
What you'll need from the store cupboard:
Pepper to taste
Instructions
1. In a heat-proof dish that fits inside saucepan, place fish and top with enchilada sauce.
2. Place a large saucepan on the medium-high fire. Place a trivet inside the saucepan and fill the pan halfway with water. Cover and bring to a boil.
3. Cover dish with foil and place on a trivet.
4. Cover pan and steam for 10 minutes. Let it rest in pan for another 5 minutes.
5. Serve and enjoy topped with pepper.

Nutrition Facts Per Serving
Calories: 257; Fat: 15.9g; Carbs: 8.9g; Protein: 19.8g

Simply Steamed Alaskan Cod

Prep time: 10 minutes, cook time: 15 minutes; Serves 2

5 Ingredients:

1-lb fillet wild Alaskan Cod
1 cup cherry tomatoes, halved
1 tbsp balsamic vinegar
1 tbsp fresh basil chopped

What you'll need from the store cupboard:

Salt and pepper to taste
5 tbsp olive oil

Instructions

1. In a heat-proof dish that fits inside the saucepan, add all ingredients except for basil. Mix well.
2. Place a large saucepan on the medium-high fire. Place a trivet inside the saucepan and fill pan halfway with water. Cover and bring to a boil.
3. Cover dish with foil and place on a trivet.
4. Cover pan and steam for 10 minutes. Let it rest in pan for another 5 minutes.
5. Serve and enjoy topped with fresh basil.

Nutrition Facts Per Serving

Calories: 495.2; Fat: 36.6g; Carbs: 4.2g; Protein: 41.0g

Steamed Ginger Scallion Fish

Prep time:10 minutes, cook time: 15 minutes; Serves

5 Ingredients:

3 tablespoons soy sauce, low sodium
2 tablespoons rice wine
1 teaspoon minced ginger
1 teaspoon garlic
1-pound firm white fish

What you'll need from the store cupboard:

Pepper to taste
4 tbsps sesame oil

Instructions

1. In a heat-proof dish that fits inside the saucepan, add all ingredients. Mix well.
2. Place a large saucepan on the medium-high fire. Place a trivet inside the saucepan and fill the pan halfway with water. Cover and bring to a boil.
3. Cover dish with foil and place on a trivet.
4. Cover pan and steam for 10 minutes. Let it rest in pan for another 5 minutes.
5. Serve and enjoy.

Nutrition Facts Per Serving

Calories: 409.5; Fat: 23.1g; Carbs: 5.5g; Protein: 44.9g

Sautéed Savory Shrimps

Prep time: 5 minutes, cook time: 15 minutes; Serves 8

5 Ingredients:

2 pounds shrimp, peeled and deveined
4 cloves garlic, minced
½ cup chicken stock, low sodium
1 tablespoon lemon juice

What you'll need from the store cupboard:

Salt and pepper
5 tablespoons oil

Instructions

1. Place a heavy-bottomed pot on medium-high fire and heat pot for 3 minutes.
2. Once hot, add oil and stir around to coat pot with oil.
3. Sauté the garlic and corn for 5 minutes.
4. Add remaining ingredients and mix well.
5. Cover and bring to a boil, lower fire to a simmer, and simmer for 5 minutes.
6. Serve and enjoy.

Nutrition Facts Per Serving

Calories: 182.6; Fat: 9.8g; Carbs: 1.7g; Protein: 25.2g

Steamed Asparagus and Shrimps

Prep time: 15 minutes, cook time: 15 minutes; Serves 6

5 Ingredients:

1-pound shrimps, peeled and deveined
1 bunch asparagus, trimmed
½ tablespoon Cajun seasoning
2 tablespoons butter
5 tablespoons oil**What you'll need from the store cupboard:**
Salt and pepper to taste

Instructions

1. In a heat-proof dish that fits inside the saucepan, add all ingredients. Mix well.
2. Place a large saucepan on the medium-high fire. Place a trivet inside the saucepan and fill the pan halfway with water. Cover and bring to a boil.
3. Cover dish with foil and place on a trivet.
4. Cover pan and steam for 10 minutes. Let it rest in pan for another 5 minutes.
5. Serve and enjoy.

Nutrition Facts Per Serving
Calories: 204.8; Fat: 15.8g; Carbs: 1.1g; Protein: 15.5g

Yummy Shrimp Fried Rice

Prep time: 10 minutes, cook time: 20 minutes; Serves 6

5 Ingredients:

4 tablespoons butter, divided
4 large eggs, lightly beaten
3 cups shredded cauliflower
1-pound uncooked medium shrimp, peeled and deveined

What you'll need from the store cupboard:

1/2 teaspoon salt
1/4 teaspoon pepper

Instructions

1. In a large skillet, melt 1 tablespoon butter over medium-high heat.
2. Pour eggs into skillet. As eggs set, lift edges, letting uncooked portion flow underneath. Remove eggs and keep warm.
3. Melt remaining butter in the skillet. Add the cauliflower, and shrimp; cook and stir for 5 minutes or until shrimp turn pink.
4. Meanwhile, chop eggs into small pieces. Return eggs to the pan; sprinkle with salt and pepper. Cook until heated through, stirring occasionally. Sprinkle with bacon if desired.

Nutrition Facts Per Serving
Calories: 172; Fat: 11g; Carbs: 3.3g; Protein: 13g

Cod with Balsamic Tomatoes

Prep time: 5 minutes, cook time: 30 minutes; Serves 4

5 Ingredients:

4 center-cut bacon strips, chopped
4 cod fillets (5 ounces each)
2 cups grape tomatoes, halved
2 tablespoons balsamic vinegar
4 tablespoons olive oil

What you'll need from the store cupboard:

1/2 teaspoon salt
1/4 teaspoon pepper

Instructions

1. In a large skillet, heat olive oil and cook bacon over medium heat until crisp, stirring occasionally.
2. Remove with a slotted spoon; drain on paper towels.
3. Sprinkle fillets with salt and pepper. Add fillets to bacon drippings; cook over medium-high heat until fish just begins to flake easily with a fork, 4-6 minutes on each side. Remove and keep warm.
4. Add tomatoes to skillet; cook and stir until tomatoes are softened, 2-4 minutes. Stir in vinegar; reduce heat to medium-low. Cook until sauce is thickened, 1-2 minutes longer.
5. Serve cod with tomato mixture and bacon.

Nutrition Facts Per Serving
Calories: 442; Fat: 30.4g; Carbs: 5g; Protein: 26g

Buttery Almond Lemon Tilapia

Prep time: 5 minutes, cook time: 10 minutes; Serves 4

5 Ingredients:

4 tilapia fillets (4 ounces each)
1/4 cup butter, cubed
1/4 cup white wine or chicken broth
2 tablespoons lemon juice
1/4 cup sliced almonds

What you'll need from the store cupboard:

1/2 teaspoon salt
1/4 teaspoon pepper
1 tablespoon olive oil

Instructions

1. Sprinkle fillets with salt and pepper. In a large nonstick skillet, heat oil over medium heat.
2. Add fillets; cook until fish just begins to flake easily with a fork, 2-3 minutes on each side. Remove and keep warm.
3. Add butter, wine and lemon juice to the same pan; cook and stir until butter is melted.
4. Serve with fish; sprinkle with almonds.

Nutrition Facts Per Serving

Calories: 269; Fat: 19g; Carbs: 2g; Protein: 22g

Cilantro Shrimp

Prep time: 5 minutes, cook time: 10 minutes; Serves 4

5 Ingredients:

1/2 cup reduced-fat Asian sesame salad dressing
1-pound uncooked shrimp (31-40 per pound), peeled and deveined
Lime wedges
1/4 cup chopped fresh cilantro

What you'll need from the store cupboard:

5 tablespoon olive oil
Salt and pepper

Instructions

1. In a large nonstick skillet, heat 1 tablespoon dressing over medium heat. Add shrimp; cook and stir 1 minute.
2. Stir in remaining dressing; cook, uncovered, until shrimp turn pink, 1-2 minutes longer.
3. To serve, squeeze lime juice over the top; sprinkle with cilantro, pepper, and salt. If desired, serve with rice.

Nutrition Facts Per Serving

Calories: 509; Fat: 39g; Carbs: 4.7g; Protein: 32g

Shrimp Spread

Prep time: 10 minutes, cook time: 0 minutes; Serves 20

5 Ingredients:

1 package (8 ounces) cream cheese, softened
1/2 cup sour cream
1 cup seafood cocktail sauce
12 ounces frozen cooked salad shrimp, thawed
1 medium green pepper, chopped

What you'll need from the store cupboard:

Pepper

Instructions

1. In a large bowl, beat the cream cheese, and sour cream until smooth.
2. Spread mixture on a round 12-inch serving platter.
3. Top with seafood sauce.
4. Sprinkle with shrimp and green peppers. Cover and refrigerate.
5. Serve with crackers.

Nutrition Facts Per Serving

Calories: 136; Fat: 10g; Carbs: 4g; Protein: 8g

Blue Cheese Shrimps

Prep time: 5 minutes, cook time: 15 minutes; Serves 6

5 Ingredients:

3 ounces cream cheese, softened

2/3 cup minced fresh parsley, divided

1/4 cup crumbled blue cheese

1/2 teaspoon Creole mustard

24 cooked jumbo shrimp, peeled and deveined

What you'll need from the store cupboard:

Pepper and salt to taste

5 tablespoon olive oil

Instructions

1. In a small bowl, beat cream cheese until smooth. Beat in 1/3 cup parsley, blue cheese, and mustard. Season with pepper and salt as desired. Refrigerate at least 1 hour.
2. Make a deep slit along the back of each shrimp to within 1/4-1/2 inch of the bottom. Stuff with cream cheese mixture; press remaining parsley onto cream cheese mixture.
3. Drizzle with olive oil last.

Nutrition Facts Per Serving

Calories: 180; Fat: 17.8g; Carbs: 1.7g; Protein: 6g

Air Fryer Seasoned Salmon Fillets

Prep time: 10 mins; Cook time: 10 mins; Serves 4

5 Ingredients:

2 lbs. salmon fillets

1 tsp. stevia

2 tbsp. mustard

1 clove of garlic, minced

1/2 tsp. thyme leaves

What you'll need from the store cupboard:

2 tsp. extra-virgin olive oil

Cooking spray

Salt and black pepper to taste

Instructions

1. Preheat your Air Fryer to 390 degrees F.
2. Season salmon fillets with salt and pepper.
3. Add together the mustard, garlic, stevia, thyme, and oil in a bowl, stir to combined well. Rub the seasoning mixture on top of salmon fillets.
4. Spray the Air Fryer basket with cooking spray and cook seasoned fillets for 10 minutes until crispy. Let it cool before serving.

Nutrition Facts Per Serving

Per Serving: Calories 238 ; Carbohydrates 10 g; Fat 14 g; Protein 18g

Seasoned Salmon with Parmesan

Prep time: 5 mins; Cook time: 20 mins; Serves 4

5 Ingredients:

2 lbs. salmon fillet

3 minced garlic cloves

¼ cup. chopped parsley

½ cup. grated parmesan cheese

Salt and pepper to taste

Instructions

1. Preheat oven to 425 degrees F. Line a baking sheet with parchment paper.
2. Lay salmon fillets on the lined baking sheet, season with salt and pepper to taste.
3. Bake for 10 minutes. Remove from the oven and sprinkle with garlic, parmesan and parsley.
4. Place in the oven to cook for 5 more minutes. Transfer to plates before serving.

Nutrition Facts Per Serving

Per Serving: Calories: 210, Fat: 12, Net Carbs: 0.6, Protein: 25

Cedar Planked Salmon with Green Onion

Prep time: 15 mins; Cook time: 20 mins; Serves 5

5 Ingredients:

3 (12 inch) untreated cedar planks
1/4 cup. chopped green onions
1 tablespoon. grated fresh ginger root
1 teaspoon. minced garlic
2 (2 pound) salmon fillets, skin removed

What you'll need from the store cupboard:

1/3 cup. olive oil
1/3 cup. mayo
1 1/2 tablespoons. rice vinegar

Instructions

1. Soak cedar planks in warm water for 1 hour more.
2. Whisk olive oil, rice vinegar, mayo, green onions, ginger, and garlic in a bowl. Marinade salmon fillets to coat completely. Cover the bowl with plastic wrap and marinate for 15 to 60 minutes.
3. Preheat an outdoor grill over medium heat. Lay planks on the center of hot grate Place the salmon fillets onto the planks and remove the marinade. Cover the grill and cook until cooked through, about 20 minutes, or until salmon is done to your liking. Serve the salmon on a platter right off the planks.

Nutrition Facts Per Serving

Per Serving: 355 calories; 27 g fat; 10 g carbohydrates; 18 g protein

Grilled Salmon Fillets with Pepper Flakes

Prep time: 10 mins; Cook time: 20 mins; Serves 4

5 Ingredients

4 (4 ounce) fillets salmon
2 tablespoons. thinly sliced green onion
1 clove garlic, minced
3/4 teaspoon. ground ginger
1/2 teaspoon. crushed red pepper flakes

What you'll need from the store cupboard:

1/4 cup olive oil
1/8 teaspoon salt
2 tablespoons mayo
2 tablespoons balsamic vinegar

Instructions

1. Add together olive oil, mayo, balsamic vinegar, green onions, garlic, ginger, red pepper flakes and salt, stir well. Pour over salmon fillets in a dish. Cover and marinate the fish in the refrigerator for 4 to 6 hours.
2. Preheat an outdoor grill with coals about 5 inches from the grate. Grease the grill grate with olive oil.
3. Remove fish from marinade and place on grill. Grill the fillets 5 inches from coals for 10 minutes per inch of thickness, measured at the thickest part. Flip halfway through cooking and serve.

Nutrition Facts Per Serving

Per Serving: 233 calories; 17.6 g fat; 2.9 g carbohydrates; 15.3 g protein

Lemon Marinated Salmon with Spices

Prep time: 10 mins; Cook time: 15 minutes; Serves 2

5 Ingredients:

2 tablespoons. lemon juice

1 tablespoon. yellow miso paste

2 teaspoons. Dijon mustard

1 pinch cayenne pepper and sea salt to taste

2 (8 ounce) center-cut salmon fillets, boned; skin on

What you'll need from the store cupboard:

1 1/2 tablespoons mayonnaise

1 tablespoon ground black pepper

Instructions

1. In a bowl, combine lemon juice with black pepper. Stir in mayonnaise, miso paste, Dijon mustard, and cayenne pepper, mix well. Pour over salmon fillets, reserve about a tablespoon marinade. Cover and marinate the fish in the refrigerator for 30 minutes.

2. Preheat oven to 450 degrees F. Line a baking sheet with parchment paper. Lay fillets on the prepared baking sheet. Rub the reserved lemon-pepper marinade on fillets. Then season with cayenne pepper and sea salt to taste.

3. Bake in the oven for 10 to 15 minutes until cooked through.

Nutrition Facts Per Serving

Per Serving: 361 calories; 28.1 g fat; 7.1 g carbohydrates; 20 g protein

Coconut Milk Sauce over Crabs

Prep time: 10 minutes, cook time: 20 minutes; Serves 6

5 Ingredients:

2-pounds crab quartered

1 can coconut milk

1 thumb-size ginger, sliced

1 onion, chopped

3 cloves of garlic, minced

What you'll need from the store cupboard:

Pepper and salt to taste

Instructions

1. Place a heavy-bottomed pot on medium-high fire and add all ingredients.

2. Cover and bring to a boil, lower fire to a simmer, and simmer for 20 minutes.

3. Serve and enjoy.

Nutrition Facts Per Serving

Calories: 244.1; Fat: 11.3g; Carbs: 6.3g; Protein: 29.3g

Simple Chicken Garlic-Tomato Stew

Prep time: 10 minutes, cook time: 45 minutes; Serves 4

5 Ingredients:

3 tbsp. coconut oil
5 cloves of garlic, minced
4 chicken breasts halves
3 roma tomatoes chopped
1 small onion chopped

What you'll need from the store cupboard:

Salt and pepper to taste
1 ½ cups water

Instructions

1. Place a large saucepan on medium-high fire and heat for 2 minutes.
2. Add 1 tbsp oil and heat for a minute.
3. Season chicken breasts generously with pepper and salt.
4. Sear for 5 minutes per side of the chicken breast. Transfer to a plate and let it rest.
5. In the same pan, add remaining oil and sauté garlic for a minute. Stir in onions and tomatoes. Sauté for 7 minutes.
6. Meanwhile, chop chicken into bite-sized pieces.
7. Deglaze pan with water and add chopped chicken. Cover and simmer for 15 minutes.
8. Adjust seasoning if needed.
9. Serve and enjoy.

Nutrition Facts Per Serving

Calories: 591; Fat: 37.5g; Carbs: 1.1g; Protein: 60.8g

Pesto Chicken

Prep time: 15 minutes, cook time: 30 minutes; Serves 4

5 Ingredients:

2 cups basil leaves
¼ cup + 1 tbsp extra virgin olive oil, divided
5 sun-dried tomatoes
4 chicken breasts
6 cloves garlic, smashed, peeled, and minced

What you'll need from the store cupboard:

Salt and pepper to taste
Water

Instructions

1. Put in the food processor the basil leaves, ¼ cup olive oil, and tomatoes. Season with salt and pepper to taste. Add a cup of water if needed.
2. Season chicken breasts with pepper and salt generously.
3. On medium fire, heat a saucepan for 2 minutes. Add a tbsp of olive oil to the pan and swirl to coat bottom and sides. Heat oil for a minute.
4. Add chicken and sear for 5 minutes per side.
5. Add pesto sauce, cover, and cook on low fire for 15 minutes or until chicken is cooked thoroughly.
6. Serve and enjoy.

Nutrition Facts Per Serving

Calories: 556; Fat: 32.7g; Carbs: 1.1g; Protein: 60.8g

Stir Fried Broccoli 'n Chicken

Prep time: 15 minutes, cook time: 20 minutes; Serves 5

5 Ingredients:

1 tbsp. coconut oil
3 cloves of garlic, minced
1 ½ lb. chicken breasts, cut into strips
¼ cup coconut aminos
1 head broccoli, cut into florets

What you'll need from the store cupboard:

Pepper to taste

Instructions

1. On medium fire, heat a saucepan for 2 minutes. Add oil to the pan and swirl to

coat bottom and sides. Heat oil for a minute.
2. Add garlic and sauté for a minute. Stir in chicken and stir fry for 5 minutes.
3. Add remaining ingredients. Season generously with pepper.
4. Increase fire to high and stir fry for 3 minutes.
5. Lower fire to low, cover, and cook for 5 minutes.
6. Serve and enjoy.

Nutrition Facts Per Serving
Calories: 263; Fat: 15.4g; Carbs: 1.8g; Protein: 28.6g

Chicken Cacciatore

Prep time: 5 minutes, cook time: 35 minutes; Serves 6

5 Ingredients:
6 chicken drumsticks, bone-in
1 bay leaf
4 roma tomatoes, chopped
½ cup black olives, pitted
3 cloves garlic, minced

What you' ll need from the store cupboard:
Salt and pepper to taste
1 cup water
1 tsp oil

Instructions
1. On high fire, heat a saucepan for 2 minutes. Add oil to the pan and swirl to coat bottom and sides. Heat oil for a minute.
2. Add garlic and sauté for a minute. Stir in tomatoes and bay leaf. Crumble and wilt tomatoes for 5 minutes.
3. Add chicken and continue sautéing for 7 minutes.
4. Deglaze the pot with ½ cup water.
5. Add remaining ingredients. Season generously with salt and pepper.
6. Lower fire to low, cover, and simmer for 20 minutes.
7. Serve and enjoy.

Nutrition Facts Per Serving
Calories: 256; Fat: 13.2g; Carbs: 9.5g; Protein: 25.3g

Whole Roasted Chicken with Lemon and Rosemary

Prep time: 120 minutes, cook time: 1 hour and 40 minutes; Serves 12

5 Ingredients:
1 whole chicken
6 cloves of garlic, minced
1 lemon, sliced
2 sprigs rosemary

What you' ll need from the store cupboard:
Salt and pepper to taste

Instructions
1. Place lemon peel, 1 rosemary sprig, and 2 cloves of smashed garlic in chicken cavity.
2. Place the whole chicken in a big bowl and rub all the spices onto the surface and insides of the chicken.
3. Place the chicken on a wire rack placed on top of a baking pan. Tent with foil.
4. Cook in a preheated 350ºF oven for 60 minutes.
5. Remove foil and continue baking until golden brown, around 30 minutes more.
6. Let chicken rest for 10 minutes.
7. Serve and enjoy.

Nutrition Facts Per Serving
Calories: 248; Fat: 17.2g; Carbs: 0.9g; Protein: 21.3g

Rotisserie Chicken with Garlic Paprika

Prep time: 120 minutes, cook time: 1 hour and 40 minutes; Serves 12

5 Ingredients:
1 whole chicken
1 tbsp. thyme
1 tbsp. paprika
6 cloves garlic
2 bay leaves

What you' ll need from the store cupboard:
1 tsp salt

½ tbsp pepper

Instructions

1. In a small bowl, mix well thyme, paprika, salt, and pepper.
2. Rub and massage the entire chicken and inside the cavity with the spices.
3. Smash and peel 6 garlic cloves and mince. Rub all over chicken and inside of the chicken.
4. Smash remaining garlic and place in the chicken cavity along with bay leaves.
5. Place chicken on a wire rack placed on top of a baking pan. Tent with foil.
6. Pop in a preheated 350°F oven and bake for 60 minutes.
7. Remove foil and continue baking for another 30 minutes.
8. Let chicken rest for 10 minutes before serving and enjoy.

Nutrition Facts Per Serving

Calories: 249; Fat: 17.2g; Carbs: 1.4g; Protein: 21.3g

Easy Asian Chicken

Prep time: 20 minutes, cook time: 16 minutes; Serves 5

5 Ingredients:

1 ½ lb. boneless chicken breasts, sliced into strips
1 tbsp ginger slices
3 tbsp coconut aminos
¼ cup organic chicken broth
3 cloves of garlic, minced

What you'll need from the store cupboard:

5 tablespoons sesame oil

Instructions

1. On high fire, heat a heavy-bottomed pot for 2 minutes. Add oil to a pan and swirl to coat bottom and sides. Heat oil for a minute.
2. Add garlic and ginger sauté for a minute.
3. Stir in chicken breast and sauté for 5 minutes. Season with coconut aminos and sauté for another 2 minutes.
4. Add remaining ingredients and bring to a boil.
5. Let it boil for 5 minutes.
6. Serve and enjoy.

Nutrition Facts Per Serving

Calories: 299; Fat: 17.6g; Carbs: 1.2g; Protein: 30.9g

Chicken Curry

Prep time: 20 minutes, cook time: 30 minutes; Serves 6

5 Ingredients:

1 ½ lb. boneless chicken breasts
2 tbsp. curry powder
2 cups chopped tomatoes
2 cups coconut milk, freshly squeezed
1 thumb-size ginger, peeled and sliced

What you'll need from the store cupboard:

Pepper and salt to taste
2 tsp oil, divided

Instructions

1. On high fire, heat a saucepan for 2 minutes. Add 1 tsp oil to the pan and swirl to coat bottom and sides. Heat oil for a minute.
2. Sear chicken breasts for 4 minutes per side. Transfer to a chopping board and chop into bite-sized pieces.
3. Meanwhile, in the same pan, add remaining oil and heat for a minute. Add ginger sauté for a minute. Stir in tomatoes and curry powder. Crumble and wilt tomatoes for 5 minutes.
4. Add chopped chicken and continue sautéing for 7 minutes.
5. Deglaze the pot with 1 cup of coconut milk. Season with pepper and salt. Cover and simmer for 15 minutes.
6. Stir in remaining coconut milk and cook until heated through, around 3 minutes.
7. Serve and enjoy.

Nutrition Facts Per Serving

Calories: 336; Fat: 22.4g; Carbs: 7.4g; Protein: 28.1g

Smoky Paprika Chicken

Prep time: 40 minutes, cook time: 10 minutes; Serves 8

5 Ingredients:

2 lb. chicken breasts, sliced into strips
2 tbsp. smoked paprika
1 tsp Cajun seasoning
1 tbsp minced garlic
1 large onion, sliced thinly

What you'll need from the store cupboard:

Salt and pepper to taste
1 tbsp. olive oil

Instructions

1. In a large bowl, marinate chicken strips in paprika, Cajun, pepper, salt, and minced garlic for at least 30 minutes.

2. On high fire, heat a saucepan for 2 minutes. Add oil to the pan and swirl to coat bottom and sides. Heat oil for a minute.

3. Stir fry chicken and onion for 7 minutes or until chicken is cooked.

4. Serve and enjoy.

Nutrition Facts Per Serving

Calories: 217; Fat: 12.4g; Carbs: 1.5g; Protein: 34g

Easy Chicken Vindaloo

Prep time: 5 minutes, cook time: 30 minutes; Serves 5

5 Ingredients:

1 lb. chicken thighs, skin and bones not removed
2 tbsp. garam masala
6 whole red dried chilies
1 onion, sliced
5 cloves of garlic, crushed

What you'll need from the store cupboard:

Pepper and salt to taste
1 tsp oil
1 cup water

Instructions

1. On high fire, heat a saucepan for 2 minutes. Add oil to the pan and swirl to coat bottom and sides. Heat oil for a minute.

2. Add chicken with skin side touching pan and sear for 5 minutes. Turn chicken over and sear the other side for 3 minutes. Transfer chicken to a plate.

3. In the same pan, sauté garlic for a minute. Add onion and sauté for 3 minutes. Stir in garam masala and chilies.

4. Return chicken to the pot and mix well. Add water and season with pepper and salt.

5. Cover and lower fire to simmer and cook for 15 minutes.

6. Serve and enjoy.

Nutrition Facts Per Serving

Calories: 206; Fat: 15.1g; Carbs: 1.4g; Protein: 15.2g

Slow Cooked Chicken Drumstick

Prep time: 5 minutes, cook time: 7 hours; Serves 12

5 Ingredients:

12 chicken drumsticks
1 ½ tbsp paprika
¼ tsp dried thyme
½ tsp onion powder
2 tbsp Worcestershire sauce

What you'll need from the store cupboard:

Salt and pepper to taste
½ cup water

Instructions

1. Place all ingredients in the slow cooker. Give a good stir to coat the entire chicken with the spices.

2. Close the slow cooker, press high settings, and cook for 7 hours.

3. Serve and enjoy.

Nutrition Facts Per Serving

Calories: 218; Fat: 12.1g; Carbs: 2.5g; Protein: 23.8g

Chili Lime Chicken

Prep time: 10 minutes, cook time: 30 minutes; Serves 5

5 Ingredients:

1 lb. chicken breasts, skin and bones removed

Juice from 1 ½ limes, freshly squeezed

1 tbsp. chili powder

1 tsp. cumin

6 cloves garlic, minced

What you'll need from the store cupboard:

Pepper and salt to taste

1 cup water

4 tablespoon olive oil

Instructions

1. Place all ingredients in a heavy-bottomed pot and give a good stir.

2. Place on high fire and bring it to a boil. Cover, lower fire to a simmer, and cook for 20 minutes.

3. Remove chicken and place in a bowl. Shred using two forks. Return shredded chicken to the pot.

4. Boil for 10 minutes or until sauce is rendered.

5. Serve and enjoy.

Nutrition Facts Per Serving

Calories: 265; Fat: 19.5g; Carbs: 1.5g; Protein: 19.3g

Fennel Shredded Chicken

Prep time: 5 minutes, cook time: 30 minutes; Serves 8

5 Ingredients:

2 lb. chicken thighs, bone-in, and skin removed

¼ cup fennel bulb

4 cloves of garlic, minced

3 tbsp. lemon juice, freshly squeezed

1 tsp. cinnamon

What you'll need from the store cupboard:

Salt and pepper to taste

½ cup water

Instructions

1. Place all ingredients in a heavy-bottomed pot and give a good stir.

2. Place on high fire and bring it to a boil for 5 minutes. Cover, lower fire to a simmer, and cook for 20 minutes.

3. Remove chicken and place in a bowl. Shred using two forks. Discard bones and return shredded chicken to the pot.

4. Boil for 5 minutes or until sauce is rendered.

5. Serve and enjoy.

Nutrition Facts Per Serving

Calories: 257; Fat: 18.8g; Carbs: 1.9g; Protein: 18.7g

Chicken and Mushrooms

Prep time: 5 minutes, cook time: 30 minutes; Serves 6

5 Ingredients:

6 boneless chicken breasts, halved

1 onion, chopped

4 cloves of garlic, minced

½ cup coconut milk

1 cup mushrooms, sliced

What you'll need from the store cupboard:

Pepper and salt to taste

½ cup water

Instructions

1. On high fire, heat a saucepan for 2 minutes. Add oil to the pan and swirl to coat bottom and sides. Heat oil for a minute.

2. Add chicken and sear for 4 minutes per side. Transfer chicken to a chopping board and chop into bite-sized chunks.

3. In the same pan, lower fire to medium and sauté garlic for a minute. Add onion and sauté for 3 minutes. Stir in mushrooms and water. Deglaze pot.

4. Return chicken to the pot and mix well. Season with pepper and salt.

5. Cover and lower fire to simmer and cook for 15 minutes.

6. Serve and enjoy.

Nutrition Facts Per Serving

Calories: 383; Fat: 11.9g; Carbs: 3.5g; Protein: 62.2g

Chicken Enchilada Dip

Prep time: 5 minutes, cook time: 5 minutes; Serves 8

5 Ingredients:

2 pounds cooked rotisserie chicken, shredded
1 can enchilada sauce
2 packages cream cheese, softened
2 green onions, sliced
1 cup low-fat mozzarella cheese

What you'll need from the store cupboard:

Salt and pepper to taste
½ cup water

Instructions

1. Place a heavy-bottomed pot on medium-high fire.
2. Add water, cream cheese, and enchilada sauce. Bring to a boil and whisk well to combine. If needed, use an immersion blender to make it creamy and smooth.
3. Once smooth, lower fire to medium and add chicken. Adjust seasoning to taste.
4. And give it one last stir.
5. Sprinkle cheese and green onions on top. Cook for another 3 minutes.
6. Turn off fire, serve, and enjoy.

Nutrition Facts Per Serving

Calories: 312; Fat: 18.3g; Carbs: 4.1g; Protein: 33.4g

Teriyaki Chicken Wings

Prep time: 5 minutes, cook time: 40 minutes; Serves 9

5 Ingredients:

3 pounds chicken wings
1 tbsp baking soda
2 cups commercial teriyaki sauce
1 tablespoon chili garlic paste
2 teaspoons ginger paste

What you'll need from the store cupboard:

salt to taste
5 tablespoons coconut oil

Instructions

1. Dry chicken wings well with paper towels.
2. Season chicken wings generously with pepper. Rub with baking soda and ½ tsp salt. Drizzle with coconut oil.
3. Evenly spread chicken wings on an oven-safe wire rack placed on top of a baking pan.
4. Bake in preheated 375ºF oven for 40 minutes or to desired crispiness.
5. Mix remaining ingredients in a bowl and brush on cooked wings.
6. Serve and enjoy.

Nutrition Facts Per Serving

Calories: 314; Fat: 15.4g; Carbs: 5.4g; Protein: 34.3g

Easy Creamy Chicken

Prep time: 20 minutes, cook time: 15 minutes; Serves 8

5 Ingredients:

5 tablespoons butter
2 cans crushed tomatoes
4 cooked chicken breasts, shredded
1 teaspoon herb seasoning mix of your choice
¼ cup parmesan cheese, grated

What you'll need from the store cupboard:

Pepper and salt to taste

Instructions

1. Place a heavy-bottomed pot on medium-high fire and melt butter. Add tomatoes.
2. Sauté for 5 minutes, season with pepper, salt, and seasoning mix.
3. Stir in chicken. Mix well.
4. Cook until heated through, around 5 minutes.
5. Serve with a sprinkle of parmesan cheese.

Nutrition Facts Per Serving

Calories: 235; Fat: 11.3g; Carbs: 2.3g; Protein: 29.5g

Chicken And Spinach

Prep time: 5 minutes, cook time: 50 minutes; Serves 8

5 Ingredients:

1-pound chicken breasts

2 jars commercial pasta sauce

2 cups baby spinach

1 onion chopped

¼ cup cheese

What you' ll need from the store cupboard:

5 tbsps oil

½ cup water

Pepper and salt to taste

Instructions

1. Place a heavy-bottomed pot on medium-high fire and heat pot for 2 minutes.
2. Add oil and swirl to coat sides and bottom of the pot. Heat oil for a minute.
3. Season chicken breasts with pepper and salt. Brown chicken for 4 minutes per side. Transfer to a chopping board and cut into ½-inch cubes.
4. In the same pot, sauté onions for 5 minutes. Add pasta sauce and season with pepper and salt. Stir in water and chicken breasts. Simmer pasta sauce for 30 minutes on low fire. Stir the bottom of the pot every now and then.
5. Mix spinach in a pot of sauce. Let it rest for 5 minutes.
6. Serve and enjoy with a sprinkle of cheese.

Nutrition Facts Per Serving

Calories: 216; Fat: 15.6g; Carbs: 6.7g; Protein: 21.2g

One Pot Chicken Alfredo

Prep time: 30 minutes, cook time: 20 minutes; Serves 4

5 Ingredients:

1-pound cooked chicken breasts, chopped

1 jar Prego Alfredo Sauce

¼ cup mozzarella cheese

½ cup bacon bits, fried and crumbled

What you' ll need from the store cupboard:

Pepper and salt to taste

2 tbsp water

Instructions

1. Add all ingredients in a pot.
2. Close the lid and bring to a boil over medium flame.
3. Allow simmering for 20 minutes.
4. Serve and enjoy.

Nutrition Facts Per Serving

Calories: 899; Fat: 64.5g; Carbs:6.5g; Protein: 53.4g

Marinara Chicken Sausage

Prep time: 15 minutes, cook time: 40 minutes; Serves 6

5 Ingredients:

1-pound Italian chicken sausage

1 bell pepper, chopped

1 jar marinara sauce

1 cup mozzarella cheese, grated

4 tablespoons oil

What you' ll need from the store cupboard:

Salt and pepper to taste

¼ cup water

Instructions

1. Place a heavy-bottomed pot on medium-high fire and heat for 2 minutes. Add oil and swirl to coat the bottom and sides of pot and heat for a minute.
2. Sauté Italian chicken sausage for 5 minutes. Transfer to a chopping board and slice.
3. In the same pot, add marinara sauce, water, bell pepper, and sliced sausage. Cover and simmer for 30 minutes. Stir the bottom of the pot every now and then. Adjust seasoning to taste.
4. Top with marinara sauce.
5. Sprinkle top with pepper, serve, and enjoy.

Nutrition Facts Per Serving

Calories: 402; Fat: 23.4g; Carbs: 4.4g; Protein: 33.9g

Easy BBQ Chicken and Cheese

Prep time: 20 minutes, cook time: 40 minutes; Serves 4

5 Ingredients:

1-pound chicken tenders, boneless

½ cup commercial BBQ sauce, keto-friendly

1 teaspoon liquid smoke

1 cup mozzarella cheese, grated

½ pound bacon, fried and crumbled

What you'll need from the store cupboard:

Pepper and salt to taste

Instructions

1. With paper towels, dry chicken tenders. Season with pepper and salt.
2. Place chicken tenders on an oven-safe dish.
3. Whisk well BBQ sauce and liquid smoke in a bowl and pour over chicken tenders. Coat well in the sauce.
4. Bake in a preheated 400°F oven for 30 minutes.
5. Remove from oven, turnover chicken tenders, sprinkle cheese on top.
6. Return to the oven and continue baking for 10 minutes more.
7. Serve and enjoy with a sprinkle of bacon bits.

Nutrition Facts Per Serving

Calories: 351; Fat: 31.5g; Carbs: 6.7g; Protein: 34.6g

Rosemary Grilled Chicken

Prep time: 60 minutes, cook time: 12 minutes; Serves 4

5 Ingredients:

1 tablespoon fresh parsley, finely chopped

1 tablespoon fresh rosemary, finely chopped

4 tablespoons olive oil

4 pieces of 4-oz chicken breast, boneless and skinless

5 cloves garlic, minced

What you'll need from the store cupboard:

Pepper and salt to taste

Instructions

1. In a shallow and large bowl, mix salt, parsley, rosemary, olive oil, and garlic. Place chicken breast and marinate in the bowl of herbs for at least an hour or more before grilling.
2. Grease grill, grate and preheat grill to medium-high fire. Once hot, grill chicken for 4 to 5 minutes per side or until juices run a clear and internal temperature of chicken is 168°F.

Nutrition Facts Per Serving

Calories: 238; Fat: 16.0g; Carbs: 1.0g; Protein: 34.0g

Chicken Jambalaya

Prep time: 20 minutes, cook time: 30 minutes; Serves 6

5 Ingredients:

½ cup celery

3 chicken breast halves, skinless and boneless, chopped to bite-sized pieces

3 tbsp garlic, minced

3 whole tomatoes, chopped

1 tbsp Cajun seasoning

What you'll need from the store cupboard:

3 cups water

4 tbsps olive oil

Pepper and salt to taste

Instructions

1. Place a pot on high fire and heat oil for 2 minutes.
2. Add chicken and garlic. Sauté for 5 minutes.
3. Add tomatoes, Cajun seasoning, salt, and pepper. Sauté for another 5 minutes.
4. Add water and simmer chicken for 10 minutes.
5. Stir in celery and continue cooking for another 5 minutes.
6. Adjust seasoning if needed.
7. Serve and enjoy.

Nutrition Facts Per Serving

Calories: 419; Fat: 22.5g; Carbs: 4.8g; Protein: 35.0g

Herbs and Lemony Roasted Chicken

Prep time: 20 minutes, cook time: 90 minutes; Serves 8

5 Ingredients:

1 3-lb whole chicken
1 tbsp garlic powder
2 lemons
2 tsp Italian seasoning
5 tbsps butter

What you'll need from the store cupboard:

1 tsp ground black pepper
1 tsp salt

Instructions

1. In a small bowl, mix well black pepper, garlic powder, mustard powder, butter, and salt.
2. Rinse chicken well and slice off giblets.

3. In a greased 9 x 13 baking dish, place chicken and add 1 ½ tsp of seasoning made earlier inside the chicken and rub the remaining seasoning around the chicken.
4. Drizzle lemon juice all over the chicken.
5. Bake chicken in a preheated 350°F oven until juices run clear, around 1 ½ hours. Occasionally, baste the chicken with its juices.

Nutrition Facts Per Serving

Calories: 260; Fat:19.0g; Carbs: 2.0g; Protein: 35.0g

Baked Chicken Pesto

Prep time:10 minutes, cook time:20 minutes; Serves 4

5 Ingredients:

2 tsp grated parmesan cheese
6 tbsp shredded reduced-fat mozzarella cheese
1 medium tomato (thinly sliced)
4 tsp basil pesto
2 boneless, skinless chicken breasts around 1-lb

What you'll need from the store cupboard:

Salt and pepper to taste

Instructions

1. In cool water, wash chicken and dry using a paper towel. Create 4 thin slices of chicken breasts by slicing horizontally.
2. Preheat oven to 400°F and then line a baking sheet with parchment or foil.

3. Put into the baking sheet the slices of chicken. Season with pepper and salt. And spread at least 1 teaspoon of pesto on each chicken slice.
4. For 15 minutes, bake the chicken and ensure that the center is no longer pink. After which remove baking sheet and top chicken with parmesan cheese, mozzarella, and tomatoes.
5. Put into the oven once again and heat for another 3 to 5 minutes to melt the cheese, then ready to serve.

Nutrition Facts Per Serving

Calories: 238; Fat: 8.0g; Carbs: 2.0g; Protein: 40.0g

Heart Healthy Chicken Salad

Prep time: 30 minutes, cook time: 45 minutes; Serves 4

5 Ingredients:

3 tbsp mayonnaise, low-fat
½ tsp onion powder
1 tbsp lemon juice
¼ cup celery (chopped)
3 ¼ cups chicken breast (cooked, cubed, and skinless)

What you'll need from the store cupboard:

Salt and pepper to taste

Instructions

1. Bake chicken breasts for 45 minutes at 350°F. Let it cool and cut them into cubes and place them in the refrigerator.
2. Combine all other ingredients in a large bowl then add the chilled chicken.
3. Mix well and ready to serve.
4. Enjoy!

Nutrition Facts Per Serving

Calories: 408; Fat: 22.0g; Carbs: 1.0g; Protein: 50.0g

Chicken Pesto

Prep time: 15 minutes, cook time: 35 minutes; Serves 8

5 Ingredients:
5 cloves of garlic
4 skinless, boneless chicken breast halves, cut into thin strips
3 tbsp grated Parmesan cheese
¼ cup pesto
1 ¼ cups heavy cream
What you'll need from the store cupboard:
10 tbsps olive oil
Pepper to taste
1/8 tsp salt
Instructions
1. On medium fire, place a large saucepan and heat olive oil.
2. Add garlic and chicken, sauté for 7 minutes, or until chicken strips are nearly cooked.
3. Lower fire and add Parmesan cheese, pesto, cream, pepper, and salt.
4. Continue cooking for 5-10 minutes more or until chicken is fully cooked. Stir frequently.
5. Once penne is cooked, drain well and pour into a large saucepan, toss to coat, and serve.

Nutrition Facts Per Serving
Calories:330; Fat: 22.0g; Carbs: 3g; Protein: 30.0g

Ginger, Chicken, And Spinach Stir Fry

Prep time: 5 minutes, cook time: 10 minutes; Serves 4

5 Ingredients:
2 cloves of garlic, minced
1 tablespoon fresh ginger, grated
1 ¼ pounds boneless chicken breasts, cut into strips
2 tablespoons yellow miso, diluted in water
2 cups baby spinach
What you'll need from the store cupboard:
2 tablespoons olive oil
Pepper and salt to taste
Instructions
1. Heat oil in a skillet over medium-high heat and sauté the garlic for 30 seconds until fragrant.
2. Stir in the ginger and chicken breasts. Season lightly with pepper and salt.
3. Cook for 5 minutes while stirring constantly.
4. Stir in the diluted miso paste.
5. Continue cooking for 3 more minutes before adding spinach.
6. Cook for another minute or until the spinach leaves have wilted.

Nutrition Facts Per Serving
Calories: 237; Fat: 10.5g; Carbs: 1.3g; Protein: 32.5g

Chicken and Mushrooms

Prep time: 5 minutes, cook time: 15 minutes; Serves 8

5 Ingredients:
1 large shallot, diced
8 chicken breasts, cubed
4 large cremini mushrooms, sliced
¼ cup yogurt
5 tablespoons olive oil
What you'll need from the store cupboard:
½ cup water
Salt and pepper to taste
Instructions
1. Heat oil in a skillet over medium flame and sauté the shallot until fragrant.
2. Stir in the chicken breasts and continue cooking for 3 minutes while stirring constantly.
3. Add the mushrooms, water, and yogurt.
4. Season with salt and pepper to taste.
5. Close the lid and bring to a boil.
6. Reduce the heat to medium-low and allow simmering for 10 minutes.

Nutrition Facts Per Serving
Calories: 512; Fat: 27.7g; Carbs: 1.5g; Protein: 55.8g

Oven-Baked Skillet Lemon Chicken

Prep time: 10 minutes, cook time: 60 minutes; Serves 4

5 Ingredients:

6 small chicken thighs

1 medium onion

1 lemon

¼ cup lemon juice, freshly squeezed

What you'll need from the store cupboard:

Salt and pepper to taste

Instructions

1. Place all ingredients in a Ziploc bag and allow to marinate for at least 6 hours in the fridge.

2. Preheat the oven to 350⁰F.

3. Place the chicken–sauce and all–into a skillet.

4. Put the skillet in the oven and bake for 1 hour or until the chicken is tender.

Nutrition Facts Per Serving

Calories: 610; Fat: 42.4g; Carbs: 6.2g; Protein: 48.2g

Tender Turkey Breast

Prep time: 10 minutes, cook time: 25 minutes; Serves 12

5 Ingredients:

4 peeled garlic cloves

4 fresh rosemary sprigs

1 bone-in turkey breast (7-pounds)

5 tablespoons olive oil

½ teaspoon coarsely ground pepper

What you'll need from the store cupboard:

¼ teaspoon salt

½ cup water

Instructions

1. Add all ingredients in a pot on high fire and bring it to a boil.

2. Once boiling, lower fire to a simmer and cook for 20 minutes.

3. Adjust seasoning to taste.

4. Serve and enjoy.

Nutrition Facts Per Serving

Calories: 390; Fat: 22.7g; Carbs: 0.8g; Protein: 35.8g

Chicken Chipotle

Prep time: 10 minutes, cook time: 25 minutes; Serves 8

5 Ingredients:

4 tablespoons McCormick grill mates' chipotle

Roasted garlic seasoning

8 garlic cloves peeled and crushed

5-pounds whole chicken

What you'll need from the store cupboard:

½ cup water

Instructions

1. Add all ingredients in a pot on high fire and bring it to a boil.

2. Once boiling, lower fire to a simmer and cook for 25 minutes.

3. Adjust seasoning to taste.

4. Serve and enjoy.

Nutrition Facts Per Serving

Calories: 613; Fat: 42.5g; Carbs: 5.7g; Protein: 52.0g

Broccoli Chicken Stew

Prep time: 5 minutes, cook time: 30 minutes; Serves 4

5 Ingredients:

1 package frozen chopped broccoli (10-ounces)

1 cup shredded sharp cheddar cheese

½ cup sour cream

¾ cup Campbell's broccoli cheese soup

4 boneless skinless chicken breasts, thawed

What you'll need from the store cupboard:

½ cup water

Instructions

1. Add all ingredients, except for broccoli in a pot on high fire and bring to a boil.
2. Once boiling, lower fire to a simmer and cook for 20 minutes, stirring frequently.
3. Adjust seasoning to taste. Add broccoli and continue cooking and stirring for another 5 minutes.
4. Serve and enjoy.

Nutrition Facts Per Serving
Calories: 511; Fat: 22.1g; Carbs: 9.7g; Protein: 63.9g

Chicken Country Style

Prep time: 5 minutes, cook time: 25 minutes; Serves 4
5 Ingredients:
3 tablespoons butter
1 packet dry Lipton's onion soup mix
1 can (14.5-ounce) Campbell's chicken gravy
4 skinless and boneless chicken breasts
What you'll need from the store cupboard:
1/3 teaspoon pepper
1 cup water
Instructions

1. Add all ingredients in a pot on high fire and bring it to a boil.
2. Once boiling, lower fire to a simmer and cook for 25 minutes.
3. Adjust seasoning to taste.
4. Serve and enjoy.

Nutrition Facts Per Serving
Calories: 380; Fat: 16.9g; Carbs: 6.8g; Protein: 53.7g

Stewed Chicken Salsa

Prep time: 10 minutes, cook time: 25 minutes; Serves 4
5 Ingredients:
1 cup shredded cheddar cheese
8-ounces cream cheese
16-ounces salsa
4 skinless and boneless thawed chicken breasts
4 tablespoons butter
What you'll need from the store cupboard:
1 cup water
Instructions

1. Add all ingredients in a pot, except for sour cream, on high fire, and bring to a boil.
2. Once boiling, lower fire to a simmer and cook for 20 minutes.
3. Adjust seasoning to taste and stir in sour cream.
4. Serve and enjoy.

Nutrition Facts Per Serving
Calories: 658; Fat: 32.6g; Carbs: 9.6g; Protein: 67.8g

Greek Chicken Stew

Prep time: 5 minutes, cook time: 30 minutes; Serves 4
5 Ingredients:
¼ cup feta cheese
Sliced and pitted Kalamata olives
1 bottle (16-ounce) ken's steak house Greek dressing with Feta cheese, olive oil, and black olives
4 boneless and skinless thawed chicken breasts
What you'll need from the store cupboard:
1 cup water

Instructions
1. Add all ingredients in a pot, except for feta, on high fire, and bring to a boil.
2. Once boiling, lower fire to a simmer and cook for 25 minutes.
3. Adjust seasoning to taste and stir in feta.
4. Serve and enjoy.

Nutrition Facts Per Serving
Calories: 818; Fat: 65.1g; Carbs: 3.2g; Protein: 54.4g

Yummy Chicken Queso

Prep time: 5 minutes, cook time: 25 minutes; Serves 4

5 Ingredients:

½ teaspoon garlic salt
4-ounce can diced drained green chiles
10-ounce can mild rotel drained
¾ cup medium queso dip
4 boneless skinless boneless fresh or thawed chicken breasts

What you'll need from the store cupboard:

5 tablespoons olive oil
1 cup water

Instructions

1. Add all ingredients in a pot on high fire and bring it to a boil.
2. Once boiling, lower fire to a simmer and cook for 20 minutes. Stir frequently.
3. Adjust seasoning to taste.
4. Serve and enjoy.

Nutrition Facts Per Serving

Calories: 500; Fat: 21.7g; Carbs: 7.2g; Protein: 56.6g

Stewed Italian Chicken

Prep time: 5 minutes, cook time: 25 minutes; Serves 4

5 Ingredients:

3 ounces Italian dressing
4 boneless skinless chicken breasts thawed
5 tablespoons olive oil

What you'll need from the store cupboard:

½ cup water
Salt and pepper to taste

Instructions

1. Add all ingredients in a pot on high fire and bring it to a boil.
2. Once boiling, lower fire to a simmer and cook for 20 minutes.
3. Adjust seasoning to taste.
4. Serve and enjoy.

Nutrition Facts Per Serving

Calories: 545; Fat: 31.0g; Carbs: 3.6g; Protein: 53.6g

Bacon Chicken Alfredo

Prep time: 20 minutes, cook time: 35 minutes; Serves 4

5 Ingredients:

4-ounces mushrooms drained and sliced
1 cup shredded mozzarella cheese
1 jar (15-ounces) Classico creamy alfredo sauce
6 slices chopped hickory bacon
4 boneless skinless chicken breasts thawed or fresh

What you'll need from the store cupboard:

Pepper and salt to taste
½ cup water

Instructions

1. Add all ingredients in a pot on high fire and bring it to a boil.
2. Once boiling, lower fire to a simmer and cook for 30 minutes, stirring every now and then.
3. Adjust seasoning to taste.
4. Serve and enjoy.

Nutrition Facts Per Serving

Calories: 976; Fat: 70.8g; Carbs: 7.7g; Protein: 75.8g

Creamy Stewed Chicken

Prep time: 5 minutes, cook time: 30 minutes; Serves 6

5 Ingredients:

10.5-ounce can cream of chicken soup
12-ounce package frozen broccoli
0.6-ounce package Italian dry mix dressing
8-ounces cream cheese
1 ½-pounds skinless, boneless chicken breasts

What you'll need from the store cupboard:

5 tablespoons olive oil

½ cup water
Pepper and salt to taste

Instructions

1. Add all ingredients in a pot on high fire and bring to a boil.

2. Once boiling, lower fire to a simmer and cook for 25 minutes, stirring every now and then.
3. Adjust seasoning to taste.

4. Serve and enjoy.
Nutrition Facts Per Serving
Calories: 350; Fat: 21.5g; Carbs: 7.0g; Protein: 31.0g

Avocado Cheese Pepper Chicken

Prep time: 5 mins; Cook time: 20 minutes; Serves 5
5 Ingredients:
¼ tsp. cayenne pepper
1½ cup. cooked and shredded chicken
2 tbsps. cream cheese
2 tbsps. lemon juice
2 large avocados, diced
What you'll need from the store cupboard:
Black pepper and salt to taste
¼ cup. mayonnaise
1 tsp. dried thyme
½ tsp. onion powder

½ tsp. garlic powder
Instructions
1. Remove the insides of your avocado halves and set them in a bowl.
2. Stir all ingredients to avocado flesh.
3. Fill avocados with chicken mix.
4. Serve and enjoy.
Nutrition Facts
Per Serving: Calories: 476, Fat: 40g, Net Carbs: 5g, Protein: 24g

Coconut Aminos Chicken Bake

Prep time: 15 mins; Cook time: 20 minutes; Serves 4
5 Ingredients:
3 green onions, chopped
4 chicken breasts
4 oz. cheddar cheese, shredded
4 bacon strips
1 oz. coconut aminos
What you'll need from the store cupboard:
2 tbsp. coconut oil
Instructions
1. Heat oil in a skillet over high heat. Add chicken breasts and cook for 7 minutes both sides.

2. In another pan over medium-high heat, sauté bacon and place to a plate lined with a paper towel and crumble it.
3. Lay the chicken in a baking dish, sprinkle with coconut aminos, bacon, shredded cheese and chopped green onions.
4. Place the baking dish in the broiler and cook on High for 5 minutes. Serve and enjoy.
Nutrition Facts Per Serving
Per Serving: Calories 570, Fat 49g, Carbs 2g, Protein 18g, Fiber 14g

Spinach Artichoke Heart Chicken

Prep time: 20 mins; Cook time: 30 minutes; Serves 4
5 Ingredients:
4 chicken breasts
1 (10 ounce) package frozen spinach
1 (4 ounce) package cream cheese, softened
½ (14 ounce) can quartered artichoke hearts, drained and chopped
¼ cup. shredded Parmesan cheese
What you'll need from the store cupboard:
¼ cup. mayonnaise
2 tbsp. olive oil
2 tbsps. grated mozzarella cheese
½ teaspoon. garlic powder
Salt to taste
Instructions
1. Place the spinach in a bowl and microwave for 2 to 3 minutes. Let chill and drain.
2. Stir in cream cheese, artichoke hearts,

Parmesan cheese, mayonnaise, garlic powder, and salt, whisk together. Cut chicken breasts to an even thickness. Spread salt and pepper over chicken breasts per side.
3. Preheat oven to 375 degrees F.
4. In a large skillet over medium-high, heat olive oil for 2 to 3 minutes. Lay chicken breasts in a large baking dish, pour spinach-artichoke mixture over chicken breasts. Place in the oven and bake at least 165 degrees F.
5. Sprinkle with mozzarella cheese and bake for 1 to 2 minutes more. Serve and enjoy.
Nutrition Facts Per Serving
Per Serving: 554 calories; 33.3 g total fat; 5.4 g carbohydrates; 56 g protein

Pork Chops and Peppers

Prep time: 5 minutes, cook time: 20 minutes; Serves 4

5 Ingredients:

4 thick pork chops
1 onion, chopped
2 cloves of garlic, minced
2 red and yellow bell peppers, seeded and julienned

What you'll need from the store cupboard:

Salt and pepper to taste
5 tablespoons oil

Instructions

1. In a large saucepan, place on medium fire and heat 1 tsp oil for 3 minutes.
2. Add pork chop and cook for 5 minutes per side. Season pork chops with salt and pepper.
3. Transfer pork chops to a plate and let it rest.
4. In the same pan, add remaining oil. Increase fire to medium-high and sauté garlic. Stir in onions and bell peppers. Sauté until tender and crisp around 5 minutes.
5. Serve pork chops topped with bell pepper mixture.

Nutrition Facts Per Serving

Calories: 245; Fat: 16.3g; Carbs: 4.3g; Protein: 23.9g

Slow Cooker Pork

Prep time: 5 minutes, cook time: 10 hours; Serves 10

5 Ingredients:

3 lb. boneless pork loin roast
¼ cup Dijon mustard
1 tsp. dried thyme leaves
2 bay leaves
5 tablespoons olive oil

What you'll need from the store cupboard:

Salt and pepper to taste
1 ½ cups water

Instructions

1. Place all ingredients in the slow cooker.
2. Season with salt and pepper and give a good stir.
3. Cover and cook on low for 10 hours.
4. Serve and enjoy.

Nutrition Facts Per Serving

Calories: 245; Fat:15.7g; Carbs: 0.4g; Protein: 30.7g

One Pot Tomato Pork Chops Stew

Prep time: 5 minutes, cook time: 30 minutes; Serves 6

5 Ingredients:

6 pork chops
1 onion, chopped
1 bay leaf
½ cup tomato paste
1 tsp oil

What you'll need from the store cupboard:

Salt and pepper to taste
1/2 cup water

Instructions

1. Place a heavy-bottomed pot on medium-high fire and heat for 2 minutes. Add oil and heat for a minute more.
2. Add pork chops and sear for 3 minutes per side. Transfer to a chopping board and slice into bite-sized pieces.
3. In the same pot, sauté onion, bay leaf, and tomato paste for a minute. Add water and deglaze the pot.
4. Return chops to the pot, season with pepper and salt.
5. Cover and simmer for 20 minutes.

Nutrition Facts Per Serving

Calories: 357; Fat: 17.5g; Carbs: 6.5g; Protein: 41.5g

Simple Pulled Pork

Prep time: 5 minutes, cook time: 25 minutes; Serves 4

5 Ingredients:

4 pork chops, deboned
1 onion, sliced
5 cloves of garlic, minced
1 tbsp soy sauce

What you'll need from the store cupboard:

1 ½ cups water
Salt and pepper to taste

Instructions

1. In a heavy-bottomed pot, add all ingredients and mix well.
2. Cover and cook on medium-high fire until boiling. Lower fire to a simmer and cook for 25 minutes undisturbed.
3. Turn off fire and let it cool a bit.
4. With two forks, shred meat.
5. Serve and enjoy.

Nutrition Facts Per Serving

Calories: 339; Fat: 17.4g; Carbs: 2.4g; Protein: 40.7g

Mushroom Pork Chops

Prep time: 5 minutes, cook time: 45 minutes; Serves 4

5 Ingredients:

4 pork chops
3 cloves of garlic, chopped
1 onion, chopped
1 lb. fresh mushrooms, sliced
4 tbsp butter

What you'll need from the store cupboard:

Salt and pepper to taste
1 tbsp water
5 tbsp oil

Instructions

1. In a large saucepan, place on medium fire and heat oil for 3 minutes. Season pork chops with salt and pepper.
2. Cook for 4 minutes per side the porkchop, until lightly browned. Transfer to a plate and let it rest.
3. In the same pan, add butter. Increase fire to medium-high and sauté garlic. Stir in onions, water, and mushrooms. Sauté until mushrooms are tender, around 7 minutes. Season with salt and pepper.
4. Serve pork chops topped with mushroom mixture.

Nutrition Facts Per Serving

Calories: 649; Fat: 47.9g; Carbs: 7.7g; Protein: 46.8g

Thai Coconut Pork

Prep time: 15 minutes, cook time: 35 minutes; Serves 7

5 Ingredients:

1 tbsp. coconut oil
1 ¼ lb. pork shoulder, cut into chunks
1 thumb-size ginger, sliced
2 ½ cups coconut milk, freshly squeezed if possible
1 lemongrass stalk, pounded

What you'll need from the store cupboard:

Salt and pepper to taste
1/2 cup water

Instructions

1. In a heavy-bottomed pot, add all ingredients except for coconut milk and mix well.
2. Cover and cook on medium-high fire until boiling. Lower fire to a simmer and cook for 25 minutes undisturbed.
3. Stir in coconut milk. Mix well and cook for another 10 minutes.
4. Serve and enjoy.

Nutrition Facts Per Serving

Calories: 435; Fat: 36.8g; Carbs: 5.6g; Protein: 22.7g

Cajun Pork

Prep time: 15 minutes, cook time: 40 minutes; Serves 8

5 Ingredients:

5 lb. pork shoulder, cut into 4 to 6 chunks
4 tbsp organic Cajun spice mix
1 bay leaf

What you'll need from the store cupboard:

2 cups water
Salt and pepper to taste

Instructions

1. In a heavy-bottomed pot, add all ingredients, including bone and mix well.

2. Cover and cook on medium-high fire until boiling. Lower fire to a simmer and cook for 30 minutes undisturbed.

3. Remove meat, transfer to a bowl, and shred with two forks. Return to pot, bring to a boil, and boil uncovered for 10 minutes until sauce is rendered.

4. Discard bay leaf, serve and enjoy.

Nutrition Facts Per Serving

Calories: 768; Fat: 50.2g; Carbs: 2.6g; Protein: 71.5g

Spicy Pork Stew with Spinach

Prep time: 15 minutes, cook time: 40 minutes; Serves 4

5 Ingredients:

1 lb. pork butt, cut into chunks
1 onion, chopped
4 cloves of garlic, minced
1 cup coconut milk, freshly squeezed
1 cup spinach leaves, washed and rinsed

What you'll need from the store cupboard:

Salt and pepper to taste
1 cup water

Instructions

1. In a heavy-bottomed pot, add all ingredients, except for coconut milk and spinach. Mix well.

2. Cover and cook on medium-high fire until boiling. Lower fire to a simmer and cook for 30 minutes undisturbed.

3. Add remaining ingredients and cook on high fire uncovered for 5 minutes. Adjust seasoning if needed.

4. Serve and enjoy.

Nutrition Facts Per Serving

Calories: 458; Fat: 34.4g; Carbs: 7.2g; Protein: 30.5g

Easy Thai 5-Spice Pork Stew

Prep time: 5 minutes, cook time: 40 minutes; Serves 9

5 Ingredients:

2 lb. pork butt, cut into chunks
2 tbsp. 5-spice powder
2 cups coconut milk, freshly squeezed
1 ½ tbsp sliced ginger
1 cup chopped cilantro

What you'll need from the store cupboard:

1 tsp oil
Salt and pepper to taste
½ cup water

Instructions

1. Place a heavy-bottomed pot on medium-high fire and heat for 2 minutes. Add oil and heat for a minute.

2. Stir in pork chunks and cook for 3 minutes per side.

3. Add ginger, cilantro, pepper, and salt. Sauté for 2 minutes.

4. Add water and deglaze the pot. Stir in 5-spice powder.

5. Cover and simmer for 20 minutes.

6. Stir in coconut milk. Cover and cook for another 10 minutes.

7. Adjust seasoning if needed.

8. Serve and enjoy.

Nutrition Facts Per Serving

Calories: 398; Fat: 30.5g; Carbs: 4.4g; Protein: 39.8g

Pork and Cabbage Soup

Prep time: 5 minutes, cook time: 50 minutes; Serves 10

5 Ingredients:

3 lb. pork butt, cut into chunks

1 thumb-size ginger, sliced

1 head cabbage, cut into quarters

1 scallion, green part only

1 small onion, chopped

What you'll need from the store cupboard:

Pepper and salt to taste

3 cups water

Instructions

1. Place all ingredients in a heavy-bottomed pot except for cabbage. Give a good stir and season with salt and pepper to taste.
2. Cover and bring to a boil. Once boiling, lower fire to a simmer and simmer for 30 minutes.
3. Add cabbage and simmer for another 10 minutes.
4. Adjust seasoning to taste.
5. Serve and enjoy.

Nutrition Facts Per Serving

Calories: 383; Fat: 24.7g; Carbs: 4.6g; Protein: 35.2g

Asian Glazed Meatballs

Prep time: 10 minutes, cook time: 20 minutes; Serves 4

5 Ingredients:

1-pound meatballs, thawed

½ cup hoisin sauce

2 tablespoons apricot jam, keto-friendly

2 tablespoons soy sauce

What you'll need from the store cupboard:

5 tablespoons coconut oil

½ teaspoon sesame oil

2 tbsp water

Instructions

1. In a nonstick saucepan, heat the coconut and sesame oil for 2 minutes.
2. Stir in meatballs and sauté for 5 minutes.
3. Add remaining ingredients and mix well.
4. Simmer for 10 minutes.
5. Serve and enjoy.

Nutrition Facts Per Serving

Calories: 368; Fat: 28.4g; Carbs: 10g; Protein: 18.1g

Dr. Pepper Pulled Pork

Prep time: 5 minutes, cook time: 45 minutes; Serves 9

5 Ingredients:

3 pounds pork loin roast, chopped into 8 equal pieces

1 packet pork rub seasoning

1 12-ounce can Dr. Pepper

½ cup commercial BBQ sauce, keto-friendly

1 bay leaf

What you'll need from the store cupboard:

1 tsp oil

2 tbsp water

Instructions

1. Place a heavy-bottomed pot on medium-high fire and heat for 2 minutes. Add oil and swirl to coat the bottom and sides of pot and heat for a minute.
2. Brown roast for 4 minutes per side.
3. Add remaining ingredients.
4. Cover and simmer for 30 minutes or until pork is fork-tender. Stir the bottom of the pot every now and then. Turn off the fire.
5. With two forks, shred pork.
6. Turn on fire to high and boil uncovered until sauce is rendered, around 5 minutes.
7. Serve and enjoy.

Nutrition Facts Per Serving

Calories: 310; Fat: 13.4g; Carbs: 4.6g; Protein: 40.9g

Pork Chops with Tomatoes and Green Beans

Prep time:5 minutes, cook time: 16 minutes; Serves 4

5 Ingredients:

4 bone-in pork chops

½ teaspoon pepper

2 cups green beans

1 ¼ cup cherry tomatoes

What you'll need from the store cupboard:

5 tablespoons olive oil

Pepper and salt to taste

Instructions

1. Season the pork with pepper and salt.
2. Heat the oil in a skillet over medium heat and sear the pork chops for 8 minutes on each side or until all sides turn lightly golden.
3. Remove from pan and set aside.
4. In the same pan, add in the olive oil and stir in the green beans and cherry tomatoes for 5 minutes or until the vegetables are done.
5. Serve the pork chop with the vegetables.

Nutrition Facts Per Serving

Calories: 503; Fat: 34.0g; Carbs: 5.3g; Protein: 41.0g

Cocoa-Crusted Pork Tenderloin

Prep time: 10 minutes, cook time: 25 minutes; Serves 2

5 Ingredients:

1-pound pork tenderloin, trimmed from fat

1 tablespoon cocoa powder

1 teaspoon instant coffee powder

½ teaspoon ground cinnamon

½ teaspoon chili powder

What you'll need from the store cupboard:

1 tablespoon olive oil

Pepper and salt to taste

Instructions

1. In a bowl, dust the pork tenderloin with cocoa powder, coffee, cinnamon, pepper, salt, and chili powder.
2. In a skillet, heat the oil and sear the meat for 5 minutes on both sides over low to medium flame.
3. Transfer the pork in a baking dish and cook in the oven for 15 minutes in a 350°F preheated oven.

Nutrition Facts Per Serving

Calories: 395; Fat: 15.0g; Carbs: 2.0g; Protein: 60.0g

Garlic Lime Marinated Pork Chops

Prep time: 10 minutes, cook time: 10 minutes; Serves 4

5 Ingredients:

4 6-ounce lean boneless pork chops, trimmed from fat

4 cloves of garlic, crushed

1 teaspoon cumin

1 teaspoon paprika

½ lime, juiced and zested

What you'll need from the store cupboard:

1 tsp black pepper

½ tsp salt

5 tablespoons olive oil

Instructions

1. In a bowl, season the pork with the rest of the ingredients.
2. Allow marinating inside the fridge for at least 2 hours.
3. Place the pork chops in a baking dish or broiler pan and grill for 5 minutes on each side until golden brown.
4. Serve with salad if desired.

Nutrition Facts Per Serving

Calories: 376; Fat: 22.9g; Carbs:2.4g; Protein: 38.5g

Pork Medallion with Herbes de Provence

Prep time: 5 minutes, cook time: 15 minutes; Serves 2

5 Ingredients:

8 ounces of pork medallion, trimmed from fat

½ teaspoon Herbes de Provence

¼ cup dry white wine

What you'll need from the store cupboard:

Freshly ground black pepper to taste

Salt to taste

Instructions

1. Season the meat with black pepper.
2. Place the meat in between sheets of wax paper and pound on a mallet until about ¼ inch thick.
3. In a nonstick skillet, sear the pork over medium heat for 5 minutes on each side or until the meat is slightly brown.
4. Remove meat from the skillet and sprinkle with herbes de Provence.
5. Using the same skillet, pour the wine and scrape the sides to deglaze. Allow simmering until the wine is reduced.
6. Pour the wine sauce over the pork.
7. Serve immediately.

Nutrition Facts Per Serving

Calories: 316; Fat: 24.0g; Carbs: 1.0g; Protein: 24.0g

Spanish Frittata

Prep time: 15 minutes, cook time: 26 minutes; Serves 6

5 Ingredients:

3 large eggs, beaten

½ chorizo sausage, sliced

½ zucchini, sliced

A dash of oregano

A dash of Spanish paprika

What you'll need from the store cupboard:

Pepper and salt to taste

3 tablespoons olive oil

Instructions

1. Preheat the air fryer for 5 minutes.
2. Combine all ingredients in a mixing bowl until well-incorporated.
3. Pour into a greased baking dish that will fit in the air fryer basket.
4. Place the baking dish in the air fryer.
5. Close and cook for 15 minutes at 350^{0}F.

Nutrition Facts Per Serving

Calories: 93; Fat: 9.4g; Carbs: 0.5g; Protein: 1.8g

Garlic Pork Chops

Prep time:10 minutes, cook time: 30 minutes; Serves 4

5 Ingredients:

1 ½ cups chicken broth

1 tablespoon butter

2 lemons, juiced

4 ¾ inch boneless pork chops

6 cloves garlic, minced

What you'll need from the store cupboard:

Salt and pepper to taste

1 tablespoon olive oil

Instructions

1. Heat the olive oil in a large pot on medium-high fire.
2. Season the pork with salt, pepper, and garlic powder.
3. Place the pork in the Instant Pot and brown the sides. Set aside.
4. Add the garlic and sauté for a minute. Add the lemon juice and chicken broth. Stir in the butter.
5. Add the pork chops back to the pan. Cover the lid and simmer for 20 minutes.
6. Serve and enjoy.

Nutrition Facts Per Serving

Calories: 355; Fat: 14.0g; Carbs: 4.8g; Protein: 50.2g

Lettuce Taco Carnitas

Prep time: 15 minutes, cook time: 40 minutes; Serves 12

5 Ingredients:

2 cups shredded Colby-Monterey jack cheese
1 can (10-ounces) green chilies and diced tomatoes, undrained
1 envelope taco seasoning
1 boneless pork shoulder butt roast (4-pounds)
Lettuce leaves

What you' ll need from the store cupboard:

Pepper and salt to taste
1 cup water

Instructions

1. Add all ingredients in a pot, except for cheese and lettuce leaves, on high fire, and bring to a boil.
2. Once boiling, lower fire to a simmer and cook for 35 minutes.
3. Adjust seasoning to taste.
4. To serve, add a good amount of shredded pork into the center of one lettuce leaf. Top it with cheese, roll, and enjoy.

Nutrition Facts Per Serving

Calories: 214; Fat: 10.4g; Carbs: 1.7g; Protein: 28.5g

Smoky Baby Back Ribs

Prep time: 5 minutes, cook time: 40 minutes; Serves 4

5 Ingredients:

1 ½ teaspoon barbecue sauce
1 ½ teaspoon hoisin sauce
½ teaspoon smoked paprika
2 ½ pounds baby back ribs
1 cup water

What you' ll need from the store cupboard:

Pepper and salt to taste

Instructions

1. Add all ingredients in a pot on high fire and bring to a boil.
2. Once boiling, lower fire to a simmer and cook for 35 minutes.
3. Adjust seasoning to taste.
4. Serve and enjoy.

Nutrition Facts Per Serving

Calories: 723; Fat: 55.0g; Carbs: 3.7g; Protein: 53.2g

Pork Chops with Cranberry Sauce

Prep time: 10 minutes, cook time: 30 minutes; Serves 6

5 Ingredients:

6-pieces bone-in pork loin chops
1 14-ounce fresh cranberries, pitted
5 tablespoons butter

What you' ll need from the store cupboard:

Salt and pepper to taste
1 cup water

Instructions

1. Add all ingredients in a pot on high fire and bring to a boil.
2. Once boiling, lower fire to a simmer and cook for 25 minutes.
3. Adjust seasoning to taste.
4. Serve and enjoy.

Nutrition Facts Per Serving

Calories: 452; Fat: 27.6g; Carbs: 9.7g; Protein: 40.6g

Spiced Baked Pork with Milk

Prep time: 10 mins; Cook time: 2h 30 minutes; Serves 4

5 Ingredients:

3 1/2 pounds boneless pork shoulder, cut into large pieces

1 tablespoon freshly ground black pepper

2 bay leaves

1/4 teaspoon cayenne pepper

2 cups almond milk

What you'll need from the store cupboard:

1 tablespoon kosher salt, or more to taste

2 tablespoons olive oil

1 lime, juiced

2 teaspoons ground cumin

1 teaspoon dried oregano

Instructions

1. Heat oil in a large pot over high heat. Cook pork with pepper and salt for 5 minutes.

2. Return all cooked pork and accumulated juice to pot. Season pork with bay leaves, cumin, dried oregano, and cayenne pepper.

3. Stir in fresh lime juice, orange zest, and milk. Bring mixture to a boil over high heat; reduce heat to low. Cover and simmer, stirring occasionally, about 2 hours.

4. Preheat oven to 450 degrees F.

5. Skim the fat to grease a baking dish. Transfer the pieces of pork to the baking dish. Drizzle about 2 more tablespoons of olive oil over the meat.

6. Bake in preheated oven for about 15 minutes until cooked through.

Nutrition Facts Per Serving

Per Serving: 325 calories; 24.1 g fat; 3.7 g carbohydrates; 22.4 g protein;

Garlic Crispy Pork Loin

Prep time: 15 mins; Cook time: 1h 5 minutes; Serves 4

Ingredients

1 quart cold water

3 cloves garlic, crushed

3 tablespoons. chopped fresh ginger

1 (2 1/2 pound) boneless pork loin roast

2 tablespoons. Dijon mustard

What you'll need from the store cupboard:

Salt and freshly ground black pepper to taste

2 teaspoons. dried rosemary

1 tablespoon olive oil

2 tablespoons stevia

1/2 teaspoon red pepper flakes

Instructions

1. Mix water, salt, 1 tbsp. stevia, garlic, ginger, rosemary and red pepper flakes in a large bowl.

2. Place pork loin in brine mixture and refrigerate for 8 to 10 hours. Remove pork from brine, pat dry, and season all sides with salt and black pepper.

3. Preheat oven to 325 degrees F.

4. Heat olive oil in a skillet over high heat. Cook pork for about 10 minutes.

5. Transfer skillet to the oven and roast for about 40 minutes.

6. Mix 2 tablespoons stevia and Dijon mustard together in a small bowl.

7. Remove pork roast from the oven and spread stevia mixture on all sides. Cook for an additional 15 minutes at 145 degrees F. Serve and enjoy

Nutrition Facts Per Serving

Per Serving: 376 calories; 18.9 g fat; 19.3 g carbohydrates; 30.7 g protein

Roasted Pork Loin with Sauce

Prep time: 20 mins; Cook time: 3 h; Serves 8

5 Ingredients:

1 teaspoon. rubbed sage
1 clove garlic, crushed
1 (5 pound) boneless pork loin
1 tablespoon almond flour
1/4 cup. water

What you'll need from the store cupboard:

1/2 teaspoon salt
1/4 cup vinegar
2 tablespoons soy sauce, low-carb
1/4 teaspoon pepper

Instructions

1. Preheat oven to 325 degrees F.
2. In a bowl, combine sage, salt, pepper, and garlic. Rub thoroughly all over pork and place it in an uncovered roasting pan on the middle oven rack.
3. Bake in the preheated oven approximately 3 hours at least 145 degrees F.
4. Meanwhile, place flour, vinegar, water, and soy sauce in a small saucepan. Heat, stirring occasionally, until mixture thicken slightly.
5. Brush roast with glaze 3 or 4 times during the last 1/2 hour of cooking. Pour remaining glaze over roast, and serve.

Nutrition Facts Per Serving

Per Serving: 472 calories; 24.6 g fat; 13.9 g carbohydrates; 45.8 g protein

Seasoned Garlic Pork Chops

Prep time: 5 mins; Cook time: 10 mins; Serves 8

5 Ingredients:

1/2 cup water
1/3 cup mayo
3 tablespoons lemon pepper seasoning
2 teaspoons minced garlic
6 boneless pork loin chops, trimmed of fat

What you'll need from the store cupboard:

1/4 cup olive oil

Instructions

1. Mix water, mayo, olive oil, lemon pepper seasoning, and minced garlic in a deep bowl.
2. Add pork chops and marinate in refrigerator at least 2 hours.
3. Preheat an outdoor grill at medium-high heat and lightly oil the grate.
4. Remove pork chops and cook on the preheated grill for 5 to 6 minutes per side at 145 degrees F.
5. Serve and enjoy.

Nutrition Facts Per Serving

Per Serving: 380 calories; 22 g fat; 2.1 g carbohydrates; 40.7 g protein

Chili Cheese Taco Dip

Prep time: 10 minutes, cook time: 25 minutes; Serves 8

5 Ingredients:

1-pound ground beef
1-pound mild Mexican cheese, grated
1 can tomato salsa
1 packet Mexican spice blend
5 tablespoons olive oil

What you'll need from the store cupboard:

Salt and pepper to taste
½ cup water

Instructions

1. Heat a nonstick saucepan over medium heat for 3 minutes. Heat the oil.
2. Sauté the ground beef until lightly golden, around 8 minutes. Season with pepper, Mexican spice blend, and salt.
3. Add remaining ingredients and give a good stir.
4. Bring to a boil, lower fire to a simmer, and simmer for 10 minutes.

Nutrition Facts Per Serving

Calories: 405; Fat:30.9g; Carbs: 3.1g; Protein: 24.8g

Italian Shredded Beef

Prep time: 5 minutes, cook time: 42 minutes; Serves 6

5 Ingredients:

3 pounds chuck roast, trimmed from excess fat and cut into chunks
1 packet Italian salad dressing mix
8 ounces pepperoncini pepper slices
1 can beef broth

What you'll need from the store cupboard:

Salt and pepper to taste
1 cup water
1 tsp oil

Instructions

1. Place a heavy-bottomed pot on medium-high fire and heat for 2 minutes. Add oil and swirl to coat the bottom and sides of pot and heat for a minute.
2. Season roast with pepper and salt. Brown roast for 4 minutes per side. Transfer to a chopping board and chop into 4 equal pieces.
3. Add remaining ingredients to the pot along with sliced beef.
4. Cover and simmer for 30 minutes or until beef is fork-tender. Stir the bottom of the pot now and then. Turn off the fire.
5. With two forks, shred beef.
6. Turn on fire to high and boil uncovered until sauce is rendered, around 5 minutes.
7. Serve and enjoy.

Nutrition Facts Per Serving

Calories: 455; Fat: 20.5g; Carbs: 6.6g; Protein: 61.5g

Bistro Beef Tenderloin

Prep time: 10 minutes, cook time: 45 minutes; Serves 7

5 Ingredients:

1 3-pound beef tenderloin, trimmed of fat
2/3 cup chopped mixed herbs
2 tablespoons Dijon mustard
5 tablespoons extra virgin olive oil

What you'll need from the store cupboard:

½ teaspoon ground black pepper
½ tsp salt

Instructions

1. Preheat the oven to 400°F.
2. Secure the beef tenderloin with a string in three places so that it does not flatten while roasting.
3. Place the beef tenderloin in a dish and rub onto the meat the olive oil, black pepper, salt, and mixed herb.

4. Place on a roasting pan and cook in the oven for 45 minutes.
5. Roast until the thermometer inserted into the thickest part of the meat until it registers 1400⁰F for medium rare.
6. Place the tenderloin on a chopping board and remove the string. Slice into 1-inch thick slices and brush with Dijon mustard.

Nutrition Facts Per Serving
Calories: 440; Fat: 22.0g; Carbs: 0.6g; Protein: 59.0g

Grilled Fennel Cumin Lamb Chops

Prep time: 10 minutes, cook time: 20 minutes; Serves 6

5 Ingredients:
6 lamb rib chops
1 clove of garlic, minced
¾ teaspoon fennel seeds, crushed
¼ teaspoon ground coriander
5 tablespoons olive oil

What you'll need from the store cupboard:
1/8 teaspoon cracked black pepper
Salt to taste

Instructions
1. Place the lamb rib chops in a shallow dish and rub onto the surface the garlic, fennel seeds, coriander, salt, and black pepper. Drizzle with olive oil. Allow to marinate in the fridge for 4 hours.
2. Heat the grill to medium and place the grill rack 6 inches above the heat source.
3. Grill the lamb chops for 10 minutes on each side or until well-done. For medium-rare lamb chops, cook for 6 to 8 minutes on each side.

Nutrition Facts Per Serving
Calories: 190; Fat: 14.1g; Carbs: 0.5g; Protein: 17.0g

Filling Beefy Soup

Prep time: 10 minutes, cook time: 15 minutes; Serves 4

5 Ingredients:
1 small onion, diced
3 cloves of garlic, minced
1-pound lean ground sirloin
3 cups low-sodium beef broth
1 bag frozen vegetables of your choice

What you'll need from the store cupboard:
5 tablespoons oil
Black pepper and salt to taste

Instructions
1. In a large saucepan, heat the oil over medium heat and sauté the onion and garlic until fragrant.
2. Stir in the lean ground sirloin and cook for 3 minutes until lightly golden.
3. Add in the rest of the ingredients and bring the broth to a boil for 10 minutes.
4. Serve warm.

Nutrition Facts Per Serving
Calories: 334; Fat: 34.0g; Carbs: 5.0g; Protein: 29.0g

Roast Rack of Lamb

Prep time: 15 minutes, cook time: 30 minutes; Serves 8

5 Ingredients:
2 1-pound French-style lamb rib roast, trimmed from fat
1 cup dry red wine
2 cloves of garlic, minced
1 tablespoon chopped rosemary
1 tsp. dried thyme

What you'll need from the store cupboard:
5 tablespoons olive oil
Pepper and salt to taste

Instructions
1. In a resealable plastic, place the lamb and add in red wine, garlic, thyme, olive oil, and rosemary. Seal the bag and turn it to coat the lamb with the spices. Marinate

1. inside the fridge for at least 4 hours while turning the bag occasionally.
2. Preheat the oven to 450°F and remove the lamb from the marinade. Reserve the juices.
3. Place the lamb bone side down on a roasting pan lined with foil.
4. Pour the reserved marinade over the roasting pan.
5. Roast for 30 minutes until the lamb turns slightly golden. Turn the lamb every 10 minutes and baste with the sauce.
6. Once cooked, take out the lamb from the oven and slice.
7. Serve.

Nutrition Facts Per Serving
Calories: 306; Fat: 20.5g; Carbs: 1.7g; Protein: 27.8g

New York Strip Steak with Mushroom Sauce

Prep time: 10 minutes, cook time: 20 minutes; Serves 2

5 Ingredients:
2 New York Strip steaks (4 ounces each), trimmed from fat
3 cloves of garlic, minced
2 ounces shiitake mushrooms, sliced
2 ounces button mushrooms, sliced
¼ teaspoon thyme

What you'll need from the store cupboard:
¼ cup water
½ tsp salt
1 tsp pepper
5 tablespoons olive oil

Instructions
1. Heat the grill to 350°F.
2. Position the grill rack 6 inches from the heat source.
3. Grill the steak for 10 minutes on each side or until slightly pink on the inside.
4. Meanwhile, prepare the sauce. In a small nonstick pan, water sauté the garlic, mushrooms, salt, pepper, and thyme for a minute. Pour in the broth and bring to a boil. Allow the sauce to simmer until the liquid is reduced.
5. Top the steaks with the mushroom sauce. Drizzle with olive oil.
6. Serve warm.

Nutrition Facts Per Serving
Calories: 528; Fat: 36.0g; Carbs: 4.0g; Protein: 47.0g

Grilled Flank Steak with Lime Vinaigrette

Prep time: 10 minutes, cook time: 10 minutes; Serves 6

5 Ingredients:
2 tablespoons lime juice, freshly squeezed
¼ cup chopped fresh cilantro
1 tablespoon ground cumin
¼ teaspoon red pepper flakes
¾ pound flank steak

What you'll need from the store cupboard:
2 tablespoons extra virgin olive oil
½ teaspoon ground black pepper
¼ tsp salt

Instructions
1. Heat the grill to low, medium heat
2. In a food processor, place all ingredients except for the cumin, red pepper flakes, and flank steak. Pulse until smooth. This will be the vinaigrette sauce. Set aside.
3. Season the flank steak with ground cumin and red pepper flakes and allow to marinate for at least 10 minutes.
4. Place the steak on the grill rack and cook for 5 minutes on each side. Cut into the center to check the doneness of the meat. You can also insert a meat thermometer to check the internal temperature.
5. Remove from the grill and allow to stand for 5 minutes.
6. Slice the steak to 2 inches long and toss the vinaigrette to flavor the meat.
7. Serve with salad if desired.

Nutrition Facts Per Serving
Calories: 65; Fat: 1.0g; Carbs: 1.0g; Protein: 13.0g

Garlic Beef & Egg Frittata

Prep time:10 minutes, cook time: 30 minutes; Serves 4

5 Ingredients:

3 eggs, beaten

3 cloves of garlic, minced

1 onion, chopped

½ pound lean ground beef

1 stalk green onion, sliced

What you'll need from the store cupboard:

2 tablespoons olive oil

A dash of salt

¼ tsp pepper

Instructions

1. Place a small cast iron pan on medium fire and heat for 2 minutes.
2. Add beef and crumble. Cook for 5 minutes.
3. Add onion and garlic, continue cooking beef until browned, around 5 minutes more. Discard any fat.
4. Season with pepper and salt.
5. Spread beef in the pan and lower fire to low.
6. Meanwhile, whisk eggs in a bowl. Pour over meat, cover, and cook for 10 minutes on low.
7. Place pan in the oven and broil on low for 3 minutes. Let it set for 5 minutes.
8. Serve and enjoy topped with green onions.

Nutrition Facts Per Serving

Calories: 294; Fat: 20.5g; Carbs: 3.8g; Protein: 22.7g

Simple Corned Beef

Prep time: 15 minutes, cook time: 1 hour and 30 minutes; Serves 6

5 Ingredients:

2 pounds corned beef brisket, cut into 1-inch cubes

2 cups water

2 onions, chopped

6 garlic cloves, smashed

What you'll need from the store cupboard:

1 cup olive oil

1 tbsp peppercorns

1 tsp salt

Instructions

1. Place all ingredients in a heavy-bottomed pot on high fire and bring to a boil.
2. Once boiling, lower fire to a simmer.
3. Simmer for 60 minutes.
4. Turn off fire and shred beef with two forks.
5. Turn on fire and continue cooking until sauce is reduced.
6. Serve and enjoy.

Nutrition Facts Per Serving

Calories: 314; Fat: 30.2g; Carbs: 0.6g; Protein: 12.1g

Beef Brisket in Mustard Sauce

Prep time: 10 minutes, cook time: 60 minutes; Serves 7

5 Ingredients:

2 ½ pounds beef brisket, cut into 2-inch cubes

½ cup onion, chopped

1 tablespoon prepared mustard

½ cup olive oil

What you'll need from the store cupboard:

Salt and pepper to taste

1 cup water

Instructions

1. Place all ingredients in a heavy-bottomed pot on high fire and bring to a boil.
2. Once boiling, lower fire to a simmer.
3. Simmer for 60 minutes.
4. Serve and enjoy.

Nutrition Facts Per Serving

Calories: 477; Fat: 39.2g; Carbs: 1.7g; Protein: 29.4g

Onion Swiss Steak

Prep time: 15 minutes, cook time: 30 minutes; Serves 6

5 Ingredients:

1 ½ pounds beef round steak, sliced
1 medium onion, sliced
2 bay leaves
¼ cup coconut oil

What you'll need from the store cupboard:

1/2 cup water
Salt and pepper to taste

Instructions

1. Place all ingredients in a heavy-bottomed pot on high fire and bring to a boil.
2. Once boiling, lower fire to a simmer.
3. Simmer for 30 minutes.
4. Serve and enjoy.

Nutrition Facts Per Serving

Calories: 308; Fat: 25.3g; Carbs: 0.9g; Protein: 19.3g

Ground Beef and Cabbage Stir Fry

Prep time: 15 minutes, cook time:20 minutes; Serves 5

5 Ingredients:

1 onion, chopped
3 cloves of garlic, minced
1 ½ pounds ground beef
1 tablespoon grated ginger
½ head cabbage, chopped

What you'll need from the store cupboard:

2 tablespoons oil
Salt and pepper to taste
1 teaspoon chili flakes (optional)

Instructions

1. In a skillet, heat oil over medium flame.
2. Sauté the onion and garlic until fragrant.
3. Stir in the ground beef and season with salt and pepper to taste. Cook and crumble for 10 minutes.
4. Add grated ginger, chopped cabbage, and chili flakes. Cover and cook for 5 minutes.
5. Stir and continue cooking for another 3 minutes or until cabbage is translucent and wilted.
6. Serve and enjoy.

Nutrition Facts Per Serving

Calories: 385; Fat: 23.7g; Carbs: 6.3g; Protein:30.6g

Moroccan Style Beef Stew

Prep time: 15 minutes, cook time: 45 minutes; Serves 8

5 Ingredients:

½ cup sliced onions
4 tablespoons garam masala
2 pounds beef roast
5 tablespoons butter
1 large bell pepper, seeded and chopped

What you'll need from the store cupboard:

2 cups water
Salt and pepper to taste
1 tablespoon oil

Instructions

1. Heat the oil in a heavy-bottomed pot over a high flame and sauté the onions for 10 minutes until lightly golden.
2. Stir in the garam masala and sear the beef roast on all sides.
3. Add remaining ingredients and bring to a boil.
4. Once boiling, lower fire to a simmer, cover, and cook for 30 minutes.
5. Serve and enjoy.

Nutrition Facts Per Serving

Calories: 350; Fat: 30.8g; Carbs: 1.2g; Protein: 25.1g

Asian-Style Beef Steak

Prep time:10 minutes, cook time: 25 minutes; Serves 6

5 Ingredients:

1 onion, sliced into rings
4 beef steaks, cut into strips
2 tablespoons lemon juice, freshly squeezed
2 tbsp soy sauce

What you'll need from the store cupboard:

1 tsp pepper
3 tablespoons oil
A dash of salt

Instructions

1. On high fire, place a nonstick pan and heat oil for 3 minutes.
2. Stir in half of the onion rings and beef steaks. Stir fry for 10 minutes.
3. Add remaining ingredients except for lemon juice and fry for another 5 minutes.
4. Serve and enjoy with lemon juice.

Nutrition Facts Per Serving

Calories: 350; Fat: 29.6g; Carbs: 0.7g; Protein: 20.4g

Keto Beefy Burritos

Prep time: 5 minutes, cook time: 25 minutes; Serves 6

5 Ingredients:

1-pound lean ground beef
6 large kale leaves
1/4 cup onion
1/4 cup low-sodium tomato puree
1/4 teaspoon ground cumin

What you'll need from the store cupboard:

1/4 teaspoon black pepper
½ tsp salt

Instructions

1. In a medium skillet, brown ground beef for 15 minutes; drain oil on paper towels.
2. Spray skillet with non-stick cooking spray; add onion to cook for 3-5 minutes, until vegetables are softened.
3. Add beef, tomato puree, black pepper, and cumin to onion/pepper mixture.
4. Mix well and cook for 3 to 5 minutes on low heat.
5. Divide the beef mixture among kale leaves.
6. Roll the kale leaves over burrito style, making sure that both ends are folded first, so the mixture does not fall out. Secure with a toothpick.

Nutrition Facts Per Serving

Calories: 412; Fat: 32.0g; Carbs: 6.0g; Protein: 25.0g

Simple Beef Curry

Prep time:10minutes, cook time:30 minutes; Serves 6

5 Ingredients:

2 pounds boneless beef chuck (cut into 1 ½ inch pieces)
1 tbsp ground turmeric
1 tsp ginger paste
6 cloves garlic, minced
1 onion, chopped

What you'll need from the store cupboard:

3 tbsp olive oil
1 cup water
Pepper and salt to taste

Instructions

1. In a saucepan, heat the olive oil over medium heat then add onion and garlic for 5 minutes.
2. Stir in beef and sauté for 10 minutes.
3. Add remaining ingredients, cover, and simmer for 20 minutes.
4. Adjust seasoning if needed.
5. Serve and enjoy.

Nutrition Facts Per Serving

Calories: 287; Fat: 16.0g; Carbs: 5.0g; Protein: 33.0g

Beefy Scotch Eggs

Prep time: 30 minutes, cook time: 25 minutes; Serves 7

5 Ingredients:
2 eggs, beaten
1-pound ground beef
2 tablespoons butter, melted
¼ cup coconut flour
7 large eggs, boiled and peeled
What you'll need from the store cupboard:
Cooking spray
Salt and pepper to taste
Instructions
1. Preheat the oven to 350ºF.

2. Place the beaten eggs, ground beef, butter, and coconut flour in a mixing bowl. Season with salt and pepper to taste.
3. Coat the boiled eggs with the meat mixture and place them on a baking sheet.
4. Bake for 25 minutes.
Nutrition Facts Per Serving
Calories: 312; Fat: 25.8g; Carbs: 1.8g; Protein: 21.4g

Beef Steak Filipino Style

Prep time: 10 minutes, cook time: 25 minutes; Serves 6

5 Ingredients:
2 tablespoons coconut oil
1 onion, sliced
4 beef steaks
2 tablespoons lemon juice, freshly squeezed
¼ cup coconut aminos
What you'll need from the store cupboard:
1 tsp salt
Pepper to taste
Instructions
1. In a nonstick fry pan, heat oil on medium-high fire.

2. Pan-fry beef steaks and season with coconut aminos.
3. Cook until dark brown, around 7 minutes per side. Transfer to a plate.
4. Sauté onions in the same pan until caramelized, around 8 minutes. Season with lemon juice and return steaks in the pan. Mix well.
5. Serve and enjoy.
Nutrition Facts Per Serving
Calories: 347; Fat: 27.1g; Carbs: 0.7g; Protein: 25.3g

Slow-Cooked Beef Moroccan Style

Prep time: 10 minutes, cook time: 8 hours; Serves 8

5 Ingredients:
½ cup apricots
½ cup sliced yellow onions
2 pounds beef roast
4 tablespoons garam masala seasoning
What you'll need from the store cupboard:
1 teaspoon sea salt
2 cups water
Instructions
1. Place onions and apricots on the bottom of Instant Pot.
2. Rub salt and garam masala all over roast beef and place roast beef on top of onions and apricots.

3. Pour water.
4. Cover, press the slow cook button, adjust cooking time to 6 hours.
5. Once done cooking, remove roast beef and shred with 2 forks.
6. Return to pot, cover, press slow cook, and adjust the time to 2 hours.
7. Serve and enjoy.
Nutrition Facts Per Serving
Calories: 275; Fat: 14.7g; Carbs: 3.0g; Protein: 31.9g

Cranberry Gravy Brisket

Prep time: 15 minutes, cook time: 25 minutes; Serves 7

5 Ingredients:
1 tablespoon prepared mustard
½ cup chopped onion
1 (8-ounce) can tomato sauce
½ cup cranberries, pitted
1 fresh beef brisket (2 ½-pounds)

What you'll need from the store cupboard:
5 tablespoons olive oil
½ teaspoon salt
¼ teaspoon pepper

Instructions
1. Add all ingredients in a pot on high fire and bring to a boil.
2. Once boiling, lower fire to a simmer and cook for 25 minutes.
3. Adjust seasoning to taste.
4. Serve and enjoy.

Nutrition Facts Per Serving
Calories: 364; Fat: 24.4g; Carbs: 9.7g; Protein: 24.9g

Beef Broccoli Stew

Prep time: 10 minutes, cook time: 40 minutes; Serves 4

5 Ingredients:
¼ cup water
1 (8-ounces) packet lee kum kee sauce for Beef Broccoli sauce packet
1 bag (14-ounces) frozen broccoli
1 ½- pounds flank steak, trimmed fat

What you'll need from the store cupboard:
5 tablespoons olive oil
Pepper and salt to taste
1 cup water

Instructions
1. Add all ingredients in a pot on high fire and bring to a boil.
2. Once boiling, lower fire to a simmer and cook for 30 minutes.
3. Adjust seasoning to taste and continue to simmer for another 5 minutes.
4. Serve and enjoy.

Nutrition Facts Per Serving
Calories: 245; Fat: 15.6g; Carbs: 2.9g; Protein: 27.7g

Beef Italian Sandwiches

Prep time: 15 minutes, cook time: 40 minutes; Serves 6

5 Ingredients:
6 Provolone cheese slices
14.5-ounce can beef broth
8-ounces giardiniera drained (Chicago-style Italian sandwich mix)
3-pounds chuck roast fat trimmed and cut into large pieces
6 large lettuce

What you'll need from the store cupboard:
Pepper and salt to taste

Instructions
1. Add all ingredients in a pot, except for lettuce and cheese, on high fire, and bring to a boil.
2. Once boiling, lower fire to a simmer and cook for 25 minutes.
3. Adjust seasoning to taste.
4. To make a sandwich, add warm shredded beef in one lettuce leaf and top with cheese.

Nutrition Facts Per Serving
Calories: 538; Fat: 36.4g; Carbs: 3.9g; Protein: 48.6g

Pizzaiola Steak Stew

Prep time: 5 minutes, cook time: 40 minutes; Serves 4

5 Ingredients:
¼ cup water
2-pounds London broil
1 medium sliced onion
1 yellow sweet sliced bell pepper
Half a jar of pasta sauce
What you'll need from the store cupboard:
Pepper and salt to taste
Instructions

1. Add all ingredients in a pot on high fire and bring to a boil.
2. Once boiling, lower fire to a simmer and cook for 35 minutes.
3. Adjust seasoning to taste.
4. Serve and enjoy.

Nutrition Facts Per Serving
Calories: 488; Fat: 20.6g; Carbs: 5.9g; Protein: 70.7g

Cherry-Balsamic Sauced Beef

Prep time: 20 minutes, cook time: 40 minutes; Serves 4

5 Ingredients:
2-lbs London broil beef, sliced into 2-inch cubes
1/3 cup balsamic vinegar
1 tsp dried thyme
What you'll need from the store cupboard:
½ teaspoon pepper
1 teaspoon salt
1 tablespoon canola oil
½ cup water

Instructions
1. Add all ingredients in a pot on high fire and bring to a boil.
2. Once boiling, lower fire to a simmer and cook for 35 minutes.
3. Adjust seasoning to taste.
4. Serve and enjoy.

Nutrition Facts Per Serving
Calories: 525; Fat: 17.2g; Carbs: 4.6g; Protein: 82.2g

Beef Enchilada Stew

Prep time: 10 minutes, cook time: 40 minutes; Serves 4

5 Ingredients:
1 cup Mexican cheese, shredded
1 can mild green chilies, drained
2 teaspoons garlic salt
1 10-ounce can La Victoria mild red enchilada sauce
2-lbs London broil beef, sliced into 2-inch cubes
What you'll need from the store cupboard:
Pepper and salt to taste

Instructions
1. Add all ingredients in a pot on high fire and bring to a boil.
2. Once boiling, lower fire to a simmer and cook for 25 minutes.
3. Adjust seasoning to taste.
4. Serve and enjoy.

Nutrition Facts Per Serving
Calories: 764; Fat: 47.4g; Carbs: 10.1g; Protein: 64.2g

Beefy BBQ Ranch

Prep time: 20 minutes, cook time: 40 minutes; Serves 4

5 Ingredients:
2-lbs London broil roast, sliced into 2-inch cubes
1 Hidden Valley Ranch seasoning mix packet
1 pound bacon
1 tablespoon barbecue powder
What you'll need from the store cupboard:
1 cup water
Pepper and salt to taste
Instructions

1. Add all ingredients in a pot on high fire and bring to a boil.
2. Once boiling, lower fire to a simmer and cook for 35 minutes.
3. Adjust seasoning to taste.

4. Serve and enjoy.
Nutrition Facts Per Serving
Calories: 642; Fat: 39.7g; Carbs: 8.4g; Protein: 65.3g

Moroccan Beef Stew

Prep time: 15 minutes, cook time: 40 minutes; Serves 4
5 Ingredients:
1 medium onion, chopped coarsely
2-lbs London broil roast, chopped into 2-inch cubes
¼ cup prunes
1 ¼ teaspoons curry powder
½ teaspoon ground cinnamon
What you'll need from the store cupboard:
½ teaspoon salt
2 cups water

Instructions
1. Add all ingredients in a pot on high fire and bring to a boil.
2. Once boiling, lower fire to a simmer and cook for 35 minutes.
3. Adjust seasoning to taste.
4. Serve and enjoy.
Nutrition Facts Per Serving
Calories: 658; Fat: 49.6g; Carbs: 8.3g; Protein:40.6g

Meatballs with Ranch-Buffalo Sauce

Prep time: 5 minutes, cook time: 30 minutes; Serves 10
5 Ingredients:
1 packet Ranch dressing dry mix
1 bottle red-hot wings buffalo sauce
1 bag frozen Rosina Italian Style Meatballs

What you'll need from the store cupboard:
5 tablespoons butter
1 cup water
Pepper and salt to taste
Instructions

1. Add all ingredients in a pot on high fire and bring to a boil.
2. Once boiling, lower fire to a simmer and cook for 25 minutes.
3. Adjust seasoning to taste.
4. Serve and enjoy.
Nutrition Facts Per Serving
Calories: 400; Fat: 27.9g; Carbs: 1.2g; Protein: 36.0g

Beefy French Onion Stew

Prep time: 15 minutes, cook time: 40 minutes; Serves 4
5 Ingredients:
½ cup sour cream
½ cup Campbell's French Onion Soup, 10.5-ounce
½ cup Campbell's chicken broth, 10.5-ounce
4 boneless center-cut pork loin chops
What you'll need from the store cupboard:
3 tablespoons butter
Pepper and salt to taste
1 cup water
Instructions

1. Add all ingredients in a pot, except for sour cream, on high fire, and bring to a boil.
2. Once boiling, lower fire to a simmer and cook for 35 minutes.
3. Adjust seasoning to taste and stir in sour cream.
4. Serve and enjoy.
Nutrition Facts Per Serving
Calories: 401; Fat: 21.5g; Carbs:8.0g; Protein: 43.9g

Mexican Ground Beef

Prep time: 15 minutes, cook time: 40 minutes; Serves 6

5 Ingredients:

1 ½-pounds ground beef

2 cups shredded cheddar cheese

1 envelope taco seasoning

1 can 10.75-ounces condensed tomato soup

1 cup sour cream

What you'll need from the store cupboard:

Pepper and salt to taste

1 cup water

Instructions

1. Add all ingredients in a pot on high fire and bring to a boil.
2. Once boiling, lower fire to a simmer and cook for 35 minutes.
3. Adjust seasoning to taste.
4. Serve and enjoy.

Nutrition Facts Per Serving

Calories: 496; Fat: 35.2g; Carbs: 3.9g; Protein: 39.1g

Old-Style Beef Stew

Prep time: 20 minutes, cook time: 40 minutes; Serves 5

5 Ingredients:

1 ½-pounds beef stew meat, cubed into 1-inch squares

16-ounce fresh cremini mushrooms

3 medium tomatoes, chopped

1 envelope reduced-sodium onion soup mix

What you'll need from the store cupboard:

5 tablespoons butter

1 cup water

Pepper and salt to taste

Instructions

1. Add all ingredients in a pot on high fire and bring to a boil.
2. Once boiling, lower fire to a simmer and cook for 25 minutes.
3. Adjust seasoning to taste.
4. Serve and enjoy.

Nutrition Facts Per Serving

Calories: 551; Fat: 27.8g; Carbs: 11.5g; Protein: 58g

Beef Stew with Vegetables

Prep time: 20 mins; Cook time: 2 hours; Serves 8

5 Ingredients:

2 pounds cubed beef stew meat

4 cubes beef bouillon, crumbled

1 teaspoon dried parsley

4 stalks celery, cut into 1 inch pieces

What you'll need from the store cupboard:

2 teaspoons cold water

1 large onion, chopped

3 tablespoons olive oil

1 teaspoon dried rosemary

1/2 teaspoon ground black pepper

Instructions

1. Heat oil in a large pot over medium heat, cook beef until tender. Pour water into the pot and bring to boil; stir in bouillon cubes until dissolved. Add in spices, then reduce heat, covered and simmer for 1 hour.

2. Add celery and onion into the pot. Pour water slowly and stir into stew. Simmer, covered, for about 1 hour.

Nutrition Facts

Per Serving: 370.2 calories; 24.2 g fat; 10.9 g carbohydrates; 27.2 g protein

Keto Ground Beef Stroganoff

Prep time: 10 mins; Cook time: 20 minutes; Serves 4

5 Ingredients:

1 pound ground beef, lean

4 oz mushrooms, sliced

1/4 cup onions, chopped or sliced (1 ounce)

1 tsp beef bouillon

1 cup sour cream

What you'll need from the store cupboard:

1 tbsp Worcestershire sauce
3 tbsp butter, divided
1-2 pinches grated nutmeg
1 tbsp chopped parsley
salt and pepper to taste
Instructions
1. In a large pan over medium heat, melt butter and add the mushrooms to spread evenly in the pan. Cook for 2 minutes, turning over for more 2 minutes' cooking.
2. Add remaining butter and onions to cook until tender. Remove the mushrooms and onions from the pan.

3. Cook the ground beef in the pan, breaking it up into small pieces, until just cooked through. Add the beef bouillon and Worcestershire sauce, stirring well.
4. Mix in the mushroom mixture and ground beef back into the pan, sprinkle the nutmeg over the top. Whisk in the sour cream and simmer gently until thickened. Add the parsley, season with salt and pepper to taste.
5. Serve with cooked cauliflower rice if desired.
Nutrition Facts
Per Serving: 468 calories; 31.7 g fat; 5.86 g carbohydrates; 23 g protein

Roast Leg of Lamb with Rosemary

Prep time: 15 mins; Cook time: 1 hour 20 mins; Serves 8
5 Ingredients:
2 tablespoons prepared Dijon-style mustard
2 tablespoons chopped fresh rosemary
1 teaspoon freshly ground black pepper
5 pounds whole leg of lamb
What you'll need from the store cupboard:
1 teaspoon lemon zest
3 cloves garlic, minced
1 teaspoon coarse sea salt
Instructions
1. Stir together the mustard, rosemary, ground black pepper, lemon zest and garlic in a bowl, mix well. Rub the mixture over lamb, cover and refrigerate overnight to marinate.

2. Preheat oven to 450 degrees F and place the lamb on a rack in a foil-lined roasting pan, season with salt.
3. Place into oven and reduce the temperature to 400 degrees F after 5 minutes. Roast for 45 minutes, or until desired doneness, 140 degrees on an instant read thermometer. Allow to rest for 10-15 minutes before serving.
Nutrition Facts
Per Serving: 553 calories; 38.7 g fat; 8.1 g carbohydrates; 40.7 g protein

Classic Meatloaf

Prep time: 15 mins; Cook time: 40 mins; Serves 3
Ingredients
1 rib celery, coarsely chopped
3 cloves garlic, coarsely chopped
2 1/2 pounds ground chuck
1 cup almond flour
Glaze Ingredients:
2 tablespoons ketchup, sugar-free
2 tablespoons Dijon mustard
hot pepper sauce to taste
What you'll need from the store cupboard:
1/2 onion, coarsely chopped
2 teaspoons salt
1 teaspoon olive oil
1/2 teaspoon cayenne pepper and ground

black pepper
1 teaspoon dried Italian herbs
Instructions
1. Preheat the oven to 325 degrees F.
2. Place the celery, onion and garlic in a food processor.
3. Place the minced vegetables into a large mixing bowl, and mix in ground chuck, Italian herbs, salt, black pepper, and cayenne pepper.
4. Whisk in the almond flour, stirring well, about 1 minute.
5. Sprinkle the olive oil into a baking dish

and place meat into the dish. Shape the ball into a loaf. Bake in the preheated oven for 15 minutes.

6. In a small bowl, mix together ketchup, Dijon mustard, and hot sauce, stirring well to combined.

7. Bake the meatloaf for 30 to 40 more minutes at least 160 degrees F.

8. Serve hot.

Nutrition Facts
Per Serving: 300 calories; 19 g fat; 10.8 g carbohydrates; 21.6 g protein

Chicken Broth Beef Roast

Prep time: 30 mins; Cook time: 2h mins; Serves 5

5 Ingredients:
2 1/2 pounds boneless beef chuck roast, cut into 2-inch cubes
2 onions, chopped
2 teaspoons caraway seeds, crushed
4 cups chicken broth, divided
2 tablespoons Hungarian paprika

What you'll need from the store cupboard:
1/2 teaspoon ground thyme
2 tablespoons balsamic vinegar
salt and ground black pepper to taste
3 cloves garlic, crushed
2 tablespoons olive oil

Instructions
1. Heat olive oil in a large skillet over high heat; cook and stir beef with salt and black pepper about 5 minutes per batch. Transfer to a large stockpot and reserve drippings in the skillet.

2. Stir onions and 1/2 teaspoon salt into the reserved drippings on Medium, and cook about 5 minutes. Transfer to the stockpot with beef.

3. Whisk the paprika, caraway seeds, black pepper and thyme in the skillet over medium heat and saute for 3 minutes.

4. Add 1 cup chicken broth and stir; transfer to the beef and onion mixture.

5. In the stockpot over high heat, stir 3 cups chicken broth into beef mixture. Add garlic, vinegar and 1/2 teaspoon salt, bring to a boil. Reduce heat to low and simmer 1 1/2 to 2 hours. Serve and enjoy.

Nutrition Facts
Per Serving: 573 calories; 41.2 g fat; 13.4 g carbohydrates; 36 g protein

Mushroom Beef Stew

Prep time: 15 mins; Cook time: 1h 30mins; Serves 5

5 Ingredients:
2 pounds beef chuck roast, cut into 1/2-inch thick strips
1/2 medium onion, sliced or diced
8 ounces sliced mushrooms
2 cups beef broth, divided

What you'll need from the store cupboard:
Salt and pepper to taste
1 tablespoon butter
2 cloves garlic, minced
1 tablespoon fresh chopped chives
1 tablespoon olive oil

Instructions
1. Heat olive oil in a large skillet over high heat. Stir in beef with salt and pepper; cook, stirring constantly, for 6-7 minutes.

Remove beef from the pan and set aside.

2. Add butter, mushrooms and onions into the pan; cook and stir over medium heat.

3. Add garlic and stir for 30 seconds. Stir in 1 cup. broth and simmer 3-4 minutes.

4. Return beef to the pan. Stir in remaining broth and chives; bring to a simmer and cook on low heat for about 1 hour, covered, stirring every 20 minutes.

5. Season with salt and pepper to taste. Serve.

Nutrition Facts
Per Serving: 307 calories; 24.5 g fat; 4.1 g carbohydrates; 15.8 g protein

Beef and Cabbage with Spice Packet

Prep time: 15 mins; Cook time: 1h 20mins; Serves 5

Ingredients

3 pounds corned beef brisket with spice packet
1 large head cabbage, cut into small wedges
1 cup diced onion
3 cups water
2 cups beef broth

Instructions

1. Place corned beef in large pot and cover with water. Add the spice packet to the corned beef.
2. Cover the pot and bring to a boil, simmering for 50 minutes.
3. Add the cabbage and onion, cook until the vegetables are almost tender.
4. Remove beef and cool for 15 minutes.
5. Transfer vegetables into a bowl and cover. Add as much broth as you want. Slice meat across the grain. Serve and enjoy.

Nutrition Facts

Per Serving: 341 calories; 23.7 g fat; 11g carbohydrates; 21 g protein

Garlicky Beef Stew

Prep time: 30 mins; Cook time: 2h 30mins; Serves 5

5 Ingredients:

4 slices bacon, cut into small pieces
2 1/2 pounds boneless beef chuck, cut into 2-inch pieces
2 onions, coarsely chopped
2 1/2 cups chicken stock, or as needed to cover

What you'll need from the store cupboard:

4 sprigs fresh thyme
4 cloves garlic, minced
1 1/2 teaspoon salt
1/2 teaspoon freshly ground black pepper, or to taste

Instructions

1. In a skillet over medium-high heat, cook bacon for 3 to 4 minutes. Turn off heat and transfer bacon into a stew pot.
2. Season beef chuck cubes with 1 teaspoon salt and black pepper to taste. Then broil beef pieces for 5 minutes on High.
3. Add beef in stew pot with bacon. Lower the heat to medium; cook and stir onions for 5 to 8 minutes; season with a large pinch of salt. Mix in the garlic, saute for 1 minute; stir in tomato paste, thyme sprigs, 1/2 teaspoon black pepper, and enough chicken broth in a skillet. Reduce heat to low and cover. Simmer stew about 2 hours.
4. Remove cover and bring stew to a boil on Medium and cook for 15 to 20 minutes.
5. Remove and discard thyme sprigs and sprinkle salt and pepper to taste.

Nutrition Facts

Per Serving: 528 calories; 24.6 g fat; 11.3 g carbohydrates; 29.4 g protein

Simple Beef Pot Roast

Prep time: 15 mins; Cook time: 3h 15mins; Serves 5

Ingredients

1 tablespoon olive oil

3 1/2 pounds beef chuck pot roast

1 cup diced onion

1/4 cup butter

What you'll need from the store cupboard:

1 teaspoon ground black pepper

2 teaspoons salt

1 cup diced celery

1 teaspoon dried rosemary

Instructions

1. Preheat the oven to 275 degrees F.
2. Pour olive oil into a large pot over medium-high heat. Season the chuck roast with salt and black pepper.
3. Brown the meat on both sides in the hot oil, and transfer to a plate.
4. Stir celery, and onion into the pot; cook and stir, about 3 minutes.
5. Add butter, and cook about 5 minutes. Then sprinkle in rosemary, stir the vegetables, and return the roast to the pot. Cover the pot with a lid.
6. Roast in the preheated oven about 2 1/2 to 3 hours. Serve hot.

Nutrition Facts

Per Serving: 507 calories; 39.2 g fat; 5.6 g carbohydrates; 31.7 g protein

Corned Beef and Cabbage

Prep time: 15 mins; Cook time: 9 hours; Serves 6

5 Ingredients:

1 onion, peeled and cut into bite-sized pieces

1 (4 pound) corned beef brisket with spice packet

6 ounces beer, low-carb

1/2 head cabbage, coarsely chopped

What you'll need from the store cupboard:

4 cups water

Instructions

1. Place the onion into a slow cooker, pour in water, and place the brisket on top of the vegetables.
2. Pour the beer over the brisket. Sprinkle on the spices. Then set the cooker on High.
3. Cook the brisket for about 8 hours. Stir in the cabbage and cook for 1 more hour.
4. Serve and enjoy.

Nutrition Facts

Per Serving: 472 calories; 19.6 g fat; 49.5 g carbohydrates; 23.6 g protein

Chocolate Hazelnut Bites

Prep time: 30 minutes, cook time: 0 minutes; Serves 9

5 Ingredients:

1 carton (8 ounces) spreadable cream cheese
1 cup (6 ounces) semisweet chocolate chips, melted
1/2 cup Nutella
2-1/4 cups graham cracker crumbs
2 cups chopped hazelnuts, toasted

What you' ll need from the store cupboard:

5 tablespoons butter

Instructions

1. Beat cream cheese, melted chocolate chips, and Nutella until blended. Stir in cracker crumbs. Refrigerate until firm enough to roll, about 30 minutes.

2. Shape mixture into 1-in. balls; roll in chopped hazelnuts. Make an indentation in the center of each with the end of a wooden spoon handle. Fill with a hazelnut. Store between layers of waxed paper in an airtight container in the refrigerator.

Nutrition Facts Per Serving

Calories: 176; Fat: 14g; Carbs: 10g; Protein: 2.7g

Choco-Chia Pudding

Prep time: 30 minutes, cook time: 5 minutes; Serves 4

5 Ingredients:

¼ cup fresh or frozen raspberries
1 scoop chocolate protein powder
1 cup unsweetened almond milk
3 tbsp Chia seeds

What you' ll need from the store cupboard:

1 tsp Stevia (optional)
5 tablespoons coconut oil

Instructions

1. Mix the chocolate protein powder and almond milk.

2. Add the chia seeds and mix well with a whisk or a fork. Add the coconut oil.

3. Flavor with Stevia depending on the desired sweetness.

4. Let it rest for 5 minutes and continue stirring.

5. Serve and enjoy.

Nutrition Facts Per Serving

Calories: 243.5; Fat: 19.6; Carbs: 10g; Protein: 11.5g

No Bake Lemon Cheese-Stard

Prep time: 20 minutes, cook time: 0 minutes; Serves 8

5 Ingredients:

1 tsp vanilla flavoring
1 tbsp lemon juice
2 oz heavy cream
8 oz softened cream cheese

What you' ll need from the store cupboard:

1 tsp liquid low carb sweetener (Splenda)
1 tsp stevia

Instructions

1. Mix all ingredients in a large mixing bowl until the mixture has a pudding consistency.

2. Pour the mixture to small serving cups and refrigerate for a few hours until it sets.

3. Serve chilled.

Nutrition Facts Per Serving

Calories: 111; Fat: 10.7g; Carbs: 1.4g; Protein: 2.2g

Keto Lemon Custard

Prep time: 20 minutes, cook time: 50 minutes; Serves 8

5 Ingredients:

1 Lemon

6 large eggs

2 tbsp lemon zest

1 cup Lakanto

2 cups heavy cream

What you'll need from the store cupboard:

None

Instructions

1. Preheat oven to 300ºF.
2. Mix all ingredients.
3. Pour mixture into ramekins.
4. Put ramekins into a dish with boiling water.
5. Bake in the oven for 45-50 minutes.
6. Let cool then refrigerate for 2 hours.
7. Use lemon slices as garnish.

Nutrition Facts Per Serving

Calories: 233; Fat: 21.0g; Carbs: 4.0g; Protein: 7.0g

Eggnog Keto Custard

Prep time: 10 minutes, cook time: 10 minutes; Serves 8

5 Ingredients:

¼ tsp nutmeg

¼ Truvia

½ cup heavy whipping cream

1 cup half and half

4 eggs

What you'll need from the store cupboard:

None

Instructions

1. Blend all ingredients together.
2. Pour evenly into 6 ramekins (microwave safe).
3. Microwave at 50% power for 4 minutes then stir thoroughly.
4. Microwave for another 3-4 minutes at 50% power then stir well again.
5. Serve either cool or hot.

Nutrition Facts Per Serving

Calories: 70; Fat: 6.0g; Carbs: 1.0g; Protein: 3.0g

White Choco Fatty Fudge

Prep time: 10 minutes, cook time: 10 minutes; Serves 6

5 Ingredients:

1/4 cup coconut butter

1/4 cup cashew butter

2 tbsp cacao butter

1/4 teaspoon vanilla powder

10–12 drops liquid stevia, or to taste

What you'll need from the store cupboard:

2 tbsp coconut oil

Instructions

1. Over low heat, place a small saucepan and melt coconut oil, cacao butter, cashew butter, and coconut butter.
2. Remove from the heat and stir in the vanilla and stevia.
3. Pour into a silicone mold and place it in the freezer for 30 minutes.
4. Store in the fridge for a softer consistency.

Nutrition Facts Per Serving

Calories: 221; Fat: 23.7g; Carbs: 1.7g; Protein: 0.2g

Lemon Gummies

Prep time: 10 minutes, cook time: 15 minutes; Serves 4

5 Ingredients:

1/4 cup fresh lemon juice

2 Tablespoons gelatin powder

2 Tablespoons stevia, to taste

½ cup half and half

What you'll need from the store cupboard:

1 Tablespoon water
Instructions
1. In a small saucepan, heat up water and lemon juice.
2. Slowly stir in the gelatin powder and the rest of the ingredients. Heating and mixing well until dissolved.
3. Pour into silicone molds.
4. Freeze or refrigerate for 2+ hours until firm.

Nutrition Facts Per Serving
Calories: 88; Fat: 7g; Carbs: 1.0g; Protein: 3.0g

Sea Salt 'n Macadamia Choco Barks

Prep time: 15 minutes, cook time: 5 minutes; Serves 10
5 Ingredients:
1 teaspoon sea salt flakes
1/4 cup macadamia nuts, crushed
2 Tablespoons erythritol or stevia, to taste
3.5 oz 100% dark chocolate, broken into pieces
What you'll need from the store cupboard:
2 Tablespoons coconut oil, melted
Instructions
1. Melt the chocolate and coconut oil over a very low heat.
2. Remove from heat. Stir in sweetener.
3. Pour the mixture into a loaf pan and place in the fridge for 15 minutes.
4. Scatter the crushed macadamia nuts on top along with the sea salt. Lightly press into the chocolate.
5. Place back into the fridge or freezer for 2 hours.

Nutrition Facts Per Serving
Calories: 84; Fat: 8.0g; Carbs: 1.0g; Protein: 2.0g

No Nuts Fudge

Prep time: 10 minutes, cook time: 4 hours; Serves 15
5 Ingredients:
¼ cup cocoa powder
½ teaspoon baking powder
1 stick of butter, melted
4 tablespoons erythritol
6 eggs, beaten
What you'll need from the store cupboard:
Salt to taste.
Instructions
1. Mix all ingredients in a slow cooker.
2. Add a pinch of salt.
3. Mix until well combined.
4. Cover pot.
5. Press the low settings and adjust the time to 4 hours.

Nutrition Facts Per Serving
Calories: 132; Fat: 12.2g; Carbs: 1.3g; Protein: 4.3g

Brownie Fudge Keto Style

Prep time: 10 minutes, cook time: 6 hours; Serves 10
5 Ingredients:
¾ cup coconut milk
1 teaspoon erythritol
2 tablespoons butter, melted
4 egg yolks, beaten
5 tablespoons cacao powder
What you'll need from the store cupboard:
None

Instructions
1. Mix all ingredients in a slow cooker and cook on low settings for 6 hours.
2. Serve and enjoy.

Nutrition Facts Per Serving
Calories: 86; Fat: 8.4g; Carbs: 1.2g; Protein: 1.5g

Coco-Ginger Fat Bombs

Prep time: 10 minutes, cook time: 10 minutes; Serves 10

5 Ingredients:

1 cup coconut oil
1 cup shredded coconut
1 teaspoon erythritol
1 teaspoon ginger powder
¼ cup water

What you'll need from the store cupboard:

None

Instructions

1. Add all ingredients and pour ¼ cup water in a saucepan on the medium-low fire.
2. Stir constantly for 10 minutes.
3. Turn off and scoop small balls from the mixture.
4. Allow to set in the fridge for 1 hour.

Nutrition Facts Per Serving

Calories: 126; Fat: 12.8g; Carbs: 2.2g; Protein: 0.5g

Brownie Mug Cake

Prep time: 5 minutes, cook time: 5 minutes; Serves 1

5 Ingredients:

1 egg, beaten
¼ cup almond flour
¼ teaspoon baking powder
1 ½ tablespoons cacao powder
2 tablespoons stevia powder

What you'll need from the store cupboard:

A pinch of salt
1 teaspoon cinnamon powder
¼ teaspoon vanilla extract (optional)

Instructions

1. Combine all ingredients in a bowl until well-combined.
2. Transfer in a heat-proof mug.
3. Place the mug in a microwave.
4. Cook for 2 minutes. Let it sit for another 2 minutes to continue cooking.
5. Serve and enjoy.

Nutrition Facts Per Serving

Calories: 159; Fat: 11.8g; Carbs: 4.1g; Protein: 9.1g

Brownies with Coco Milk

Prep time: 10 minutes, cook time: 6 hours; Serves 10

5 Ingredients:

¾ cup coconut milk
1 teaspoon erythritol
2 tablespoons butter, melted
4 egg yolks, beaten
5 tablespoons cacao powder

What you'll need from the store cupboard:

Instructions

1. In a bowl, mix well all ingredients.
2. Lightly grease your slow cooker with cooking spray and pour in batter.
3. Cover and cook on low for six hours.
4. Serve and enjoy.

Nutrition Facts Per Serving

Calories: 86; Fat: 8.4g; Carbs: 1.2g; Protein: 1.5g

Keto Nut Bark

Prep time: 20 minutes, cook time: 40 minutes; Serves 8

5 Ingredients:

1 pound (4 cups) chopped walnuts
1-1/2 teaspoons ground cinnamon
½ cup butter, melted
1 packet stevia powder
½ cup coconut oil

What you'll need from the store cupboard:

None

Instructions

1. Preheat oven to 350°F. Coat a 13x9-in. baking dish with cooking spray. Combine walnuts and cinnamon.
2. Mix all ingredients until well combined.

3. Press on a baking sheet and flatten with a rolling pin.
4. Allow to harden in the fridge before breaking into barks.

Nutrition Facts Per Serving
Calories: 648; Fat: 68g; Carbs: 7.9g; Protein: 9g

Choco-Coco Bars

Prep time: 15 minutes, cook time: 10 minutes; Serves 12

5 Ingredients:
1/3 cup Virgin Coconut Oil, melted
2 cups shredded unsweetened coconut
2 droppers Liquid Stevia
2 droppers of Liquid Stevia (or enough sweetener to equal 1/4 cup)
3 squares Baker's Unsweetened Chocolate (3 ounces chocolate)

What you'll need from the store cupboard:
1 tablespoon oil

Instructions
1. Lightly grease an 8x8-inch silicone pan.
2. In a food processor, process shredded unsweetened coconut, coconut oil, and Stevia until it forms a dough. Transfer to prepared pan and press on the bottom to form a dough. Place in the freezer to set.
3. Meanwhile, in a microwave-safe Pyrex cup, place chocolate, coconut oil, and Stevia. Heat for 10-second intervals and mix well. Do not overheat, just until you have mixed the mixture thoroughly. Pour over dough.
4. Return to the freezer until set.
5. Serve and enjoy.

Nutrition Facts Per Serving
Calories: 222; Fat: 22.0g; Carbs: 4.0g; Protein: 2.0g

Fast 'n Easy Cookie in a Mug

Prep time: 10 minutes, cook time: 5 minutes; Serves 1

5 Ingredients:
1 tablespoon butter
3 tablespoons almond flour
1 tablespoon erythritol
1 egg yolk
1/8 teaspoon vanilla extract

What you'll need from the store cupboard:
A dash of cinnamon
A pinch of salt

Instructions
1. Mix all ingredients in a microwave-safe mug.
2. Nuke in the microwave for 3 minutes.
3. Let it rest for a minute.
4. Serve and enjoy.

Nutrition Facts Per Serving
Calories: 180; Fat: 17.8g; Carbs: 1.4g; Protein: 3.5g

Coconut Raspberry Bars

Prep time: 10 minutes, cook time: 20 minutes; Serves 12

5 Ingredients:
1 cup coconut milk
3 cups desiccated coconut
1/3 cup erythritol powder
1 cup raspberries, pulsed

What you'll need from the store cupboard:
½ cup coconut oil or other oils

Instructions
1. Preheat oven to 380ºF.
2. Combine all ingredients in a mixing bowl.
3. Pour into a greased baking dish.
4. Bake in the oven for 20 minutes.
5. Let it rest for 10 minutes.
6. Serve and enjoy.

Nutrition Facts Per Serving
Calories: 170; Fat: 14.7g; Carbs: 8.2g; Protein: 1.5g

Cream Cheese 'n Coconut Cookies

Prep time: 10 minutes, cook time: 17 minutes; Serves 15

5 Ingredients:
1 Egg
1/2 cup Butter softened
1/2 cup Coconut Flour
1/2 cup Erythritol or other sugar substitutes
3 tablespoons Cream cheese, softened

What you'll need from the store cupboard:
1 teaspoon Vanilla extract
1/4 teaspoon salt
1/2 teaspoon baking powder

Instructions
1. In a mixing bowl, whisk well erythritol, cream cheese, and butter.
2. Add egg and vanilla. Beat until thoroughly combined.
3. Mix in salt, baking powder, and coconut flour.
4. On an 11x13-inch piece of wax paper, place the batter. Mold into a log shape and then twist the ends to secure. Refrigerate for an hour and then slice into 1-inch circles.
5. When ready, preheat oven to 350°F and line a baking sheet with foil. Place cookies at least 1/2-inch apart.
6. Pop in the oven and bake until golden brown, around 17 minutes.
7. Serve and enjoy.

Nutrition Facts Per Serving
Calories: 88; Fat: 8.0g; Carbs: 3.0g; Protein: 1.0g

Lemon 'n Cashew Bars

Prep time: 10 minutes, cook time: 25 minutes; Serves 12

5 Ingredients:
¼ cup cashew
¼ cup fresh lemon juice, freshly squeezed
¾ cup coconut milk
¾ cup erythritol
1 cup desiccated coconut

What you'll need from the store cupboard:
1 teaspoon baking powder
2 eggs, beaten
2 tablespoons coconut oil
A dash of salt

Instructions
1. Preheat oven to 350°F and lightly grease an 8x8-inch square pan.
2. Combine all ingredients thoroughly in a mixing bowl.
3. Pour batter in prepared pan and bake for 20-25 minutes.
4. Serve and enjoy.

Nutrition Facts Per Serving
Calories: 118; Fat: 10.2g; Carbs: 3.9g; Protein: 2.6g

Vanilla Jello Keto Way

Prep time: 10 minutes, cook time: 6 minutes; Serves 6

5 Ingredients:
1 cup heavy cream
1 teaspoon vanilla extract
2 tablespoons gelatin powder, unsweetened
3 tablespoons erythritol

What you'll need from the store cupboard:
1 cup boiling water

Instructions
1. Place the boiling water in a small pot and bring to a simmer.
2. Add the gelatin powder and allow to dissolve.
3. Stir in the rest of the ingredients.
4. Pour the mixture into jello molds.
5. Place in the fridge to set for 2 hours.

Nutrition Facts Per Serving
Calories: 105; Fat: 7.9g; Carbs: 5.2g; Protein: 3.3g

Coconut Milk Pudding

Prep time: 10 minutes, cook time: 5 minutes; Serves 2

5 Ingredients:
½ teaspoon vanilla extract
1 cup coconut milk
1 tablespoon gelatin, unsweetened
2 teaspoons erythritol
3 egg yolks, beaten
What you'll need from the store cupboard:
4 tablespoons MCT or coconut oil
Instructions

1. Add all ingredients in a pot.
2. Bring to a simmer, mix continuously, and cook for 3 minutes.
3. Transfer to a bowl and refrigerate for an hour.
4. Serve and enjoy.

Nutrition Facts Per Serving
Calories: 529; Fat: 49.7g; Carbs: 9.2g; Protein: 8.3g

Smarties Cookies

Prep time: 10 mins; Cook time: 10 mins; Serves 8

5 Ingredients:
1/4 cup. butter
1/2 cup. almond flour
1 tsp. vanilla essence
12 oz. bag of smarties
What you'll need from the store cupboard:
1 cup. stevia
1/4 tsp. baking powder
Instructions
1. Sift in flour and baking powder in a bowl, then stir through butter and mix until well combined.
2. Whisk in stevia and vanilla essence , stir until thick.
3. Then add the smarties and use your hand to mix and divide into small balls.
4. Bake until completely cooked, about 10 minutes. Let it cool and serve.

Nutrition Facts Per Serving
Per Serving: Calories 239; Carbohydrates 11.89 g; Fat 20.77 g; Protein 3.7 g; Fiber 1.9 g

Crispy Zucchini Chips

Prep time: 10 mins; Cook time: 20 mins; Serves 5

5 Ingredients:
1 large egg, beaten
1 cup. almond flour
1 medium zucchini, thinly sliced
3/4 cup Parmesan cheese, grated
Cooking spray
Instructions
1. Preheat oven to 400 degrees F. Line a baking pan with parchment paper.
2. In a bowl, mix together Parmesan cheese and almond flour.
3. In another bowl whisk the egg. Dip each zucchini slice in the egg, then the cheese mixture until finely coated.
4. Spray zucchini slices with cooking spray and place in the prepared oven.
Bake for 20 minutes until crispy. Serve.

Nutrition Facts Per Serving
Per Serving: Calories 215.2; Carbohydrates 6 g; Fat 16.6 g; Protein 10.8 g

Spicy Cheese Crackers

Prep time: 10 mins; Cook time: 10 mins; Serves 4

5 Ingredients:
3/4 cup almond flour
1 egg
2 tablespoons cream cheese
2 cups shredded Parmesan cheese
1/2 teaspoon red pepper flakes

What you'll need from the store cupboard:
1 tablespoon dry ranch salad dressing mix

Instructions
1. Preheat oven to 425 degrees F.
2. Combine Parmesan and cream cheese in a microwave safe bowl and microwave in 30 second intervals. Add the cheese to mix well, and whisk along the almond flour, egg, ranch dressing mix, and red pepper flakes, stirring occasionally.
3. Transfer the dough in between two parchment-lined baking sheets. Form the dough into rolls by cutting off plum-sized pieces of dough with dough cutter into 1-inch square pieces, yielding about 60 pieces.
4. Place crackers to a baking sheet lined parchment. Bake for 5 minutes, flipping halfway, then continue to bake for 5 minutes more. Chill before serving..

Nutrition Facts Per Serving
Per Serving: Calories 235; Carbohydrates 4 g; Fat 18 g; Protein 17 g

Blackberry Cheese Vanilla Blocks

Prep time: 10 mins; Cook time: 20 mins; Serves 5

5 Ingredients:
½ cup blackberries
6 eggs
4 oz mascarpone cheese
1 tsp vanilla extract
4 tbsp stevia

What you'll need from the store cupboard:
8 oz melted coconut oil
½ tsp baking powder

Instructions
1. Except for blackberries, blend all ingredients in a blender until smooth.
2. Combine blackberries with blended mixture and transfer to a baking dish.
3. Bake blackberries mixture in the oven at 320°F for 20 minutes. Serve.

Nutrition Facts Per Serving
Per Serving: Calories 199; Carbohydrates 4 g; Fat 15 g; Protein 12 g

Coconut Macadamia Nut Bombs

Prep time: 5 mins; Cook time: 0 mins; Serves 4

5 Ingredients:
2 packets stevia
5 tbsps unsweetened coconut powder
10 tbsps coconut oil
3 tbsps chopped macadamia nuts
Salt to taste

Instructions
1. Heat the coconut oil in a pan over medium heat. Add coconut powder, stevia and salt, stirring to combined well; then remove from heat.
2. Spoon mixture into a lined mini muffin pan. Place in the freezer for a few hours.
3. Sprinkle nuts over the mixture before serving

Nutrition Facts Per Serving
Per Serving: Calories: 143 ,Fat: 15.2 g, Net Carbs: 1.1 g, Protein: 0.4 g

Chicken Cabbage Soup

Prep time: 5 minutes, cook time: 30 minutes; Serves 6

5 Ingredients:

1 can Italian-style tomatoes
3 cups chicken broth
1 chicken breast
½ head of cabbage, shredded
1 packet Italian seasoning mix

What you'll need from the store cupboard:

Salt and pepper to taste
1 cup water
1 tsp oil

Instructions

1. Place a heavy-bottomed pot on medium fire and heat for a minute. Add oil and swirl to coat the bottom and sides of the pot.
2. Pan fry chicken breast for 4 minutes per side. Transfer to a chopping board and cut into ½-inch cubes.
3. Add all ingredients to the pot and stir well.
4. Cover and bring to a boil, lower fire to a simmer, and cook for 20 minutes.
5. Adjust seasoning to taste, serve, and enjoy.

Nutrition Facts Per Serving

Calories: 248; Fat: 9.3g; Carbs: 5.6g; Protein: 34.1g

Corn and Bacon Chowder

Prep time: 20 minutes, cook time: 23 minutes; Serves 8

5 Ingredients:

½ cup bacon, fried and crumbled
1 package celery, onion, and bell pepper mix
2 cups full-fat milk
½ cup sharp cheddar cheese, grated

What you'll need from the store cupboard:

5 tablespoons butter
Pepper and salt to taste
1 cup water

Instructions

1. In a heavy-bottomed pot, melt butter.
2. Saute the bacon and celery for 3 minutes.
3. Turn fire on to medium. Add remaining ingredients and cook for 20 minutes until thick.
4. Serve and enjoy with a sprinkle of crumbled bacon.

Nutrition Facts Per Serving

Calories: 210.5; Fat: 13.6g; Carbs: 4.4g; Protein: 16.6g

Creamy Cauliflower Soup

Prep time: 5 minutes, cook time: 20 minutes; Serves 4

5 Ingredients:

1 cauliflower head, chopped
½ cup onions, chopped
4 cups chicken broth
1 tablespoon butter
1 cup heavy cream

What you'll need from the store cupboard:

Pepper and salt to taste

Instructions

1. Place all ingredients in a pot on medium-high fire, except for the heavy cream.
2. Season with salt and pepper to taste.
3. Give a good stir to combine everything.
4. Cover and bring to a boil, and simmer for 15 minutes.
5. With an immersion blender, blend well until smooth and creamy.
6. Stir in heavy cream and continue simmering for another 5 minutes. Adjust seasoning if needed.
7. Serve and enjoy.

Nutrition Facts Per Serving

Calories: 531; Fat: 30.8g; Carbs: 7.3g; Protein: 53.9g

Tomato Hamburger Soup

Prep time: 10 minutes, cook time: 25 minutes; Serves 8

5 Ingredients:

1-pound ground beef
1 can V-8 juice
2 packages frozen vegetable mix
1 can condensed mushroom soup
2 teaspoon dried onion powder

What you'll need from the store cupboard:

5 tablespoons olive oil
Salt and pepper to taste
1 cup water

Instructions

1. Place a pot over medium flame and heat for 2 minutes. Add oil and heat for a minute.
2. Sauté the beef until lightly browned, around 7 minutes. Season with salt, pepper, and onion powder.
3. Add the mushroom soup and water.
4. Give a good stir to combine everything.
5. Cover and bring to a boil, lower fire to a simmer and cook for 10 minutes.
6. Stir in vegetables. Cook until heated through around 5 minutes. Adjust seasoning if needed.
7. Serve and enjoy.

Nutrition Facts Per Serving

Calories: 227; Fat: 14.8g; Carbs: 10g; Protein: 18.1g

Bacon Chowder

Prep time: 5 minutes, cook time: 15 minutes; Serves 6

5 Ingredients:

1-pound bacon strips, chopped
1/4 cup chopped onion
1 can (12 ounces) evaporated milk
1 sprig parsley, chopped

What you'll need from the store cupboard:

5 tablespoons butter
1/4 teaspoon salt
1/4 teaspoon pepper

Instructions

1. In a large skillet, cook bacon over medium heat until crisp, stirring occasionally. Remove with a slotted spoon; drain on paper towels. Discard drippings, reserving 1-1/2 teaspoons in the pan. Add onion to drippings; cook and stir over medium-high heat until tender.
2. Meanwhile, place all ingredients Bring to a boil over high heat. Reduce heat to medium; cook, uncovered, 10-15 minutes or until tender. Reserve 1 cup potato water.
3. Add milk, salt and pepper to the saucepan; heat through. Stir in bacon and onion.

Nutrition Facts Per Serving

Calories: 322; Fat: 31.9g; Carbs: 5.4g; Protein: 10g

Mexican Soup

Prep time: 5 minutes, cook time: 25 minutes; Serves 4

5 Ingredients:

1-pound boneless skinless chicken thighs, cut into 3/4-inch pieces
1 tablespoon reduced-sodium taco seasoning
1 cup salsa
1 carton (32 ounces) reduced-sodium chicken broth

What you'll need from the store cupboard:

4 tablespoons olive oil

Instructions

1. In a large saucepan, heat oil over medium-high heat. Add chicken; cook and stir 6-8 minutes or until no longer pink. Stir in taco seasoning.
2. Add remaining ingredients; bring to a boil. Reduce heat; simmer, uncovered, 5 minutes to allow flavors to blend. Skim fat before serving.

Nutrition Facts Per Serving

Calories: 281; Fat: 16.5g; Carbs: 5.6g; Protein: 25g

Mushroom Soup

Prep time: 10 minutes, cook time: 35 minutes; Serves 8

5 Ingredients:

1-pound baby portobello mushrooms, chopped

2 tablespoons olive oil

1 carton (32 ounces) reduced-sodium beef broth

2 cups heavy whipping cream

What you'll need from the store cupboard:

4 tablespoons butter

1/2 cup water

Instructions

1. In a Dutch oven, sauté mushrooms in oil and butter until tender.
2. Add the contents of seasoning packets, broth, and water. Bring to a boil.
3. Reduce heat; cover and simmer for 25 minutes.
4. Add cream and heat through.

Nutrition Facts Per Serving

Calories: 280; Fat: 26g; Carbs: 3.6g; Protein: 8g

Rustic Beef Soup

Prep time: 5 minutes, cook time: 20 minutes; Serves 4

5 Ingredients:

3 cups beef broth

2 cups frozen mixed vegetables

1 teaspoon ground mustard

Beef roast

What you'll need from the store cupboard:

1 teaspoon water

Pinch of salt

Instructions

1. In a large saucepan, combine all the ingredients.
2. Bring to a boil.
3. Reduce heat; simmer, uncovered, for 15-20 minutes or until barley is tender.

Nutrition Facts Per Serving

Calories: 450; Fat: 24g; Carbs: 8g; Protein: 51g

Coconut Cauliflower Soup

Prep time: 10 minutes, cook time: 26 minutes; Serves 10

5 Ingredients:

1 medium onion, finely chopped

3 tablespoons yellow curry paste

2 medium heads cauliflower, broken into florets

1 carton (32 ounces) vegetable broth

1 cup coconut milk

What you'll need from the store cupboard:

2 tablespoons olive oil

Instructions

1. In a large saucepan, heat oil over medium heat. Add onion; cook and stir until softened, 2-3 minutes.
2. Add curry paste; cook until fragrant, 1-2 minutes.
3. Add cauliflower and broth. Increase heat to high; bring to a boil. Reduce heat to medium-low; cook, covered, about 20 minutes.
4. Stir in coconut milk; cook an additional minute.
5. Remove from heat; cool slightly.
6. Puree in batches in a blender or food processor.
7. If desired, top with minced fresh cilantro.

Nutrition Facts Per Serving

Calories: 111; Fat: 8g; Carbs: 10g; Protein: 3g

Clam Chowder

Prep time: 0 minutes, cook time: 10 minutes; Serves 5

5 Ingredients:

1 can (10-3/4 ounces) condensed cream of celery soup, undiluted

2 cups half-and-half cream

2 cans (6-1/2 ounces each) minced/chopped clams, drained

1/4 teaspoon ground nutmeg

What you'll need from the store cupboard:

5 tablespoons butter

Pepper to taste

Instructions

1. In a large saucepan, combine all ingredients. Cook and stir over medium heat until heated through.

Nutrition Facts Per Serving

Calories: 251; Fat: 14g; Carbs: 3.8g; Protein: 10g

Butternut and Kale Soup

Prep time: 20 minutes, cook time: 30 minutes; Serves 10

5 Ingredients:

1 package (19-1/2 ounces) Italian turkey sausage links, casings removed

½ medium butternut squash (about 3 pounds), peeled and cubed

2 cartons (32 ounces each) reduced-sodium chicken broth

1 bunch kale, trimmed and coarsely chopped (about 16 cups)

1/2 cup shaved Parmesan cheese

What you'll need from the store cupboard:

6 tablespoons butter

Water

Salt to taste

Instructions

1. In a stockpot, cook sausage over medium heat until no longer pink, breaking into crumbles, 8-10 minutes.

2. Add squash and broth; bring to a boil. Gradually stir in kale, allowing it to wilt slightly between additions. Return to a boil.

3. Reduce heat; simmer, uncovered, until vegetables are tender, 15-20 minutes. Top servings with cheese.

Nutrition Facts Per Serving

Calories: 118; Fat: 5g; Carbs: 5.3g; Protein: 13g

Creamy Soup with Greens

Prep time: 15 minutes, cook time: 20 minutes; Serves 6

5 Ingredients:

½-pounds collard greens, torn to bite-sized pieces

5 cups chicken broth

2 cups broccoli florets

1 cup diced onion

What you'll need from the store cupboard:

3 tablespoon oil

4 tablespoons butter

Salt and pepper to taste

Instructions

1. Add all ingredients to the pot and bring to a boil.

2. Lower fire to a simmer and simmer for 15 minutes while covered.

3. With an immersion blender, puree soup until creamy.

4. Adjust seasoning to taste.

5. Serve and enjoy.

Nutrition Facts Per Serving

Calories: 548; Fat: 33.5g; Carbs: 6.5g; Protein: 50.6g

Simplified French Onion Soup

Prep time: 5 minutes, cook time: 30 minutes; Serves 5

5 Ingredients:

3 large onions, sliced
2 bay leaves
5 cups Beef Bone Broth
1 teaspoon dried thyme
1-oz Gruyere cheese, sliced into 5 equal pieces

What you'll need from the store cupboard:

Pepper to taste
4 tablespoons oil

Instructions

1. Place a heavy-bottomed pot on medium-high fire and heat pot for 3 minutes.
2. Add oil and heat for 2 minutes. Stir in onions and sauté for 5 minutes.
3. Lower fire to medium-low, continue sautéing onions for 10 minutes until soft and browned, but not burned.
4. Add remaining ingredients and mix well.
5. Bring to a boil, lower fire to a simmer, cover and cook for 5 minutes.
6. Ladle into bowls, top with cheese.
7. Let it sit for 5 minutes.
8. Serve and enjoy.

Nutrition Facts Per Serving

Calories: 208; Fat: 16.8g; Carbs: 9.9g; Protein: 4.3g

Quail Eggs and Winter Melon in a Soup

Prep time: 15 minutes, cook time: 40 minutes; Serves 6

5 Ingredients:

1-pound pork bones
4 cloves of garlic, minced
1 onion, chopped
1 winter melon, peeled and sliced
10 quail eggs, pre-boiled and peeled

What you'll need from the store cupboard:

Pepper and salt to taste
6 cups water, divided
Chopped cilantro for garnish (optional)

Instructions

1. Place a heavy-bottomed pot on medium-high fire.
2. Add 5 cups water and pork bones. Season generously with pepper.
3. Bring to a boil, lower fire to a simmer, cover and cook for 30 minutes. Discard bones.
4. Add remaining ingredients except for the cilantro. Cover and simmer for another 10 minutes.
5. Adjust seasoning to taste.
6. Serve and enjoy with cilantro for garnish.

Nutrition Facts Per Serving

Calories: 65; Fat: 3.0g; Carbs: 5.6g; Protein: 4.0g

Mushroom-Broccoli Soup

Prep time:10 minutes, cook time: 20 minutes; Serves 4

5 Ingredients:

1 onion, diced
3 cloves of garlic, diced
2 cups mushrooms, chopped
2 heads of broccoli, cut into florets
1 cup full-fat milk

What you'll need from the store cupboard:

3 cups water
Pepper and salt to taste

Instructions

1. Place a heavy-bottomed pot on medium-high fire and heat for 3 minutes.
2. Add onion, garlic, water, and broccoli. Season generously with pepper and salt.
3. Cover and bring to a boil. Once boiling, lower fire to a simmer and let it cook for 7 minutes.
4. With a handheld blender, puree mixture until smooth and creamy.
5. Stir in mushrooms and milk, cover, and simmer for another 8 minutes.
6. Serve and enjoy.

Nutrition Facts Per Serving

Calories: 58.2; Fat: 1.0g; Carbs: 8.5g; Protein: 3.8g

Creamy Squash Bisque

Prep time: 15 minutes, cook time: 25 minutes; Serves 8

5 Ingredients:
½ tablespoon turmeric powder
½ teaspoon cumin
½ cup onion, chopped
2 medium-sized kabocha squash, seeded and chopped
1 cup coconut milk

What you'll need from the store cupboard:
3 tablespoons oil
1 cup water
Pepper and salt to taste

Instructions
1. Place a heavy-bottomed pot on medium-high fire and heat for 3 minutes.
2. Add oil to the pot and swirl to coat sides and bottom of the pot. Heat for 2 minutes.
3. Place squash in a single layer and season generously with pepper and salt.
4. Sprinkle turmeric, cumin, and onion. Add water.
5. Cover and bring to a boil. Once boiling, lower fire to a simmer and let it cook for 10 minutes.
6. With a handheld blender, puree squash. Stir in coconut milk and mix well. Cook until heated through, around 5 minutes.
7. Serve and enjoy.

Nutrition Facts Per Serving
Calories: 218; Fat: 18.1g; Carbs: 10.9g; Protein: 3.1g

South Dublin Libraries
www.southdublinlibraries.ie

Chicken Taco Soup

Prep time: 15 minutes, cook time: 45 minutes; Serves 6

5 Ingredients:
1-pound boneless chicken breast
1 tbsp taco seasoning
3 medium tomato chopped
1 medium onion chopped
2 Tablespoons garlic minced

What you'll need from the store cupboard:
5 cups water
Salt and Pepper to taste
Sour cream or tortilla chips for topping (optional)

Instructions
1. Add all ingredients in a heavy-bottomed pot except for garnish if using.
2. Bring to a boil, lower fire to a simmer, cover and cook for 30 minutes.
3. Remove chicken and shred. Return to the pot. Adjust seasoning with pepper and salt to taste.
4. Serve and enjoy with topping.

Nutrition Facts Per Serving
Calories: 98; Fat: 2.0g; Carbs: 5.0g; Protein: 15.0g

Spaghetti Squash Cream Soup

Prep time: 25 mins; Cook time: 35 minutes; Serves 4

5 Ingredients:
6 tablespoons chopped onion
1 cup butter
6 cups peeled and cubed spaghetti squash
4 cubes chicken bouillon
2 (8 ounce) packages cream cheese

What you'll need from the store cupboard:
3 cups water
1/4 teaspoon ground black pepper
1/8 teaspoon ground cayenne pepper
1/2 teaspoon dried marjoram

Instructions
1. Melt the butter in a large saucepan and cook onions until soft. Add squash, bouillon, marjoram, black pepper, cayenne pepper and water, bring to a boil and cook until squash is tender, about 20 minutes.
2. Use an immersion blender to puree the soup and cheese until smooth. Pour it back into the saucepan and stir often until warmed through.

Nutrition Facts Per Serving
Per Serving: 418.6 calories; 33.4 g fat; 8.2 g carbohydrates; 21.3 g protein

Chicken and Cauliflower Rice Soup

Prep time: 30 mins; Cook time: 20 mins; Serves 8

5 Ingredients:

2 cooked, boneless chicken breast halves, shredded

2 (12 ounce) packages Steamed Cauliflower Rice

1/4 cup celery, chopped

1/2 cup onion, chopped

4 garlic cloves, minced

What you'll need from the store cupboard:

Salt and ground black pepper to taste

2 teaspoons poultry seasoning

4 cups chicken broth

½ cup butter

2 cups heavy cream

Instructions

1. Heat butter in a large pot over medium heat, add onion, celery and garlic cloves to cook until tender. Meanwhile, place the riced cauliflower steam bags in the microwave following directions on the package.

2. Add the riced cauliflower, seasoning, salt and black pepper to butter mixture, saute them for 7 minutes on medium heat, stirring constantly to well combined.

3. Bring cooked chicken breast halves, broth and heavy cream to a broil. When it starts boiling, lower the heat, cover and simmer for 15 minutes.

Nutrition Facts Per Serving

Per Serving: 415 calories; 30 g total fat; 6 g carbohydrates; 27 g protein

Spicy Chicken Bean Soup

Prep time: 15 mins; Cook time: 1h 20mins; Serves 8

5 Ingredients:

8 skinless, boneless chicken breast halves

5 cubes chicken bouillon

2 (14.5 ounce) cans peeled and diced tomatoes

1 (8 ounce) container sour cream

1 cups frozen cut green beans

What you'll need from the store cupboard:

3 tablespoons. olive oil

Salt and black pepper to taste

1 onion, chopped

3 cloves garlic, chopped

1 cups frozen cut green beans

Instructions

1. Heat olive oil in a large pot over medium heat, add onion, garlic and cook until tender. Stir in water, chicken, salt, pepper, bouillon cubes and bring to boil, simmer for 1 hour on Low. Remove chicken from the pot, reserve 5 cups broth and slice.

2. Stir in the remaining ingredients in the pot and simmer 30 minutes. Serve and enjoy..

Nutrition Facts Per Serving

Per Serving: 275.1 calories; 15.3 g total fat; 7.6 g carbohydrates; 26.5 g protein

Appendix 1: Measurement Conversion Chart

Volume Equivalents(Liquid)

US STANDARD	US STANDARD(OUNCES)	METRIC(APPROXIMATE)
2 TABLESPOONS	1 fl.oz.	30 mL
1/4 CUP	2 fl.oz.	60 mL
1/2 CUP	4 fl.oz.	120 mL
1 CUP	8 fl.oz.	240 mL
1 1/2 CUP	12 fl.oz.	355 mL
2 CUPS OR 1 PINT	16 fl.oz.	475 mL
4 CUPS OR 1 QUART	32 fl.oz.	1 L
1 GALLON	128 fl.oz.	4 L

Volume Equivalents (DRY)

US STANDARD	METRIC (APPROXIMATE)
1/8 TEASPOON	0.5 mL
1/4 TEASPOON	1 mL
1/2 TEASPOON	2 mL
3/4 TEASPOON	4 mL
1 TEASPOON	5 mL
1 TABLESPOON	15 mL
1/4 CUP	59 mL
1/2 CUP	118 mL
3/4 CUP	177 mL
1 CUP	235 mL
2 CUPS	475 mL
3 CUPS	700 mL
4 CUPS	1 L

Weight Equivalents

US STANDARD	METRIC (APPROXIMATE)
1/2 OUNCE	15g
1 OUNCE	30g
2 OUNCE	60g
4 OUNCE	115g
8 OUNCE	225g
12 OUNCE	340g
16 OUNCES OR 1 POUND	455g

Temperatures Equivalents

FAHRENHEIT (F)	CELSIUS(C) (APPROXIMATE)
250	121
300	149
325	163
350	177
375	190
400	205
425	218
450	232

Lightning Source UK Ltd.
Milton Keynes UK
UKHW030341221120
373825UK00009B/496

9 781952 613029